Social Protection in Southern Africa

A new generation of innovative social protection strategies is emerging in southern Africa. Although cash transfers are most prevalent, some countries' strategies include combinations of interventions such as food, livelihood inputs and support, asset building, public works and social services. The strategies vary in their commitment to social rights, their institutional and funding arrangements, the reach, scope and design of the programmes, and the behavioural conditions attached to grant access. The proliferation of national social protection in the Global South has been widely supported by governments, international agencies and non-governmental organisations (NGOs).

This book offers researchers and policymakers much to think about when considering the rapid growth of social protection in southern Africa, the challenges this presents and the opportunities it offers for social development and economic growth. Hence, the book is a contribution to scholarship and policy debate on how to solve intractable social development problems in Africa and elsewhere.

This book was originally published as a special issue of *Development Southern Africa*.

Leila Patel is Professor of Social Development Studies and Director of the Centre for Social Development in Africa, University of Johannesburg, South Africa. She has published widely on social welfare, social protection, gender and social development in the African context.

James Midgley is the Harry and Riva Specht Professor of Public Social Services at the School of Social Welfare, University of California, and Visiting Professor, Centre for Social Development in Africa, University of Johannesburg, South Africa. He has published widely on issues of social development, social protection and international social welfare.

Marianne Ulriksen is affiliated to the Centre for Social Development in Africa, University of Johannesburg, South Africa, as a Senior Research Fellow. Currently residing in Tanzania, Marianne's research includes: comparative politics, political economy of welfare policy development, social protection, poverty and inequality, mineral wealth and resource mobilisation, and state-citizens relations.

Social Protection in Southern Africa
New Opportunities for Social Development

Edited by
Leila Patel, James Midgley and
Marianne Ulriksen

LONDON AND NEW YORK

First published 2014
by Routledge
2 Park Square, Milton Park, Abingdon, Oxon, OX14 4RN

and by Routledge
711 Third Avenue, New York, NY 10017

Routledge is an imprint of the Taylor & Francis Group, an informa business

© 2014 Taylor & Francis

All rights reserved. No part of this book may be reprinted or reproduced or utilised in any form or by any electronic, mechanical, or other means, now known or hereafter invented, including photocopying and recording, or in any information storage or retrieval system, without permission in writing from the publishers.

Trademark notice: Product or corporate names may be trademarks or registered trademarks, and are used only for identification and explanation without intent to infringe.

British Library Cataloguing in Publication Data
A catalogue record for this book is available from the British Library

ISBN 13: 978-0-415-72725-9

Typeset in Times New Roman
by Taylor & Francis Books

Publisher's Note
The publisher accepts responsibility for any inconsistencies that may have arisen during the conversion of this book from journal articles to book chapters, namely the possible inclusion of journal terminology.

Disclaimer
Every effort has been made to contact copyright holders for their permission to reprint material in this book. The publishers would be grateful to hear from any copyright holder who is not here acknowledged and will undertake to rectify any errors or omissions in future editions of this book.

Contents

Citation Information — vii

1. Introduction: Social protection in southern Africa: New opportunities for social development
   Leila Patel, James Midgley & Marianne Ulriksen — 1

2. Social development and social protection: New opportunities and challenges
   James Midgley — 2

3. Trajectories of social protection in Africa
   Stephen Devereux — 13

4. Social protection, redistribution and economic growth
   David Piachaud — 24

5. The politics of social protection expenditure and financing in southern Africa
   Marianne Ulriksen — 39

6. 'Growing' social protection in developing countries: Lessons from Brazil and South Africa
   Armando Barrientos, Valerie Møller, João Saboia, Peter Lloyd-Sherlock & Julia Mase — 54

7. Gender and child sensitive social protection in South Africa
   Leila Patel, Tessa Hochfeld & Jacqueline Moodley — 69

8. The contribution of non-formal social protection to social development in Botswana
   Rodreck Mupedziswa & Dolly Ntseane — 84

9. Social protection in Lesotho: Innovations and reform challenges
   Marius Olivier — 98

10. Are social protection programmes child-sensitive?
    Scelo Zibagwe, Themba Nduna & Gift Dafuleya — 111

11. Tackling child poverty in South Africa: Implications of *ubuntu* for the system of social grants
    Adam Whitworth & Kate Wilkinson — 121

CONTENTS

12. The South African disability grant: Influence on HIV treatment outcomes and household well-being in KwaZulu-Natal
Lucia Knight, Victoria Hosegood & Ian M Timæus — 135

Index — 149

Citation Information

The chapters in this book were originally published in *Development Southern Africa*, volume 30, issue 1 (March 2013). When citing this material, please use the original page numbering for each article, as follows:

Chapter 1
Editorial: Social protection in southern Africa: New opportunities for social development
Leila Patel, James Midgley & Marianne Ulriksen
Development Southern Africa, volume 30, issue 1 (March 2013)
p. 1

Chapter 2
Social development and social protection: New opportunities and challenges
James Midgley
Development Southern Africa, volume 30, issue 1 (March 2013)
pp. 2–12

Chapter 3
Trajectories of social protection in Africa
Stephen Devereux
Development Southern Africa, volume 30, issue 1 (March 2013)
pp. 13–23

Chapter 4
Social protection, redistribution and economic growth
David Piachaud
Development Southern Africa, volume 30, issue 1 (March 2013)
pp. 24–38

Chapter 5
The politics of social protection expenditure and financing in southern Africa
Marianne Ulriksen
Development Southern Africa, volume 30, issue 1 (March 2013)
pp. 39–53

Chapter 6
'Growing' social protection in developing countries: Lessons from Brazil and South Africa
Armando Barrientos, Valerie Møller, João Saboia, Peter Lloyd-Sherlock & Julia Mase
Development Southern Africa, volume 30, issue 1 (March 2013) pp. 54–68

Chapter 7
Gender and child sensitive social protection in South Africa
Leila Patel, Tessa Hochfeld & Jacqueline Moodley
Development Southern Africa, volume 30, issue 1 (March 2013) pp. 69–83

Chapter 8
The contribution of non-formal social protection to social development in Botswana
Rodreck Mupedziswa & Dolly Ntseane
Development Southern Africa, volume 30, issue 1 (March 2013) pp. 84–97

Chapter 9
Social protection in Lesotho: Innovations and reform challenges
Marius Olivier
Development Southern Africa, volume 30, issue 1 (March 2013) pp. 98–110

Chapter 10
Are social protection programmes child-sensitive?
Scelo Zibagwe, Themba Nduna & Gift Dafuleya
Development Southern Africa, volume 30, issue 1 (March 2013) pp. 111–120

Chapter 11
Tackling child poverty in South Africa: Implications of ubuntu for the system of social grants
Adam Whitworth & Kate Wilkinson
Development Southern Africa, volume 30, issue 1 (March 2013) pp. 121–134

Chapter 12
The South African disability grant: Influence on HIV treatment outcomes and household well-being in KwaZulu-Natal
Lucia Knight, Victoria Hosegood & Ian M Timæus
Development Southern Africa, volume 30, issue 1 (March 2013) pp. 135–147

Please direct any queries you may have about the citations to clsuk.permissions@cengage.com

Introduction
Social protection in southern Africa: New opportunities for social development

A new generation of innovative social protection strategies is emerging in southern Africa. Similar developments can be seen in Latin America and Asia. Although cash transfers are most prevalent, some country strategies include combinations of interventions such as food, livelihood inputs and support, asset building, public works and social services. The strategies vary in their commitment to social rights, their institutional and funding arrangements, the reach, scope and design of the programmes, and the behavioural conditions attached to grant access. A new paradigm is apparent in developing countries aiming to achieve redistribution through various types of social protection intervention. Some of these interventions target households more than individuals and take a productivist or developmental perspective. The proliferation of national social protection in the Global South has been widely supported by governments, international agencies and non-governmental organisations (NGOs).

Social protection is now firmly on the southern African development agenda, but much remains for policymakers to consider: the conceptual, theoretical and paradigmatic issues, the relevance to Africa of Eurocentric welfare state approaches for social protection, and the possible alternatives, the effects of various types of programmes on redistribution and economic growth, the ways that countries in the region can finance their social protection and how their interests shape their spending priorities. Lessons can be learnt from the diversity of social protection strategies being deployed in both low and middle income countries. Comparative studies of arrangements in the Global South can offer insights into what social protection is and how it works. Cross-country studies of South Africa and Brazil, both middle income countries, might help us understand the paradigm shift in this field and how these two countries differ. More research can be done on the gendered nature of care and how social protection helps or hinders progress towards gender equality and better lives for children. Social protection tends to favour statutory programmes and neglect the way non-formal provision by families, communities and NGOs can be linked to formal state provision – this is a matter for further investigation. And we might look in particular at what Lesotho, one of Africa's poorest countries, has achieved in social protection reform.

This special issue of *Development Southern Africa* offers researchers and policymakers much to think about when considering the rapid growth of social protection in southern Africa, the challenges this presents and the opportunities it offers for social development and economic growth. The papers are the product of an international symposium convened by the Centre for Social Development in Africa at the University of Johannesburg in May 2011. We offer them as a contribution to scholarship and policy debate on how to solve some of the region's most intractable social development problems.

Leila Patel, James Midgley & Marianne Ulriksen

Social development and social protection: New opportunities and challenges

James Midgley[1]

The growing interest in social protection in the interdisciplinary field of development studies presents new challenges and opportunities. However, to respond effectively, development scholars should be cognisant of the extensive research that has been undertaken over many years in the interdisciplinary field of social policy into what is known as 'social security'. They have hitherto neglected this research, but it can make a significant contribution to their own work. At the same time, they have a rare opportunity to inform social policy research, which has historically relied on a Eurocentric 'welfare state' approach that is of limited relevance to the developing world. By forging closer links between these two fields, we can address the challenges facing social protection more effectively.

1. Introduction

The growing interest in social protection and social security in social development studies and development studies more generally is welcome but somewhat surprising. Although social development emerged in the 1950s as a distinct subfield of development studies concerned with what is often referred to as the 'social' aspects of development, neither practitioners nor scholars working in the field have previously paid much attention to social protection and social security, which have been associated with consumption rather than developmental activities and are generally viewed in development circles as better suited to the Western countries.

As is well known, the situation has changed. The creation of conditional cash transfer schemes in Brazil, Mexico and other Latin American countries, the redesign and expansion of social assistance in South Africa, the introduction of universal old-age pensions in Botswana, Lesotho and Namibia and the launching of the National Rural Employment Guarantee Scheme in India have all contributed to the new interest in social protection in development circles. Although a rapidly burgeoning descriptive literature on social protection by social development scholars is now available, there is a need to reflect on wider meta-theoretical issues that focus, for example, on defining, conceptualising, measuring and theorising social protection. This is not an irrelevant academic exercise but an essential part of formulating successful policy interventions and enhancing the programmatic effectiveness of social protection policies.

In this article I provide a broad introduction to the papers in this special issue by contrasting the recent interest in social protection in social development with the more established body of social security literature in social policy. This literature has evolved over many decades and has generally but not exclusively focused on statutory

---

[1]Harry & Riva Specht Professor, School of Social Welfare, University of California, Berkeley, and Visiting Professor, Centre for Social Development in Africa, University of Johannesburg, South Africa.

income maintenance in the Western world. I suggest that social development scholars concerned with social protection today have much to learn from this work. I also suggest that those studying social security from the social policy perspective have much to learn from the research into social protection that is being undertaken by social development scholars. Unfortunately, there has been relatively little exchange of research findings, conceptual ideas and policy lessons between those working in these two fields. Social policy scholars remain largely ignorant of the work being done on social protection in development studies, and similarly, social development scholars make surprisingly few references to the social policy literature. Nevertheless, there are fruitful opportunities for closer collaboration as well as possibilities to address significant challenges.

I begin by discussing research into social security in the field of social policy. I then contrast the social policy approach with the emerging work being done on social protection in social development, which, as noted earlier, forms a special area within the wider field of development studies. I then discuss a number of issues and concerns that provide opportunities for reciprocal policy learning. Finally, I consider the prospect of fostering closer collaboration and forging a comprehensive unified perspective on social protection.

2. The academic study of social protection

Systematic scholarly work in social protection and social security is a fairly recent trend dating back to the early decades of the 20th century. This work is associated with the introduction of statutory income maintenance programmes in Europe in the late 19th and early 20th centuries and with the creation of the International Labour Organization (ILO) in 1919. One early example of an academic study of social protection is Beatrice and Sidney Webb's history of the English Poor Law, which was published in two volumes in 1927 and 1929 (Webb & Webb, 1927, 1929). Another example is a pioneering book by Barbara Armstrong (1932), a Berkeley law professor, which reported on European social insurance and other innovations such as minimum wages and statutory employer mandates. Her work helped to shape the retirement insurance provisions of the 1935 Social Security Act in the US. Another important early publication was Karl de Schweinitz's (1943) extensive historical review of English social security measures, which included both the Poor Law and developments in social insurance. These and other early publications transcended earlier polemical tracts that either advocated or deprecated the provision of government assistance to those in need. They also laid the foundation for a plethora of subsequent studies of social security in the latter half of the 20th century.

2.1 The social policy perspective

The rapid expansion of statutory social services in a number of Western countries during the middle decades of the 20th century focused academic interest on government social security schemes, which were at the core of these 'welfare state' innovations. As scholars in disciplines as varied as history, economics, law, government and sociology documented and studied these innovations, interdisciplinary collaboration increased and more books and specialist journal articles on social security were published. This development was bolstered by the ILO and the International Social Security Association, which encouraged the publication of research into social security.

Another development was the creation in a number of universities in Britain and other English-speaking countries of interdisciplinary academic departments concerned with the study of social policy. One of the most important was the Department of Social Science and Administration at the London School of Economics, which was established in 1950 with Richard Titmuss as its first professorial head. Similar departments were created at other universities in Britain, notably at Liverpool and Birmingham. There were comparable developments in other English-speaking countries such as Australia and Canada, although in the US the study of social policy emerged within professional postgraduate schools of public policy and social work. Since then, the academic study of social policy has evolved steadily and is today pursued at universities in many parts of the world.

Initially, the subject of social policy was concerned with training administrators who would manage social services, but its vocational commitment was transcended by attempts to address wider policy issues, enhance the quality and rigour of research and articulate broad theoretical perspectives. Titmuss himself was not much concerned with the technical aspects of social service management and focused instead on the conceptual and normative issues that legitimated collective welfare provision. Perhaps his most significant contribution was to formulate a paradigmatic normative approach based on social democratic beliefs that continues to influence the way social policies are investigated and interpreted today (Midgley, 2009). Since those formative years, social policy has attained a commendable level of theoretical sophistication that is revealed in the construction of numerous typologies of welfare systems, the formulation of explanatory theories and analyses of prevailing normative perspectives on social security.

The social policy approach to the study of social security has a number of distinctive features. These include a concern with statutory provisions, and chiefly with social insurance and social assistance, which are widely regarded as the core components of the social security system. Universal tax funded child benefit and pension schemes have also featured prominently, but less attention has been given to employer mandates and income subsidies through the fiscal system. However, there is growing interest in these provisions and in the role of statutory mandated retirement accounts managed by commercial providers.

The preoccupation with statutory social security exhibited by scholars working within the social policy tradition is also the result of the adoption of international treaties and human rights instruments. Among the most important of these are the ILO's Social Security Minimum Standards Convention of 1952, the UN's Universal Declaration on Human Rights of 1948 and the UN International Covenant on Economic, Social and Cultural Rights of 1966. These and similar instruments reflect a view of social security as a collective rather than individual responsibility based on notions of social rights, redistribution and social solidarity. They have inspired a widely accepted definition of social security as involving the provision of resources by the state to maintain or supplement peoples' incomes that have been interrupted, terminated or reduced by contingencies such as sickness, unemployment, disability, retirement, maternity or the death of the household's primary wage earner.

Because of their concern with government provision, those who study social security from a social policy perspective have generally paid little attention to non-statutory income maintenance and support programmes, or to familial and community social support networks and the role of non-profit and faith-based organisations. The rapidly expanding commercial sector, which is not always viewed positively in social policy circles, has also received limited attention – except of course from those who oppose social security privatisation.

A related feature of the social policy approach is its macro-focus on the nation state and particularly the so-called 'welfare state'. International comparisons of social security policies and programmes have generally used the nation state as a unit of analysis, and social protection activities at the household or community level have received relatively little attention. Also, when undertaking international comparative research, social policy scholars have focused largely, although not exclusively, on the Western countries. Although comparative research in the field was already well developed by the 1980s, it was primarily concerned with Europe and North America, and initially little attention was paid to the developing countries of the Global South. Formative academic publications dealing with social security in the developing world by MacPherson (1982), Midgley (1984) and Ahmad et al. (1991) were usually regarded as exotic and of marginal relevance. Although the situation has changed as more studies of social security policies and programmes in Asia and Latin America and to some extent Africa have been published, these generally conform to social policy's macro and the Eurocentric 'welfare state' approach.

2.2 The social development perspective

Like social policy, the interdisciplinary field of development studies emerged in the years following World War II and also had a formative vocational commitment to train administrators who could implement the public policies of the newly independent developing countries. Many of these programmes grew out of older university based training courses designed to prepare officials for colonial service, but after the war they catered primarily for civil servants from the developing world. The British government played a major role in promoting and funding these training activities, but similar opportunities were provided at a number of universities in other Western countries. These activities gave rise to the first interdisciplinary development studies centres, which have played a significant role in research and policy formulation in the development field.

The involvement of scholars from different disciplines in development studies made a major contribution to the field's intellectual evolution. Although development studies retained a strong commitment to practical policy concerns, like social policy, this *interdisciplinary field* developed a research agenda and offered new conceptual frameworks for studying the development process. However, unlike social policy, which adopted a statist approach, diverse competing conceptual and normative interpretations soon emerged in the field. This is revealed in the very different ways development has been defined by scholars who used statist, populist, Marxist, feminist, market liberal and other interpretations. Similarly, development studies did not focus exclusively on the nation state. Unlike social policy – which neglected the role of households, communities and non-profit organisations in social welfare – development studies ranged simultaneously over these institutions to examine their diverse contribution to the development process.

This broader scope gave rise to specialised subfields such as social development, which, as Midgley (1995) documented, emerged in the 1950s. Social development had a strong practical bent and originally focused primarily on local community development projects in India and Africa. In the 1960s these activities were augmented by the introduction of social planning at the national level, which, it was argued, should complement economic planning. Leading development economists such as Myrdal (1957, 1970) and Seers (1969) promoted this idea, arguing that development policy should be concerned not only with economic growth but also with improvements in health, nutrition, education and standards of living. It was in this context that social development acquired greater significance within the field of development studies, and, with the support of the UN and other multilateral agencies, efforts to promote social development eventually resulted in the World Summit on Social Development of 1995 and the adoption of the Millennium Development Goals in 2000.

Today, social development's concern with the social dimensions of economic development finds expression in a variety of interventions. These operate at different levels and range from household-based microenterprises to community-based sanitary and water supply initiatives, as well as national level programmes such as literacy education and national social planning. As noted earlier, social protection was not previously considered to be an integral part of social development, but it has recently become a major topic of interest in development circles.

There are several reasons why social protection was neglected in social development's formative years. Income transfers were widely regarded as an expensive luxury that developing countries could not afford, and they were believed to detract from development priorities, which required investment rather than consumption expenditure. These programmes were also seen as a legacy of the colonial period that had little relevance to more appropriate interventions such as participatory community development and gender projects. Accordingly, as noted earlier, the handful of books on social security in the Global South that had been published by the 1980s attracted little attention. However, as social protection programmes in the Global South have expanded, and as innovations in Brazil, India, Mexico, South Africa and elsewhere have been documented, social protection is now regarded as an important social development intervention. These programmes are also important for challenging the market liberal, Washington Consensus perspective promoted by the IMF and the World Bank. Recent social protection innovations are also noteworthy for expanding coverage well beyond the limited safety net and social funds approaches previously adopted by these organisations (Hall & Midgley, 2004).

Because the study of social protection by social development academics is still of recent origin, it is perhaps premature to attempt a sketch of its key features. Nevertheless, some of these can be identified. First, with regard to nomenclature, social development scholars have adopted the term 'social protection' rather than the better known term 'social security'. Although social protection has also been used from time to time in social policy circles, social security has generally been preferred. Reasons for the preference for social protection in development studies are obscure but it seems to serve as an umbrella term that covers a wider range of programmes than those associated with social security's income maintenance function, namely social insurance, social assistance and universal social allowances. As will be shown, these include food for work programmes, microfinance, cooperative benefit associations, faith-based initiatives and microinsurance. Second, the social protection approach transcends the statutory focus that dominates social policy inquiry into social security. Many social protection programmes in the developing world have been initiated by non-profit organisations often supported by international donors. However, this does not mean that governments are not involved – on the contrary, many social protection innovations have been introduced and are managed by governments. Third, as suggested earlier, the social protection approach is also distinctive in that it transcends the macro-focus of the social policy approach to focus on innovations at the household, neighbourhood and community levels. This is compatible with social development's historical interest in community-based interventions.

3. Policy exchanges and policy learning: Opportunities and challenges

Although social policy and social development researchers have much to share, exchanges between them have been limited. Nevertheless, it is clear that they have much to learn from each other. This will not only promote the helpful exchange of information but also foster mutual efforts to address the many challenges facing the field today. The following are just a few topics and issues that would benefit from a closer collaboration between those who study social security from a social policy perspective and those who study social protection from a social development perspective.

One topic that would benefit from mutual discussion is nomenclature. The term 'social security' is favoured by social policy scholars while the term 'social protection' has been widely adopted in social development circles. Of course, the latter term is also used in social policy, but a number of other terms such as income security, income protection, economic security, income transfers, social insurance, social assistance, cash transfers and tax funded universal benefits are also in circulation. Unfortunately, no standardised definition of social protection has emerged in the social development literature, and a wide variety of interventions are loosely described as comprising social protection schemes. Although this issue may be regarded as a semantic quibble, it has implications for research and for policy formulation. It is desirable that terminologies be standardised for research purposes and that politicians, government administrators, international donors and planners are not confused by imprecise terminologies when seeking to introduce or expand these programmes. Social development scholars would benefit from reviewing the way terminologies are used in social policy, where a significant degree of standardisation has been achieved largely through recourse to international instruments such as the ILO conventions.

An arguably more important topic for debate concerns the way that social security and social protection are conceptualised. Although much of the literature is descriptive, normative assumptions are often implicit in statements about the need for social protection, and these should be more systematically articulated and debated. Some social development scholars, including Sabates-Wheeler & Devereux (2007), have sought to analyse conceptual issues by identifying key normative preferences, but much more needs to done to clarify the normative assumptions that underpin the field and examine their relevance for policy.

Because of social development's engagement with households, communities and states, it is not surprising that very different normative perspectives can be identified in the social development literature. These differences are not as marked in the social policy literature where, as was noted earlier, most social policy scholars view social security as a collective means for maintaining income. In the social development literature, on the other hand, some authors suggest that social protection programmes should be designed primarily to help households manage risk while others believe that they should be concerned with poverty reduction. Yet others contend that these programmes should promote social rights, solidarity and equality. The latter view favours income transfers through the agency of the state, while the former encourages access to microfinance and microinsurance provided by non-governmental and commercial carriers.

The World Bank's risk management framework, which emerged in the late 1990s in the wake of its widely discussed book *Averting the Old Age Crisis* (1994), had an unmistakably individualistic focus that underpinned its social funds and social safety net approaches. Both shifted responsibility away from collective provisions through the state to households, communities and non-profit organisations. Since then, much of the social protection literature has focused on non-statutory provision and the way households manage risk. Today, studies by economists have largely viewed social protection through the lens of household risk management (Townsend, 1994; Dercon, 2005). Since these approaches are conducive to the promotion of market-based approaches and the increasing involvement of commercial providers in social protection, they should be critically reviewed in the light of alternative perspectives such as that advocated by Sabates-Wheeler & Devereux (2007). A dialogue with colleagues in social policy who have undertaken quite extensive theoretical work in the field would be mutually beneficial. Certainly, attempts to institutionalise an approach that affirms the role of collective provision, social rights and redistribution in social protection would benefit from a dialogue of this kind.

Another topic for debate is the affordability of social protection. Although this has not been viewed as a matter for concern in social development circles – partly because these programmes are often financed by international donors – funding may become a critical issue in the future. The replication of Latin American conditional cash transfers in Asian and African countries under the direction of the World Bank and the regional development banks involves loans that need to be repaid. The question of funding is certainly a major topic in social policy in Western countries today, where the affordability of social security schemes has been vigorously questioned. Market liberals and others who oppose government intervention argue that it is simply not possible for social security in these countries to meet the needs of the growing elderly population, unemployed people, families with children and other deserving groups without imposing unsustainable taxes and damaging the economy. This argument has resonated with politicians and increasingly with voters who have been persuaded that sacrifices are needed to promote economic growth. These arguments have become even more trenchant as many Western governments have imposed significant budget cuts in the wake of the recent Great Recession.

It is true that the expansion of statutory programmes in middle income countries experiencing economic growth such as Brazil, China, Mexico and South Africa involves comparatively modest costs. But it is likely that critical voices will more frequently be raised to question the economic wisdom of these expenditures. The question of affordability will also be raised as the populations of many developing countries age and as more elderly people need retirement income protection. This has already happened in China (Frazier, 2010). Sharing information on the issue of funding and more carefully assessing the costs of social protection, particularly with reference to creating an affordable social protection floor (Cichon & Hagemejer, 2007), would be mutually beneficial. Social policy researchers have a good deal of experience of this issue, which can be of benefit to social development scholars.

At the same time, these scholars have experience of studying low-cost interventions that will be of interest and value to social policy scholars.

Another topic that would benefit from mutual discussion is the divergent focus of social security and social protection programmes. As noted earlier, social security schemes generally have a macro-focus while social protection programmes are often directed at households and local communities. Sharing views on this issue is important because it could promote the integration of the two approaches. It could also help to address the issues of limited coverage and social exclusion that characterise social security in many developing countries. As has been extensively documented, national social security schemes have largely provided coverage to workers in the formal sector of the economy and ignored the needs of the rural majority (Hall & Midgley, 2004; Van Ginneken, 2007, 2010). Those in the urban informal sector have also been excluded, as have women, who have derived few benefits from the formal social security system. Although it has long been argued that the formal system will gradually extend coverage as the modern economy expands, this has only been the case in a small number of countries. There is growing recognition that policy innovations that address the problem of exclusion are urgently needed. The experience of implementing social protection programmes in local communities and involving grassroots associations, women's groups and faith-based organisations can inform policymakers and promote the goal of extending coverage to all, a goal that is vigorously promoted by the ILO (Reynaud, 2002).

An important topic that will be of particular interest to social policy scholars is the role of social protection innovations that address the unique needs of people in the developing world. These may also have relevance to Western countries. For many years it was assumed that the developing countries would benefit from replicating policy innovations from the West. Today, innovations from the developing world are increasingly being examined for their wider international relevance, and some have been adopted in Western countries. By exchanging information about these and other social protection innovations, policymakers could enhance policy transfers and make more extensive and fruitful programmatic adaptations.

One obvious example is microfinance. The Grameen Bank and the activities of other microfinance organisations such as the Foundation for International Community Assistance (FINCA) and ACCION International have attracted a good deal of attention in the West, and some of these have sponsored operations in countries such as the US. Conditional cash transfers are also of interest. Following a visit to Mexico by New York Mayor Michael Bloomberg, the city introduced a demonstration project based on the Mexican *Oportunidades* programme known as Opportunity NYC-Family Rewards. Also relevant are social protection innovations that accommodate diverse cultural beliefs and practices. Although not widely reported in the literature, a number of Islamic countries have modified their conventional social security schemes to accommodate religious beliefs. Non-governmental Islamic associations have formalised the collection of *zakat* (alms) contributions in Pakistan and Saudi Arabia, and in Indonesia they have developed social protection measures based on Islamic teaching (Sirojudin & Midgley, 2011). Considering the challenges of providing income protection to culturally diverse immigrant communities, these innovations should be of interest to social policy scholars in Western countries. Another important innovation is microinsurance, which has become a major topic of interest in social development but has as yet attracted little attention from social security scholars in the

West. The term refers to programmes operated by organisations that collect small regular premiums from poor people and pay benefits when certain contingencies arise (Loewe, 2006; Midgley, 2011). Disability and death benefits are among the most common, but microhealth insurance schemes have also been established. Opportunities for insurance-linked retirement savings are also being provided. These and other social protection innovations will be of interest and potential policy relevance to social policy scholars.

A final topic that I discuss here is the set of developmental implications of social security and social protection. The question of the affordability of social security, which I mentioned earlier, has been linked to the argument that social security transfers have a negative effect on economic development. This argument is not new, but it has been widely accepted in recent years and has supported the claim that individuals and families need to make their own arrangements to meet their income protection needs. The continued expansion of statutory programmes will, it is argued, inevitably retard economic growth, with disastrous consequences. Although this argument has been countered by a number of social policy scholars who have drawn on empirical research to show that the expansion of statutory income protection programmes has not had a negative economic effect, this research has been largely ignored (Midgley, 2008).

Social development research into the economic impact of social protection has adopted a more proactive approach showing that, if properly configured, these programmes function as social investments that contribute positively to economic development. Originally, research of this kind focused on the way health, nutrition and education improved the productivity of the labour force, but more recent studies have shown that innovative social investment programmes such as conditional cash transfers have a direct impact on human capital formation and thus on economic development. For example, Rawlings (2005) has shown that conditional cash transfer schemes in several Latin American countries significantly increased school attendance. Similarly, studies of South Africa's social assistance grants (Patel & Triegaardt, 2008) reveal that these programmes improve nutritional standards and promote school attendance, contributing positively to human capital formation. Research conducted in South Africa also shows that social assistance benefits are often used to fund microenterprises and that the 'pension days' at which social assistance benefits are distributed are characterised by thriving markets at which a variety of locally produced commodities are bought and sold. Social policy scholars have much to learn from this research when formulating arguments to support their contention that social security is not a wasteful consumption expenditure but a positive investment that contributes to development.

4. Conclusion: Enhancing policy exchanges

In this paper I have argued that closer links should be forged between academics in the interdisciplinary field of social policy who have undertaken extensive research into what is known as 'social security' and those in the social development field who have focused on what is called 'social protection'. Although they share a common commitment to enhancing the well-being of the world's peoples, reducing poverty and creating a more just and equal society, they differ on what policies and programmes might best achieve this. As I have shown, the social policy perspective is primarily concerned with statutory social security schemes in Western 'welfare states', while the social development perspective has given more priority to household and community-based interventions in the developing world.

Nevertheless, I contend that these two perspectives have much to learn from each other. Besides sharing common interests, they would find that there are a number of topics that present fruitful opportunities for policy learning as well as addressing challenges. I have discussed some of these in this paper and I have suggested that closer collaboration would have useful policy implications. Collaboration and mutual policy exchanges could also generate a unified 'one world' perspective that has global relevance and could be helpful to policymakers and practitioners working in very different economic, social and cultural environments. Although social protection has evolved in different ways in different societies, and should be suited to local conditions, efforts should be redoubled to foster a unitary perspective that transcends academic boundaries to produce concepts and principles of global relevance.

Because academics working in social policy and development studies have not collaborated extensively in the past, more opportunities for mutual exchanges should be created. Certainly both would benefit from becoming more aware of each other's work. As I have noted earlier, social policy scholars are largely unfamiliar with the social development literature and remain largely unaware of the now quite frequent publication of papers on social protection in mainstream development studies journals. Similarly, the sizable body of literature on social security in social policy is seldom cited by those working in the social development field. Efforts to enhance the awareness and ultimately the integration of this knowledge should be enhanced. More opportunities should also be created for joint research and publication.

Collaboration could also be fostered by increased academic visits and exchanges. Although these are well developed in social policy, international academic exchanges between scholars in the Western countries are much more common than exchanges between scholars in the developing world, or between those from high income and low income countries. Funding opportunities that foster exchanges of this kind should be more systematically explored. This could also promote joint research projects that could integrate knowledge from the two fields. Finally, international gatherings such as the symposium held at the University of Johannesburg in May 2011 should be convened with greater frequency. Events of this kind provide an excellent opportunity to exchange ideas, share research findings and address the many challenges of formulating effective social protection policies and programmes that will enhance the well-being of the world's people.

References

Ahmad, E, Dreze, J, Hills, J & Sen, A (Eds), 1991. Social Security in Developing Countries. Clarendon Press, Oxford.

Armstrong, BN, 1932. Insuring the Essentials: Minimum Wage plus Social Insurance – A Living Wage Program. Macmillan, New York.

Cichon, M & Hagemejer, K, 2007. Changing the development policy paradigm: Investing in a social security floor for all. International Social Security Review 60(2/3), 169–96.

Dercon, S, 2005. Risk, insurance and poverty. In Dercon, S (Ed.), Insurance Against Poverty. Oxford University Press, New York, pp. 9–37.

de Schweinitz, K, 1943. England's Road to Social Security. University of Pennsylvania Press, Philadelphia, PA.

Frazier, MW, 2010. Socialist Insecurity: Pensions and the Politics of Uneven Development in China. Cornell University Press, Ithaca, NY.

Hall, A & Midgley, J, 2004. Social Policy for Development. SAGE, London.

Loewe, M, 2006. Downscaling, upgrading, or linking? Ways to realize micro-insurance. International Social Security Review 59(2), 37–59.

MacPherson, S, 1982. Social Policy in the Third World: The Dilemmas of Underdevelopment. Harvester, Brighton.

Midgley, J, 1984. Social Security, Inequality and the Third World. Wiley, New York.

Midgley, J, 1995. Social Development: The Developmental Perspective in Social Welfare. SAGE, London.

Midgley, J, 2008. Social security and the economy: Key perspectives. In Midgley, J & Tang, KL (Eds), Social Security, the Economy and Development. Palgrave Macmillan, New York, pp. 51–82.

Midgley, J, 2009. The institutional approach to social policy. In Midgley, J & Livermore, M (Eds), Handbook of Social Policy. SAGE, Thousand Oaks, CA, pp. 181–94.

Midgley, J, 2011. From mutual aid to microinsurance: Strengthening grassroots social security in the developing world. Social Development Issues 33(1), 1–12.

Myrdal, G, 1957. Rich Lands and Poor: The Road to World Prosperity. Harper, New York.

Myrdal, G, 1970. The Challenge of World Poverty. Penguin, Harmondsworth.

Patel, L & Triegaardt, J, 2008. South Africa: Social security, poverty and development. In Midgley, J & Tang, KL (Eds), Social Security, the Economy and Development. New York, Palgrave Macmillan, pp. 85–109.

Rawlings, LB, 2005. A new approach to social assistance: Latin America's experience with conditional cash transfer programmes. International Social Security Review 58(2/3), 133–62.

Reynaud, E, 2002. The Extension of Social Security Coverage: The Approach of the International Labour Office. ILO, Geneva.

Sabates-Wheeler, R & Devereux, S, 2007. Social protection for transformation. IDS Bulletin 38(3), 23–28.

Seers, D, 1969. The meaning of development. International Development Review 11(4), 1–6.

Sirojudin & Midgley, J, 2011. Grassroots social security in Indonesia: The role of Islamic associations. In Midgley, J & Hosaka, M (Eds), Grassroots Social Security in Asia: Mutual Associations, Microinsurance and Social Welfare. Routledge, New York, pp. 123–35.

Townsend, R, 1994. Risk and insurance in village India. Econometrica 62(4), 539–92.

Van Ginneken, W, 2007. Extending social security coverage: Concepts, global trends and policy issues. International Social Security Review 60(2/3), 39–59.

Van Ginnekin, W, 2010. Social security coverage extension: A review of recent evidence. International Social Security Review 63(1), 57–76.

Webb, B & Webb, S, 1927. English Law History: Part I, The Old Poor Law. Longmans Green, London.

Webb, B & Webb, S, 1929. English Law History: Part II, The Last Hundred Years. Longmans Green, London.

World Bank, 1994. Averting the Old Age Crisis. Policies to Protect the Old and Promote Growth. World Bank, Washington, DC.

Trajectories of social protection in Africa

Stephen Devereux[1]

Social protection in contemporary Africa is the product of several strands of social policy, from European social security systems to humanitarian relief interventions. Contributory social security mechanisms such as unemployment insurance and pensions were imported to Africa during the colonial period, but cover only a minority of formally employed workers. Food aid alleviates hunger but does not resolve problems of chronic food insecurity. Cash transfers are being promoted as an alternative to food aid, but have been criticised for being ineffective against price inflation and underwriting neoliberal economic policies. Some programmes link social transfers to public works employment and microfinance, with the aim of 'graduating' participants off social protection. This article argues instead for a 'social contract' approach – recognising the right to social protection, empowering passive beneficiaries to become entitled claimants, and introducing social audits to hold duty-bearers accountable for effective and equitable delivery of citizen-driven social protection policies.

1. Introduction

Social protection in Africa today is woven from several strands of complex and diverse pre-colonial, colonial and post-colonial histories. This article explores two of these strands – European social security provision and humanitarian relief interventions – to develop an argument about the limitations and potential of the evolving discourse, in terms of delivering effective and comprehensive social protection.

This paper makes its argument in three steps. First I demonstrate that the current social protection policy agenda in Africa is not indigenous but largely imported. I identify two specific trajectories of social protection in Africa (there may also be others). One trajectory started with the adaptation of European social security models, which were first applied to the formally employed workforce in African countries in the form of contributory pensions and unemployment insurance and have more recently been extended to the informal and self-employed sectors in the form of targeted cash transfer programmes such as 'social pensions'. The other trajectory started with ad hoc humanitarian responses by the international community to food security shocks in Africa and developed towards quasi-institutionalised social assistance and social insurance mechanisms such as public works programmes for the seasonally underemployed and weather-indexed insurance for farmers.

In the second step I argue that attempts to graft these imported models onto domestic policy agendas have failed to recognise that the economic and social structures of African countries are fundamentally different from those of Europe, resulting in grossly inadequate coverage and programmatic responses that fail to meet the actual social protection needs of local populations. In the third step I propose an alternative model, based on the construction of a rights-based 'social contract' for social

---

[1] Research Fellow, Centre for Social Protection, Institute of Development Studies, Brighton, UK.

protection at national level, which would generate a third trajectory – from largely unaccountable and often externally financed social assistance projects towards accountable, nationally owned social protection systems.

2. Antecedents

Formal social security systems originated in Europe as one set of policy responses to the 'great transformation' (Polanyi, 1944) during the 18th and 19th centuries. The emergence of the modern nation-state and of 'self-regulating markets' as organising institutions of liberal economies was associated with dramatic economic transitions and social dislocation. Industrialisation triggered a mass movement of rural populations to towns and cities, to work in factories and offices. Urbanisation was accompanied by the commodification of labour, which meant that labour power previously devoted to growing food for the family was now dedicated to producing profits for employers.

'Social protectionism', understood here as an 'intervention in the market economy in order to secure the cultural and social integrity of humankind and/or society (e.g. welfare-state redistribution and the regulation of the economy)' (Drahokoupil, 2004:837), evolved to protect society against the negative consequences of market forces. Drahokoupil (2004) identifies two contradictory readings of social protectionism in Polanyi's *The Great Transformation*. The 'balancing principle' reading is that social protection insulates society against self-regulating markets – it is a necessary counter-balance to economic liberalism and can produce a sustainable equilibrium. The alternative 'market pathology' reading sees social protection as an interference in the functioning of the self-regulating market that will lead inevitably to its destruction. This tension can also be framed in terms of class struggle – if 'self-regulating markets' serve the interests of capital, 'social protectionism' serves the needs of labour. In the contemporary social protection discourse, the tension between economic and social concerns manifests itself in complaints (from economists, business, ministries of finance) about 'dependency syndrome' and the 'unaffordability' or 'unsustainability' of labour market interventions and social welfare programmes.

Urbanisation and industrialisation had two important implications for social reproduction and the 'demand' for and 'supply' of social protection. On the demand side, urbanised former farmers lost their access to subsistence through own production and became dependent on the labour market for survival. Instead of relying on rainfall and harvests for their food and income, they now relied on regular payments in the form of wages or salaries from employers, with which they purchased food and other essentials from commodity markets. On the supply side, in pre-industrial societies informal social protection, according to Polanyi, was organised according to the behavioural principles of reciprocity, redistribution and householding, but these principles were displaced by the economic rules of the market. Traditional informal providers of social protection – kin and community – were undermined by the disruption of community bonds, the weakening of affective relationships and the *anomie* of urban lifestyles.

Similar concerns about the dialectical relationship between 'formal' and 'informal' social protection have pervaded policy debates for decades. In South Africa, where social pensions were extended to urban Africans in 1944, rural Africans were excluded for some years because the 1943 Social Security Commission argued against providing benefits that would 'conflict with or break down their traditional food sharing habit' (Devereux, 2007:543).

Responsibility for guaranteeing subsistence to individuals and families who could not support themselves shifted away from relatives and neighbours and became the responsibility of the market and the state. A complex array of formal social protection instruments was devised to ensure the reproduction of the labour force. Adults with labour capacity need (contributory) social security for periods when they are not working – unemployment insurance, retirement pensions and paid maternity and sick leave. Dependants who are not working – children, older persons, people living with disabilities – need state-funded (non-contributory) social welfare if their private support systems are inadequate. The foundations of this model were devised in Bismarck's Germany in the 1880s, institutionalised in the UK following the recommendations of the 1942 'Beveridge Report', which argued for a social insurance system that would guarantee a minimum standard of living 'below which no one should be allowed to fall', and later evolved into the range of 'welfare state regimes' (Esping-Andersen, 1990) now found across the European Community.

This model was also exported across much of Africa, Asia and Latin America by European administrators during the colonial era of the late 19th and early 20th centuries. In Africa, the earliest social security systems were introduced in South Africa and North Africa. Although based on employee contributions, agricultural and self-employed workers were sometimes encouraged to join (e.g. in Egypt and Tunisia), with incentives such as lower contribution rates. In francophone West Africa, voluntary retirement plans for civil servants during the colonial period became compulsory schemes based on defined benefits after independence. In former British colonies, provident funds for public sector workers were also introduced after independence, usually as compulsory savings schemes to provide insurance against unemployment or retirement. Some countries, especially those affected by armed conflict (such as Somalia) do not yet have institutionalised social security systems, while others (such as the Democratic Republic of the Congo) have seen theirs destroyed by internal instability (Bailey & Turner, 2002).

But how well do European models of social security map onto the African context? Arguably, not well at all. In most African countries, the urban and industrial transitions have not yet happened. Most Africans still live in rural areas where they depend on farming for a living and on relatives or neighbours when their livelihood fails (i.e. householding, reciprocity and redistribution). Both these features present challenges to the European social security model. First, in industrialised economies the majority of workers are employed in a 'standard employment relationship', with written contracts that entitle them to a regular income from which contributions to social security can be automatically deducted. A minority of people live in poverty, do not have access to regular paid work and depend on social welfare. In African countries this economic structure is reversed: a minority have contractual employment, but the majority live outside the formal sector, with no job security, irregular and unpredictable incomes and no opportunity to make regular social security contributions. Coverage of national social security schemes or contributory provident funds reaches only the few who have a 'standard employment relationship' in the public and private sectors – typically, less than 15% of the population. A major challenge is to 'extend social security to all', in contexts where most of the working population are either self-employed farmers or pursuing a meagre and often precarious living in the informal sector.

Second, rural livelihoods are very different from urban livelihoods. Seasonality brings predictable cycles of hard work and under-employment, full and empty granaries, low food prices when the harvest has been reaped and high prices when the crops are still in the field. Rural people know what it is to face the annual 'hungry season'. Farmers face food crises, usually triggered by adverse weather events. Poor smallholders with only a little land and struggling to afford seeds and fertiliser face persistently low yields and chronic hunger. Recognising that problems in accessing inputs and food are both symptoms of low income – or 'entitlement failure', in Sen's phrase (1999) – many African governments have introduced cash transfers rather than food aid as a solution to chronic poverty and food insecurity. But whether cash transfers are the most effective policy response to the inherent variability and unpredictability of rural African livelihoods remains open to question.

Third, labour markets are more complex in Africa than in Europe, and are becoming more so. The notion that people are either contractually employed or unemployed does not hold where there are high levels of informal employment and self-employment. Moreover, labour markets across the world are becoming increasingly 'informalised' (Standing, 2008) and it is not just the unemployed who are vulnerable but also casual, seasonal and other low-paid workers. Innovative thinking is needed to extend social security coverage and 'decent work' principles (ILO, 2006) to vulnerable workers of all kinds, and also to defend the employment contracts and associated rights to social security that are being eroded by labour market 'flexibilisation'.

A further impetus for social protection in Africa was dissatisfaction with decades of humanitarian relief, especially emergency food aid. Humanitarian relief is not targeted at individuals on the basis of their employment status; instead, it provides temporary assistance to families who have lost their livelihood, for instance following a drought that destroys harvests. Unlike social security, which is rules-based, humanitararian relief is entirely discretionary. Critics of emergency food aid argue that while it alleviates the symptoms of food insecurity, it does little to address the underlying causes (Clay et al., 1998). Similarly, evaluations of project food aid (food-for-work, supplementary feeding, school feeding schemes) in many countries have found little or no discernible impact on chronic food insecurity, though it should be noted that food-for-work and school feeding schemes also have broader developmental objectives. A stronger criticism is that decades of food aid in Africa have merely perpetuated the demand for food aid – by weakening farmers' incentives to grow food, inhibiting market development, distorting consumer preferences, enabling donors to institutionalise surplus disposal, and allowing aid-dependent governments to neglect investment in agriculture and rural livelihoods (Barrett & Maxwell, 2005).

On the other hand, food aid does respond directly to real food security needs. Whether cash transfers can buy food security in a self-provisioning agrarian economy depends on the functioning of local markets. If access to food is restricted at household level but not at local or national level, cash works (it restores access to food when entitlements fail), but if food availability is constrained at local or national level, then cash works less well (and food aid works better).

Cash transfers have recently been introduced as a drought response in several African countries, with varying success. In some cases where drought has caused food production to collapse, cash transfers have been effective in replacing access to food through production (growing one's own food) with access to food through markets (buying food). In drought and other emergency scenarios in Africa cash transfers can even help to strengthen weak markets, by providing an incentive for traders to bring food from surplus to deficit areas. In other countries, cash transfers have worked less well. In Malawi, Lesotho and Swaziland, emergency cash transfers were supplemented with food aid, to ensure that drought-affected households had some access to food if local markets failed. Also, the value of the cash transfer was benchmarked against the cost of a basic food basket, and in the Food and Cash Transfers project in Malawi it was adjusted every month as local food prices rose and fell. In non-emergency contexts, many PSNP (Productive Safety Net Programme) participants in Ethiopia who had initially received cash transfers chose to revert to food aid or cash plus food in 2007, when food prices started rising faster than the value of the cash transfer (Sabates-Wheeler & Devereux, 2010). In neighbouring northern Kenya, participants in the Hunger Safety Net Programme have seen the purchasing power of their cash transfers drop by two thirds since the programme started in 2008, because of rapid and uncompensated food price inflation.

Notwithstanding the persistence of food aid, especially in emergency situations, social protection in Africa has become dominated by regular cash transfers to targeted vulnerable households in rural communities, a modality that is reminiscent of an incipient social welfare system. Looked at this way, the 'cash versus food' debate, which has preoccupied the social protection discourse in Africa until recently, can with hindsight be reinterpreted as a struggle between the social welfare lobby and the food security lobby within development policy, with food aid being negatively characterised as backward-looking, self-serving (surplus disposal by donors) and paternalistic (denying beneficiaries choice), while cash transfers are positively characterised as forward-looking, progressive and 'modern'. The displacement of food aid by cash transfers is not just a technical choice between alternative modalities: it signifies a broader move away from a humanitarian approach towards a welfarist approach. In a sense, the hegemony of cash transfers is a victory for the 'modernisation' and commodification of social protection in Africa.

3. Ideological critiques

Although they have been widely adopted and evidence of their benefits is accumulating, large-scale social transfer programmes in Africa have been subjected to ideological criticism from both the right and the left. Critiques from the right resonate with social welfare debates in Europe. Handouts, especially to able-bodied adults, are predicted to create perverse incentives for behavioural change – people who could and should be self-reliant might choose free support from the state instead ('dependency syndrome'), or even adjust their behaviour in order to qualify for humanitarian relief or social assistance ('moral hazard'). Examples would be if farmers in Ethiopia stopped farming in expectation of receiving food aid, or if young women in South Africa deliberately fell pregnant in order to receive the Child Support Grant (CSG).

Studies have in fact been conducted on both these scenarios, but there is little empirical evidence for dependency syndrome or moral hazard in either case (Devereux, 2010).

In rural Ethiopia, food aid is not guaranteed or predictable and is usually inadequate to meet a family's food needs, so no rational farmer would stop farming in the hope of being given enough food aid, and promptly, to compensate for lost production and to smooth consumption (Little, 2008). The incentive to alter behaviour rises with the value and predictability of the transfer, so regular social welfare programmes such as the CSG are stronger candidates for 'leakages' to people who do not really need them than are ad hoc emergency relief interventions. In South Africa, anecdotal claims that teenage fertility has increased since the CSG was introduced in 1998 have been refuted by an empirical study that showed that teenage pregnancies had in fact stabilised by 1998, that only 20% of teenagers with children receive the CSG, and that trends in fertility among teenagers were similar across all socio-economic groups, including those who would not qualify for the CSG (Makiwane & Udjo, 2006).

Critiques from the left question the political motivation for social protection, especially in countries pursuing neoliberal economic policies, where delivering social transfers to the poorest citizens is often interpreted as a palliative measure designed to quell social unrest and deflect calls for alternative economic models or radical political reforms. Countries with high levels of inequality – such as South Africa, Namibia and Botswana, which all have well-developed social protection systems – are especially susceptible to this criticism. South Africa's post-apartheid blend of neoliberal economic policies and progressive social policies has justifiably been described as a 'strange and often incoherent mix of policies and interventions' (Seekings & Nattrass, forthcoming:23). Neoliberalism reproduces economic growth and prosperity for a minority alongside chronic poverty and unemployment for the majority, who receive compensation in the form of social grants – a nominal level of redistribution that contains but does not substantially reduce either headcount poverty or income inequality (Leibbrandt & Woolard, 2010) and serves to legitimise the economic growth strategy.

When South Africa's extensive social grants system is discussed as a possible model for other African countries, the phrase 'South African exceptionalism' is often heard – especially in the context of affordability, since South Africa (like Botswana and Namibia) is undeniably wealthier and has a higher revenue base than, say, Ethiopia or Malawi. But South Africa is also a more urbanised, less agrarian society – which explains why the European model of social security plus social grants seems more appropriate at first glance. The problem is that the South African economy is not structured like a European economy. Most significant is the fact that unemployment in South Africa does not affect just a residual minority – an extremely high proportion (30 to 40%) of adults are unemployed, and most of them have no access to social insurance (the Unemployment Insurance Fund has limited coverage) or to social assistance (the Extended Public Works Programme also has limited coverage). Social grants are designed to reach non-working vulnerable groups such as the young (the CSG), older persons (the Old Age Pension) and people with disabilities (the Disability Grant) – but many unemployed or underpaid adults end up depending on these grants: in other words, they become dependent on dependants. This is not the intention, but it is the inevitable consequence of a hybrid blend of neoliberal economic policies and progressive social policies. In other southern Africa countries where non-contributory social pensions have been introduced, including much poorer countries such as Lesotho and Swaziland, dependence of working-age adults on these transfers has also been observed.

4. Labour market linkages

A comprehensive and sustainable approach to social protection needs to address failures in the labour market as well as provide social welfare for the non-working poor. A statistical decomposition of household incomes in South Africa reveals that wealthier citizens survive mainly on wage or salary income, while the poorest survive mainly on social grants (Leibbrandt & Woolard, 2010). This raises a fundamental question. Does the rapid and dramatic expansion of social grants indicate successful social policy or a failure of labour market policy? South Africa is applauded globally for the scope and generosity of its social grants system, but a radical critique might argue that these grants effectively underwrite an unemployment rate of over 30%, rather than compelling the government to make more sustained efforts to tackle the structural causes of poverty, by intervening directly in the labour market to reduce unemployment.

That is not to say that the employed are guaranteed access to social security. In South Africa workers' rights have been extended in recent years through progressive labour legislation to ensure decent working conditions, a statutory minimum wage and access to social security, including unemployment insurance. Perversely, these positive trends have been accompanied by accelerated casualisation of vulnerable sectors of the workforce, such as domestic workers and farm workers, as employers take steps to evade the costs of meeting their obligations under the law, leaving many workers less protected than before.

Interventions such as the PSNP in Ethiopia and the VUP (Vision 2020 Umurenge Programme) in Rwanda seem to have discovered an elegant solution to the reality that social protection needs to compensate for both a failure of labour markets – with the concomitant loss of access to social security – and a failure of most African governments to deliver social welfare to their poor non-working citizens. In effect, these programmes deliver both a labour market intervention for working adults and social grants for the dependent poor. The PSNP and VUP both offer temporary employment (public works) for unemployed or underemployed adults – though without the social security and decent working conditions of a 'standard employment relationship' – and unconditional transfers (direct support) for poor individuals who cannot work. The unconditional transfers were always intended to be a 'residual' component. In Ethiopia, this residualism was codified in an informal rule of thumb – in the 1990s, a public works programme called the Employment Generation Scheme was complemented by Gratuitous Relief, but the two were supposed to be delivered in a ratio of 80:20. The assumption was that most dependants were resident in households with working adults who could be employed in public works activities. In the PSNP, 'full family targeting' is applied, meaning that payments are made in direct proportion to household size, allowing working adults to earn cash or food for themselves as well as their non-working dependants.

Moreover, employment in public works was never intended to be a permanent feature of the PSNP or VUP. Instead, public works participants are supposed to 'graduate' within three to five years, by reaching a level of food security or self-reliance where they no longer need access to subsidised employment. But the debate about graduation is confused. Firstly, when the International Food Policy Research Institute (IFPRI) designed graduation thresholds for Ethiopia's PSNP, they converted household asset values into cash and concluded that a household had graduated when the value of its assets exceeded a threshold value. This approach is evidence of a fundamental misunderstanding about the nature of agrarian livelihoods in Africa. A calculation of the poverty headcount in a panel survey in Ethiopia showed very different rates at different times of year – because of seasonality, poverty is substantially higher before the main annual harvest than after (Dercon & Krishnan, 1998). This is mirrored in findings from the nutrition literature, where adult body weights and child malnutrition rates are often reported as varying seasonally, but poverty surveys in Africa never record different poverty rates for the 'hungry season' and the 'post-harvest' season. Yet calculating the value of a household's assets at one point in time (which point in time?) says nothing about the ability of the household to withstand seasonal stress and its resilience against future shocks, which should be a key indicator of success for a social protection intervention. The preoccupation with graduation reveals a contradiction between establishing an effective and permanent safety net against cyclical seasonality and occasional crises, and a linear (but unrealistic) vision of economic growth where poor people are assisted to move smoothly up the income ladder until they are no longer poor, at which point the safety net can simply be removed.

A second limitation of graduation thinking is that it places too much pressure on cash transfers and public works to solve the structural problems that generate and perpetuate poverty and food insecurity in rural Africa. The assumption was that the vicious cycles of dependency and disincentives associated with food aid would be converted into virtuous cycles of asset accumulation and income growth through cash transfers and the infrastructure created by public works projects. But this ignores the precarious nature of livelihoods, the thinness of commodity markets and near-absence of financial intermediation, the failure by governments and donors to invest in agriculture over several decades, and the grossly inadequate asset base (in terms of land, livestock and inputs) that most farming families face. Also, despite its proponents' expectation that recipients will invest cash transfers in assets and inputs for more productive and sustainable livelihoods, in contexts of chronic and seasonal hunger, where the transfer covers only part of the family's food needs, it is inevitable that most of these transfers will be consumed. Indeed, the fact that substantial proportions of even small cash transfers are invested in agriculture, education and other productive purposes, as evidence shows, is quite remarkable.

Recognising this challenge, the PSNP added 'other food security programmes' and then the 'household asset building programme' to the menu of public works and direct support, with the aim of helping PSNP participants to generate supplementary streams of income, for instance, by keeping bees to produce and sell honey. This intervention has proved difficult to implement at scale, and the limited number of livelihood options supported means that local markets tend to be flooded quickly, so relatively few participants have successfully graduated through this route. In Rwanda, instead of livelihood packages, VUP participants are offered access to low-interest loans through the Ubudehe Credit Scheme, either as individuals or in small groups. Access to the scheme requires a business plan that demonstrates how the loan will be used to generate enough income to repay the loan within one year and generate sustainable streams of income thereafter. This component was launched in 2010 and there is no evidence yet to show whether it is facilitating large-scale graduation.

Even if working adults who participate in public works and/or take an asset building package do achieve a level of income and assets that allows them to leave the PSNP better off than when they entered it, most direct support beneficiaries by definition have no prospect of ever graduating. Although the 80:20 rule of thumb has been applied on the PSNP, the scale of the programme means that approximately one million Ethiopians are currently receiving direct support transfers. Despite its antipathy to social welfare and its fears of generating long-term dependency on social transfers, the government of Ethiopia does recognise the imperative to address the needs of these people, as well as those of public works participants who have not yet graduated when the current phase of the PSNP ends in 2014. Options for transferring the direct support caseload from the PSNP to the Ministry of Labour and Social Assistance are being seriously considered (Devereux & Teshome, 2009). Whether the same trajectory will be followed in Rwanda and other African countries where cash transfers and public works are compensating for the absence of social welfare provisioning and labour market failures remains to be seen.

5. Social contracts for social protection

The preceding discussion has identified two complementary functions of social protection: as social assistance in the absence of fully fledged social welfare systems, and as a labour market intervention in the absence of fully fledged social security or insurance mechanisms. Nonetheless, social protection does not completely compensate for the limited coverage of social welfare and social security in contemporary Africa. Two related deficits in the design and delivery of social protection need to be addressed: the absence of social contracts and the fact that most social protection is supply-led rather than demand-driven.

The first challenge is not, as is often asserted, to build political will for social protection but rather to construct a social contract for social protection in each country – which immediately problematises the dominant role of donors and international non-governmental organisations (NGOs) in designing, delivering and financing social protection in much of Africa. A rights-based approach has some merits in establishing a social contract, but rights must be realised. The terms 'rights-holder' and 'duty-bearer' are useful for identifying the actors involved and their roles and responsibilities, but a politician's signature on a document such as the 1948 Universal Declaration of Human Rights, the 1966 International Covenant of Economic, Social and Cultural Rights or the 2006 Livingstone Declaration on social protection means nothing until it produces a real programme that delivers real benefits. Central to a social contract approach is the establishment of enforceable claims to social protection. If citizens have a right to demand protection from the state, for instance, they cannot be told they have 'graduated' and be removed prematurely from social protection programmes.

Terminology matters. The term 'beneficiary' is too passive and paternalistic (beneficiaries do not necessarily get their benefits in full and on time, and they might benefit more from a different or better designed programme – beneficiaries are rarely consulted about their priorities). The term 'client' is too closely associated with the commodification of social protection, whereas social protection should be about social solidarity and collective responsibility, which is obscured by the language of consumers and markets. The term 'claimant' carries several positive connotations. First, claimants are entitled to receive certain prescribed social protection benefits (grants and/or services), rather than a vaguely defined 'right to social protection' that governments can easily evade through recourse to the cop-out clause of 'progressive realisation'. Second, if social protection benefits are not delivered to people who are entitled to receive them, mechanisms can (and should) be established to enable these people to claim them. These mechanisms include social audits, rights committees, grievance procedures, or even taking the government to court. Here the constructively adversarial role of domestic civil society can be powerful, and in South Africa civil society activism has achieved notable successes in extending the access and scope of interventions such as the CSG (Proudlock, 2011). Conversely, the 2009 decision by the Ethiopian government to pass the 'NGO law', effectively barring NGOs from campaigning for any rights at all, is a blow to the formation of a social contract between the state and its citizens and relegates civil society participation in social protection to the role of implementing agencies or service providers.

A third argument for the term 'claimant' and for enforceable claims is not just that eligible individuals should receive specified social grants and services but that these should be delivered in full, on time and at minimum inconvenience (e.g. in terms of distance to pay-points, queuing time, access costs and security risks). Poor and vulnerable people are entitled to be treated with dignity and sensitivity. So the claim should cover not only the benefit but also the way it is delivered, and the claimant should be able to hold the duty-bearer to account on both aspects. This approach is more real, more enforceable, more defined and broader than an abstract right to social protection. In Africa, where most governments have signed up to the right to social protection but social protection is often delivered in the form of projects funded by external donors and implemented by international NGOs, an enforceable claim bridges the gap between unaccountable donors and unenforceable rights.

Finally, seeing social protection as an enforceable claim requires the transfer of certain powers from those who deliver benefits such as social grants to those who receive them. This goes beyond allowing beneficiaries to participate, or consulting them; it implies empowering them as claimants. Lessons can be drawn from recent innovations in India, where social audits 'create a collaborative and constructive platform for participatory governance of social protection programs ... provide the most vulnerable with a "voice" to assert their "rights" [and] hold the village and local administration accountable' (Vij, 2011:2).

Elements of empowerment are filtering into some African programmes. The Cash and Food Transfer Pilot Project in Lesotho, which delivered cash or food to drought-affected households in 2007/08, set up help desks where people who believed they were eligible but had been excluded could lodge their complaint. The Hunger Safety Net Programme in Kenya has established a rights charter that specifies the responsibilities of administrators and beneficiaries, and rights committees to whom both included and excluded people can complain if they feel badly treated or overlooked by the programme (Devereux & White, 2010). South Africa's new National Development Plan argues for introducing social audits to its social grants programmes, 'not only because this would enhance the effectiveness of these programmes, but also because it would empower poor and vulnerable citizens and deepen the process of democratic inclusion' (NPC, 2011:347). These are small but significant first steps towards making social protection in Africa not just more comprehensive, but more responsive, accountable and citizen-driven.

References

Bailey, C & Turner, J, 2002. Social Security in Africa. ILO (International Labour Office), Geneva.
Barrett, C & Maxwell, D, 2005. Food Aid After Fifty Years: Recasting its Role. Routledge, London.

Clay, E, Pillai, N & Benson, C, 1998. Food aid and food security in the 1990s: Performance and effectiveness. ODI Working Paper 113, Overseas Development Institute, London.

Dercon, S & Krishnan, P, 1998. Changes in poverty in rural Ethiopia 1989–1995: Measurement, robustness tests and decomposition. Working Paper Series 98-7, Centre for the Study of African Economies, Oxford.

Devereux, S, 2007. Social pensions in southern Africa in the twentieth century. Journal of Southern African Studies 33(3), 539–60.

Devereux, S, 2010. Dependency and graduation. Frontiers of Social Protection Brief 5, Regional Hunger and Vulnerability Programme, Johannesburg.

Devereux, S & Teshome, A, 2009. Options for Direct Support in Ethiopia: From Productive Safety Net Programme to Social Protection System. Report commissioned by DfID (Department for International Development), Ethiopia. Institute of Development Studies, Brighton.

Devereux, S & White, P, 2010. Social protection in Africa: Evidence, politics and rights. Poverty and Public Policy 2(3), 53–77.

Drahokoupil, J, 2004. Re-inventing Karl Polanyi: On the contradictory interpretations of social protectionism. Czech Sociological Review 40(6), 835–49.

Esping-Andersen, G, 1990. The Three Worlds of Welfare Capitalism. Polity Press, Cambridge.

ILO (International Labour Organization), 2006. Social security for all: Investing in global social and economic development. Issues in Social Protection. Discussion Paper 16, ILO, Geneva.

Leibbrandt, M & Woolard, I, 2010. Trends in inequality and poverty over the post-apartheid era: What kind of a society is emerging? Paper presented at Conference on Overcoming Inequality and Structural Poverty in South Africa: Toward Inclusive Growth and Development, 20–22 September, Johannesburg.

Little, P, 2008. Food aid dependency in northeastern Ethiopia: Myth or reality? World Development 36(5), 860–74.

Makiwane, M & Udjo, E, 2006. Is the Child Support Grant Associated with an Increase in Teenage Fertility in South Africa? Evidence from National Surveys and Administrative Data. HSRC (Human Sciences Research Council), Pretoria.

NPC (National Planning Commission), 2011. National Development Plan: Vision for 2030. Government Printer, Pretoria.

Polanyi, K, 1944. The Great Transformation. Rinehart, New York.

Proudlock, P, 2011. Lessons learned from the campaigns to expand the Child Support Grant in South Africa. In Handa, S, Devereux, S & Webb, D (Eds), Social Protection for Africa's Children. Routledge, London, pp. 149–75.

Sabates-Wheeler, R & Devereux, S, 2010. Cash transfers and high food prices: Explaining outcomes on Ethiopia's productive safety net programme. Food Policy 35(4), 274–85.

Seekings, J & Nattrass, N, forthcoming. Policy, politics and poverty in South Africa. Mimeo, University of Cape Town, Cape Town.

Sen, A, 1999. Development as Freedom. Oxford University Press, Oxford.

Standing, G, 2008. Economic insecurity and global casualisation: Threat or promise? Social Indicators Research 88(1), 15–30.

Vij, N, 2011. Building capacities for empowerment: The missing link between social protection and social justice. Case of social audits in Mahatma Gandhi National Rural Employment Guarantee Act in India. Paper presented at Conference on Social Protection for Social Justice, 13–15 April, Institute of Development Studies, Brighton, UK.

Social protection, redistribution and economic growth

David Piachaud[1]

Social protection has conventionally been associated with redistribution and equity. This paper examines the effects of different types of social protection on economic growth. It looks at the possible effects on human capital formation, on physical investment and innovation, on the local economy and on the macroeconomy, discusses these effects in theory and reviews empirical evidence of such effects. It considers the widely varying impacts that different types of social protection can have on the distribution of incomes and on economic growth. The paper concludes that, in analysing, assessing and planning social protection, it is crucially important to consider the potential drawbacks – and the benefits.

1. Introduction

This paper is concerned with the effects of social protection. Here the use of the term 'social protection' follows the United Nations Research Institute for Social Development definition:

> As a key component of social policy, social protection is concerned with preventing, managing and overcoming situations that adversely affect people's wellbeing. It helps individuals maintain their living standard when confronted by contingencies such as illness, maternity, disability or old age; market risks, such as unemployment; as well as economic crises or natural disasters. (UNRISD, 2010:135)

The most obvious effect of social protection is that it redistributes income between members of the society. This may benefit those less well off, those exposed to certain contingencies or certain groups in society. Social protection schemes may also affect people's social and economic behaviour, which may in turn affect economic growth. These redistributional and growth effects may be thought of as, respectively, static and dynamic. Redistribution involves moving a fixed quantity of resources between people. If such redistribution affects economic growth, it influences the availability of resources and income levels in the future. Although redistribution has received the most attention, in the long run the effects on growth are most important for overall income levels, and differences in effects on growth at different income levels determine long-run distributional effects.

The relationship between the development of social security and economic development has been given little attention, whether in the social policy or the economic development literature. One notable exception is the work edited by Midgley & Tang (2009); in it, Midgley examines the concept and origin of social security and, drawing on his earlier

---
[1] Professor of Social Policy, Centre for Analysis of Social Exclusion (CASE), London School of Economics, UK.

work (Midgley, 1984), provides a typology or classification. The country case studies show the different ways in which social security has developed, or not, and how social security has been affected by and has affected economic development. The study is of pioneering importance in challenging the widely held assumption that social security impedes economic development. Midgley and Tang's approach is based on comparing national experiences. In this paper, the focus is on the processes or mechanics of the relationship between social protection and economic growth.

In discussing the distributional and growth effects of social protection, it is important to recognise that there is no one entity that is 'social protection'. This may seem contradicted by recent reports from the OECD (2009) and the European Report on Development (2010) and major academic studies from Barrientos & Hulme (2008) and Ellis et al. (2009) – all of which have 'social protection' in their title. But the term 'social protection' is used, often loosely, to cover many different types of schemes. Clarity about what is under discussion is essential. It is also essential to consider costs as well as benefits. Redistribution involves some gains and some losses. Assuming that the cost can be met miraculously or from external sources is not at all helpful; every scheme has an opportunity cost.

The effects of social protection schemes depend on the social and economic context in which they operate: one size does not fit all. The objective here is to highlight and hopefully clarify some important issues that have been largely neglected in the past.

The paper proceeds as follows. Section 2 differentiates types of social protection, Section 3 describes a range of possible behavioural effects, Section 4 discusses theories of economic growth and considers how social protection may affect growth, Section 5 surveys empirical international evidence of the effects of social protection on growth, Section 6 discusses the redistributive effects and possible implications for economic growth of different types of social protection, and Section 7 concludes.

2. Types of social protection

Social protection in many industrialised economies has become frighteningly complex, requiring highly skilled advisers to advise claimants and undermining any sense of understanding and social solidarity supporting the social security system.

Most social protection falls into one of three types. These are:

- *Selective social assistance for the relief of poverty:* Such assistance – often also called a safety net, a minimum income guarantee, a make-up level, an income top-up and many other names – is principally designed to relieve poverty. Negative income taxes and some tax credit schemes are also a form of social assistance. Income tax is usually paid by those with income above a certain level; in negative tax schemes, payments (or negative taxes) are made to those with incomes below certain levels. Such schemes are usually administered by tax authorities rather than social welfare agencies. For all these forms of social assistance eligibility is based on a test of income (and in some cases capital).
- *Social insurance:* This form of social protection is usually for contingencies such as retirement, unemployment or sickness although it can be for other risks such as crop failure. Eligibility usually depends on contributions. It may be financed on a funded or a pay-as-you-go basis. It may involve some cross-subsidy to lower income groups, to those caring for children or to people living with disabilities.

- *Universal categorical benefits:* These are benefits paid to people in certain circumstances without tests of income or capital. One type of universal benefit is a basic income grant (BIG), also known as a citizen's income or 'demogrant'. It has been advocated by some as a replacement for all other social protection arrangements that would provide all citizens with a basic income, without any test of means, paid for out of taxation. Other universal benefits are restricted to only certain categories of people – including children, pensioners or people living with disabilities.

These three benefit types do not exhaust the range of social protection. Benefits can be both categorical and means-tested, as with the South African Child Support Grant. Social insurance can operate alongside social assistance, as occurs in the UK. Partial basic income grants have been advocated subject to tests of eligibility. Finance can come from diverse sources in different proportions with different degrees of progressivity. Any redistributional policy can only be assessed by taking into account both who benefits and who pays.

There are other important features that characterise and distinguish other aspects of social protection. These include:

- *Conditionality:* How far benefits depend on meeting conditions relating to work, such as job search behaviour or accepting reasonable employment, to educational attendance of children, to health checks or other requirements.
- *The form of benefits:* Whether they are paid in cash, food, food stamps or other ways.
- *The payment of benefits:* Whether they are paid monthly or weekly and whether they are paid to heads of household, wage earners, mothers or other people.
- *The administrative structure:* Whether benefits are assessed according to national or local rules, administered by government or agencies, what languages they are administered in, the accessibility of offices, the rights to obtain advice or appeal and many other important administrative aspects.

Here only the variations in types and finance of social protection are considered since these are most directly relevant to redistribution and economic growth.

3. Behavioural effects

This section sets out the range of possible effects – sometimes referred to as incentive effects – that social protection policies have on individuals, households, the wider society, the economy and the nation. In later sections these possible effects are discussed in relation to the different types of social protection and the different means of finance.

Claims about possible negative behavioural effects, which have been given considerable prominence in the discipline of economics, include the assertion that social protection may discourage private protection by the individual or family, thus discouraging work effort, saving and family support. Moreover, if the financing of social protection requires higher taxation or contributions it may discourage work effort or saving.

Behavioural effects may be negative or positive, depending on wider considerations. Such effects are:

- *Effects on household formation and household separation:* Social protection may help individuals to live together with others or on their own, or hinder them from doing so.

- *Effects on child-bearing*: Child support grants could encourage more births, yet if families become more prosperous as a result, they may decide to have fewer children.
- *Effects on survival and mortality:* Social protection may enable more people to survive famine, yet if the population grows as a result, income per head may be lower, leading to increased mortality rates.
- *Effects on family and community provision:* With more individual protection, families and the wider community may be encouraged to make greater provision without the fear of having to take on total responsibility; on the other hand, they may think less is needed from them and reduce their support.

Some behavioural effects are likely to be positive. Social protection may:

- Promote private consumption, for example improving nutrition.
- Promote investment in human capital and increase the return on past investment in human capital through education and health programmes.
- Enable people to maintain contact with the labour market, which they may not be able to do if they become destitute.
- Promote the local economy.
- Maintain employment and the level of aggregate demand in the economy and keep down unemployment. Social protection may perform the role of automatic economic stabiliser.
- Promote confidence in the future and thereby encourage savings and investment.
- Promote social cohesion and stability.
- Promote trust in the government.
- Encourage growth in the economy as a result of reducing poverty and inequality.

To summarise, social protection may have negative or positive (or neutral) behavioural effects. A balanced assessment of behavioural effects is crucial. These effects clearly depend on the form of social protection.

4. Social protection and economic growth in theory

The relationship between social protection and economic growth has received remarkably little attention from social scientists. For example, the important recent books on social protection by Barrientos & Hulme (2008) and Ellis et al. (2009) barely mention possible effects on growth.

If social protection simply achieves a redistribution of income between individuals and households and has no effect on behaviour in the short or long run, it may reduce poverty and inequality yet will have no effect at all on economic growth. However, there can be little doubt that if social protection involves a substantial redistribution of income it has a significant effect on economic growth.

The influence of social protection on economic growth cannot be discussed without first examining what is meant by economic growth and how it is to be measured. Conventionally, economic growth is measured by estimating the change in aggregate national production or income and adjusting for price changes (and adjusting for population change to obtain per capita growth). This method measures *aggregate* economic growth. A very different measure is to take all the income units and measure their change of income and then take the *average* of these changes. If all units experienced the same growth, the aggregate and average growth rates would of course be the same. In a very unequal economy such as that of South Africa, it is possible for income to increase in the top decile but to fall in all other deciles and still record positive growth overall. If, however, growth was pro-poor, i.e. higher for the poor, the *average* growth rate would exceed the *aggregate* growth rate. It is therefore important to consider possible effects on economic growth not only in aggregate but also at different income levels.

Theories of economic growth have changed markedly over time. In the late 1940s and 1950s, the Harrod-Domar model focused on the rate of saving and capital accumulation. In the 1960s and 1970s, Solow stressed the importance of technical progress and Kaldor emphasised the importance of investment for technical progress. In the 1980s and 1990s, Romer and others pointed to the importance of endogenous growth, with technical advancement coming from people developing ideas, experimenting and looking for niche markets; there are externalities from new ideas and techniques.

All these theories are relevant to the discussion of how social protection could affect economic growth. It may also be useful to distinguish five types of capital that are relevant to economic growth: physical, financial, human, social, and natural or environmental. With the possible exception of the last, all these types of capital could be affected by social protection.

How then can social protection affect economic growth?

One answer is that it will inevitably *reduce* economic growth. Economics is sometimes known as 'the dismal science'. Such is the dominance of free market ideology in most economists' thinking that any intervention in the market, including social protection, is assumed to be potentially damaging and to have only one possible effect, and that is to reduce the rate of economic growth. The greater the intervention, the more dire the effect. Such an assumption, or belief system, is rarely thought to need any empirical justification. Where justification is offered, it is often by reference to massively interventionist systems such as the 'iron rice bowl' system of pre-reform China in which social equalisation was imposed, together with rigid central planning of production, with negative effects on economic growth. Yet evidence from such extremes tells us nothing about the effects of more moderate and practical attempts at relieving poverty or reducing inequality.

In essence, social protection could:

- Protect and encourage human capital formation.
- Encourage investment and innovation.
- Promote the local economy and make use of local knowledge.
- Have positive effects on the society and economy.

4.1 The protection and encouragement of human capital formation

At the extreme, social protection keeps people alive. When a person dies their education and skills die with them. As John Donne wrote, 'Any man's death diminishes me'. Without adequate income a child's education may be interrupted, a curable disease may be left untreated. Social protection could complement human capital formation and help preserve it. The adage 'Give a man a fish and feed him for a day. Teach a man to fish and feed him for a lifetime' is simple and appealing. It suggests education should take absolute priority over social protection. The reality is much more complex; feeding children may be a prerequisite for improving education.

4.2 Encouragement of investment and innovation

Whether struggling to feed themselves and their families or providing shelter, the poor are engaged in complex investment decisions – what to plant and when, whether to raise a goat or some chickens, whether to spend time rebuilding mud walls, whether to spend money acquiring a tin roof. When consumption is barely adequate for subsistence, reducing it further in order to invest is hard. Investment decisions made by the poor are critical. Far more depends on their investment decisions than on those of the wealthy.

Increasing income security may encourage risk-taking and promote investment in physical and human capital. Those on the lower income levels risk actual starvation if they make risky investments. Those on the higher income levels merely have to wait before replacing their car or manage without a second home. When those on the lower income levels are protected, their ability to invest – even in just the basics such as tools, seeds or a bicycle – is increased. Further, it is the poorest for whom the marginal efficiency of capital (the return on an investment) is likely to be the highest.

This can be illustrated with a simple example. Consider a possible investment in, say, a new variety of seed. The investment has a 90% probability of success (increasing income by half) and a 10% probability of failure (that income will fall by half). Table 1 shows the effects on A and B, who have respective initial incomes of 100 and 200 each. The average effect is the effect on income adjusted for the probabilities of gains and losses – in this case an attractive 40% gain on average. If A relies totally on the crop produced by this new seed variety, however, and the amount needed for survival is 60, then using the new seed involves a 10% risk of starving to death – hardly an attractive investment. If a social protection scheme boosts A's income by 10, the downside risk is no longer starvation and the innovation is far more likely to be adopted.

Risks are inevitable for all. But, as Drèze & Sen (1991:3) write:

> The lives of billions of people are not merely nasty, brutish and short, they are also full of uncertain horrors. An epidemic can wipe out a community, a famine can decimate a nation, unemployment can plunge masses into extreme deprivation, and insecurity in general plagues a large part of mankind with savage persistence.

Table 1: Risk and investment

	Initial income	Failure	Success	Average income
A	100	50	150	140
B	200	100	300	280
A + social protection	100 + 10	60	160	150

The poorer a person is, the worse the consequences of adverse events. By reducing the possible adverse consequences of risky investment behaviour, social protection can encourage innovation and thereby promote economic growth.

4.3 Promoting the local economy and using local knowledge

Social protection allows people to spend money on what they want, and since their desires are based on local knowledge, their spending could aid the local economy with local multiplier effects. Providing social protection to the poorest is most likely to have the highest local multiplier effects as extra income is spent on local products produced by other low income earners. By contrast, many interventions designed to help the poor consist of doing things for the poor, to the detriment of the local economy. The distribution of international food aid for example generally undermines local agriculture. Teachers, doctors and other professionals who live in the more prosperous urban areas and provide their services in rural areas do not boost the local economy in the process. Yet this is an inevitable consequence of the top-down provision of services.

Injecting spending power into poorer areas has a number of benefits including the real possibility of a multiplier effect, which could eventually culminate in a higher level of prosperity for the community and greater transparency. As Bryden (2010:253–4) writes:

> [T]here is a general issue of the gap between economic power and political democracy which applies at all levels of society and government, always made worse by inequality between citizens in income, wealth and education. With any given pattern of material inequality, the mechanisms of control at the local level are potentially more effective and less disastrous, since they are often more transparent and subject to scrutiny.

4.4 Macro effects

Poverty and inequality can undermine social cohesion and social stability. Lack of economic demand can lead to unemployment and economic depression. Responding to social needs through social protection can increase trust in and support for the government. The promotion of social justice can boost general confidence in the future and, as a result, investment in the economy and in the social fabric may increase. Through all these routes, social protection can encourage economic growth.

5. Evidence of the effects of social protection on economic growth

In theory, then, social protection could have positive consequences for economic growth, particularly in poor communities, and these benefits could outweigh the adverse effects predicted by many economists. But of course what really matters is what happens in practice. While empirical evidence to substantiate likely benefits is limited, research shows that there are indeed some positive connections. When considering the positive connections discussed below, it needs to be kept in mind, however, that generalisation about social protection is dangerous, as different types can have very different consequences and what seems effective in one context may not necessarily be effective in another.

5.1 Human capital

The most obvious effect of extra income is on food intake:

> Not surprisingly, if poor households receive extra income, they increase their food expenditure and calorie consumption significantly. Empirical evidence – for example, for Bolivia, Brazil, Chile, Côte d'Ivoire, Ghana, India, Indonesia, Pakistan, Philippines, Malaysia, Nicaragua and Peru – also indicates the positive effects of family income change on child schooling. (Ranis et al., 2000:198)

How extra income is spent depends on the recipient of this income:

> Where women control cash income, it appears that expenditure patterns are geared relatively more toward Human Development inputs, such as food and education. For example, among Gambian households, the larger the proportion of food under women's control, the larger household calorie consumption. (Ranis et al., 2000:198)

In South Africa, it was found that:

> Over a quarter of Black South African children under age 5 live with a pension recipient. ... pensions received by women had a large impact on the anthropometric status of girls ..., but little effect on that of boys. In contrast [there was no] similar effect for pensions received by men. (Duflo, 2000:i)

A recent study of the impact of the South African Child Support Grant found that:

> Early life receipt of the CSG (in the first two years of life) ... improves height-for age scores for children whose mothers have more than eight grades of schooling. Since children's cognitive development depends on receiving appropriate nutrition in the first few years of life, this result provides important evidence of the CSG's role as an investment in human capabilities – a critical determinant of multi-dimensional poverty reduction ... Children who enrolled in the CSG at birth completed significantly more grades of schooling than children who were enrolled at age six, and received higher scores on a math test ... Analysis of adolescent risky behaviours provides evidence of the CSG's impact in significantly reducing six main risky behaviours – sexual activity, pregnancy, alcohol use, drug use, criminal activity and gang membership. (DSD, SASSA & UNICEF, 2012:iii–iv)

When looking at the effects of social grants on human capital, most studies have focused on conditional cash transfers (CCTs), where the social protection is granted subject to the existence of certain human capital related behavioural aspects. Bastagli (2010:9–10) provides a comprehensive summary of these studies, with a particular focus on Latin America, where CCTs were developed:

> Studies show that, in some countries, CCTs improved intermediate education and health indicators in terms of service utilisation. ... CCTs have been successful in increasing rates of school enrolment and attendance and in reducing dropout rates. In Mexico, *PROGRESA* [a government social assistance programme] led to increases in enrolment in secondary school, reductions in repetition and dropout rates in primary and secondary school and in years of schooling completed. In Nicaragua ... [CCTs] led to an

increase in school enrolment of 13 percentage points. Impacts on school enrolment in both countries are higher for poorer children, suggesting that CCTs help reduce inequalities, beyond income measures. However, there is no evidence of significant CCT effects on learning. For Mexico ... longer exposure to *Progresa/ Oportunidades* has a positive impact on grades of schooling attained, but no effects on achievement tests.

CCTs have led to improvements in health care service use. Studies reveal positive effects on the use of preventive infant care, check-ups during pregnancy, after birth and in early childhood.

It is not always clear whether the effects of CCTs can be ascribed to the extra income or to the conditions that need to be in place in order for the transfers to be made. However, the laxity with which the conditions are often enforced does indicate that the effects can largely be ascribed to the extra income. As Bastagli (2010:9) writes:

> The monitoring of conditionalities, involving the regular collection and transmission of information on beneficiary behaviour, has not been consistently implemented as envisaged by programme regulation ... In practice, responses to non-compliance in some countries were not implemented or were only gradually administered as regular monitoring was stepped up. In Brazil, the first cancellation of *Bolsa Familia* benefits as a result of conditionality non-compliance took place in 2007, that is, four years after the launch of the programme.

5.2 Investment

There is a large amount of literature on the impact of risk on the economic behaviour of low income households. The OECD's explanation (2009:21) is perhaps most clear:

> In order to reduce their vulnerability to unmanageable risks poor households often engage in low productivity and low profitability economic activities, only because they are also less risky than high productivity/ profitability alternatives. For example, poor farmers may adopt safer but lower yielding crop varieties, helping prevent a slide into absolute destitution but also foreclosing promising opportunities to break free from poverty ... As a result, vulnerability to poverty is a major brake on human and economic development. In particular, lack of reliable risk management mechanisms is a major barrier to contributions by the poor to the growth process.

5.3 Local economy

A study of a pilot basic income grant scheme in Namibia showed that:

> Income has risen in the community since the introduction of the BIG by more than the amount of the grants. There is strong evidence that more people are now able to engage in more productive activities and that the BIG fosters local economic growth and development. Several small enterprises started in [the central Namibian village of] Otjivero, making use of the BIG money being spent in the community. (Basic Income Grant Coalition, 2008:10)

By contrast, official development assistance has been criticised for focusing on the urban and industrial sectors, thereby increasing economic inequality between urban and rural areas. Food aid from overseas may undermine local farmers.

The great variety of agricultural conditions means that generalisations made by experts from distant cities or from abroad may be inappropriate. As Johnston wrote (in Riddell, 1987:240):

> Given the complexity of the issues of agricultural development and the lack of knowledge concerning the distinctive and extremely heterogeneous characteristics of African agriculture, it is important to recognize that ignorance and uncertainty with respect to the design and implementation of agricultural strategies are unavoidable and serious handicaps.

While this 'negative' evidence of the limitations of external support does not prove that local knowledge is superior, it certainly indicates that social protection channelled through the local economy may be of greater benefit than external assistance. A Department for International Development review of cash transfers cited the following evidence:

> In Ethiopia, 15 percent of participants in the Productive Safety Net Programme ... used their transfers to invest in farming, and 8 percent purchased livestock. In Zambia, the Kalomo Social Cash Transfer Scheme led to an increase in the ownership of goats from 8.5 percent of households to 41.7 percent. It also led to four times more households engaging in investment activity, and a doubling of the amounts invested. In Malawi, a study of the Dowa Emergency Cash Transfer ... programme found economic multiplier impacts exceeding two kwacha for every kwacha disbursed. In Paraguay, CCT beneficiary households invested between 45 and 50 percent more in agricultural production. The programme also increased the probability that households would acquire livestock by 6 percent. In Mexico, on average 12 percent of transfers from the *Progresa/ Oportunidades* programme were invested in productive activities such as microenterprises and agriculture. Average rates of return were 18 percent. The transfers allowed households to overcome credit constraints. The secure income may have made them more willing to take on riskier (but potentially more rewarding) investments. (DFID, 2011:36)

5.4 Macro effects

There is much evidence that inequality – which social protection tends to reduce – is harmful to economic growth. As Ranis et al. (2000:203) argue:

> Recent empirical evidence suggests that the distribution of assets and income has an effect on economic growth, with a more equal distribution favouring higher rates of growth ... [A]n unequal distribution of income may be associated with greater political and economic instability, more likely to interrupt economic progress.

Another review of the evidence concludes:

> Macro-level studies ... provide robust evidence that initial income inequality and subsequent growth are inversely related, and that better income and wealth distribution helps growth. (Mkandawire, 2004:9)

But this evidence is not undisputed. A meta-analysis by De Dominicis et al. of 22 studies containing 254 estimates of the link between economic growth and inequality, as measured by the Gini coefficient, concludes that:

> In the empirical literature, the majority of cross-sectional studies have found a negative correlation between income inequality and growth. However, the negative effect disappears when the models are estimated using panel datasets and associated estimation techniques. (De Dominicis et al., 2006:21)

There is a further problem in that causation may run in two directions – inequality can affect growth, but growth can affect inequality.

It is almost impossible to say with certainty how social protection affects trust in government, social stability and general confidence in the future – all factors that affect economic growth. What can be said, going on the experience of industrialised nations, is that some degree of social equity is essential for social, economic and political stability, which in turn has formed the basis of economic growth. Social protection has been the principal means of achieving this equity. Without social protection, the political ramifications of unabated poverty would have severely curtailed the development of modern industrialised economies; social amelioration has been central to political legitimation. Yet separating social protection from the many other factors involved in estimating its precise contribution is probably impossible and has certainly never been achieved.

6. Types of social protection and their potential effects

It was stated in the Introduction that generalisations about 'social protection' are almost entirely devoid of meaning and that costs, or financing, must be considered alongside benefits. This section reviews the different types of social protection and clarifies the issues they raise for redistribution and economic growth. The types are those outlined in Section 2, although they cover many variants.

Social assistance policies can be divided into two broad categories:

- *Safety net or minimum income schemes:* These schemes bring the income up to some minimum, with a 100% withdrawal or tax rate – i.e. those with zero income receive the minimum and those with the minimum from earnings or other sources receive zero.
- *Tapered or negative income tax type schemes:* Those who earn some income retain a portion of this, often 50%, until the benefit is tapered to zero.

Social insurance policies are generally based on contributions and confined to those in the formal, waged economy. The contingencies covered have in most countries been old age, unemployment and sickness.

Universal categorical benefits can be divided into two principal types:

- Those paid to all, such as a basic income grant.
- Those paid only to certain categories of people, such as all children or all people over a certain age.

How then do the redistributive effects and possible behavioural and economic growth consequences of these types of social protection differ? This depends, of course, on how the social protection is financed; here it is assumed that it is financed out of taxation.

If behavioural effects are not taken into account, there is no doubt that targeted social assistance policies – safety net and to a lesser extent tapered or negative income tax schemes – are the most effective means of tackling poverty and reducing inequality.

Social insurance, if confined to those in formal employment, is likely to exclude the majority of southern Africa's poorest citizens and is therefore extremely ineffective as a means of tackling poverty. Universal categorical benefits are redistributive providing they are paid for only by those in the highest income levels. Since children or older people may be significantly worse off than the general population, benefits targeted at them may be more redistributive.

In terms of behavioural effects and impact on economic growth, the different types of social protection are likely to have hugely different impacts.

Social assistance policies lead to strong disincentive effects for those directly involved. With the most targeted scheme (safety net policies), it makes no difference to net income whether original income is at the minimum level or is zero. There is, in effect, a 100% tax rate on any earnings up to the minimum level. With a tapered, negative tax scheme the tax rate is 50%. Thus, inevitably, schemes of this type will have major effects on behaviour. If, as is likely, work effort is reduced, economic growth will be reduced over the long term.

Social insurance schemes are essentially redistributive between stages of the life-cycle, between the employed and the unemployed, and between the healthy and the sick. There are no clear-cut or predictable effects on work effort or economic growth.

Universal categorical benefits have no dramatic incentive effects on the recipients, but the taxes levied on them can have some effects.

Overall, the social protection policies that seem most likely to be effective in tackling poverty while encouraging positive effects on human capital formation, investment and the local economy are universal categorical benefits focused on categories whose members are most likely to be poor; these universal categorical benefits policies should be funded by progressive taxation.

7. Conclusions

'Social protection' can mean many things. It can help poor people or it can benefit prosperous people. It can accelerate economic growth or it can destroy incentives and discourage growth. It has been argued that it can result in very different redistributive effects and that the implementation of social protection can have very different consequences for economic growth.

It might, therefore, be helpful if the term 'social protection' was never used again and, instead, specific types of schemes were clearly described – but this is not likely to happen. It would certainly be better if at all times schemes were presented as redistributive, with some gaining and some losing. And, most important of all, the behavioural effects need to be considered.

It has been argued that some types of social protection have positive behavioural effects that promote economic growth. The ready, and facile, assumption that has long been the conventional wisdom in the discipline of economics – that any form of social protection undermines the 'animal spirits' of the free market and damages economic growth – lacks any serious foundation. On the other hand, to assume that just any form of social protection is good is equally unjustifiable. The primary purposes of social protection have always been, and must remain, to reduce poverty, to relieve those suffering most severely from 'the slings and arrows of outrageous fortune' and create a more just society. Social protection has not been, and should not be, conceived of as primarily a policy to promote economic growth. Yet in the long run the dynamic effect that social protection has on economic growth – and the disaggregated effects on the growth of incomes of different groups – is as crucial to social justice as the more immediate redistributive effect.

This conclusion is not new, nor is it sufficient for social protection, or indeed any social policy, to be adopted. As Mkandawire (2004:9) has written:

> [R]ecognition of the transformative and productivity-enhancing quality of measures that contribute to social development does not necessarily lead to their adoption, not even in democratic political settings where numbers would tend to favour the poor. Even the widespread recognition of 'social capital' has not been sufficient to place social policy at the core of development policies.

Why do 'social' policies continue to be seen as luxuries – desirable if and when they can be afforded – but not priorities or fundamental to economic performance? Few central bankers, economics ministers or professional economists show much interest in social protection. (John Maynard Keynes, as distinguished an economist as any in the last century, was one of the few who did.) There are four possible reasons. First, there is the mystique of the market and the implication that whatever distribution results from it must be for the best and that any interference will be damaging. Second, there is a prevalent view that social protection is only concerned with social 'casualties', the 'losers' and 'also-rans' in the economic race. Third, there is the suspicion that social protection is subverted or abused in practice. Fourth, there is the top-down detachment of the prosperous: the business community, economists and politicians who do not think the economic life of the poor is as important as theirs. Whatever the reasons for neglecting the economic importance of social protection, this paper has sought to show that such neglect is unjustified, indeed wholly wrong.

It does not follow that *any* form of social protection is right or good. As discussed in Section 6, different forms of social protection have entirely different effects on poverty and inequality and are likely to have very different effects on economic growth. What remains true is that there is considerable uncertainty about the effects of social protection, particularly its effects on economic growth. Although much evidence has been cited on the possible positive effects of certain types of social protection, this evidence cannot be transposed across time and place to predict future effects with any confidence. What this suggests is the need to experiment and to evaluate such experiments, in order to learn about actual effects on redistribution and on economic growth. Without experiments, separating the effects of social protection from all the other changes that occur in an economy is almost impossible. Yet experiments are expensive and difficult – particularly because many think that social protection, if it is to be fair and socially just, must be available to all. However, since, as is argued here, the effects of social protection on economic growth are uncertain, there is a real need to experiment and learn. In the long run that will make the greatest contribution to fairness and social justice.

If priority is given to targeting any social protection at the poorest, as social assistance schemes do, then this inevitably reduces incentives to individual effort – and can destroy them altogether. Thus concentrating social protection only on the poorest may superficially appear to be the fairest policy, but in the long run, through the effects on incentives and on economic growth, it is almost certainly a misguided polity. Equally, concentrating social insurance on those with stable, formal employment is likely to be of little help to most of the poor. Thus basing social protection on either income testing or insurance principles seems an unproductive route for progress. In southern Africa, universal categorical benefits appear to be the most promising basis for progress, with a focus on children probably being the most effective way of tackling poverty.

In the last few years, colossal sums have been taken from the public purse to bail out banks in many countries around the world; this is a form of social protection for the wealthiest in society that some see as robbery by the banks. How far the bail-out was necessary and desirable is beyond the scope of this paper. But if there is a case for protecting banks, how much stronger is the case for developing social protection as a central component of a more cohesive and faster-growing economy?

On the basis of both economic theory and the available evidence, the importance of social protection for both redistribution *and* economic growth means that it should be central not only to social but also to economic policy. The contribution social protection can make to economic growth is crucial.

References

Barrientos, A & Hulme, D, 2008. Social Protection for the Poor and Poorest. Palgrave Macmillan, Basingstoke.

Basic Income Grant Coalition, 2008. Towards a Basic Income Grant for All. Basic Income Grant Coalition, Namibia.

Bastagli, F, 2010. Poverty, inequality and public cash transfers: Lessons from Latin America. Paper prepared for the Conference on Experiences and Lessons from Social Protection Programmes Across the Developing World: What Role for the EU?, organised by the European Report on Development, 17–18 June, Paris.

Bryden, J, 2010. Local development. In Hart, K, Laville, J-L & Cattani, A (Eds), The Human Economy. Polity Press, Cambridge.

De Dominicis, L, De Groot, H & Florax, R, 2006. Growth and inequality: A meta-analysis. Tinbergen Institute Discussion Paper No. 2006-064/3, Social Science Research Network. http://ssrn.com/abstract=921332 Accessed 19 November 2012.

DFID (Department for International Development), 2011. Cash Transfers, Evidence Paper: Policy Division 2011. DFID, London.

Drèze, J & Sen, A, 1991. Public Action for social security: Foundations and strategy. In Ahmad, E, Drèze, J, Hills, J & Sen, A (Eds), Social Security in Developing Countries. Clarendon Press, Oxford.

DSD, SASSA & UNICEF (Department of Social Development, South African Social Security Agency & United Nations Children's Fund), 2012. The South African Child Support Grant Impact Assessment. UNICEF South Africa, Pretoria.

Duflo, E, 2000. Grandmothers and granddaughters: Old age pension and intra-household allocation in South Africa. Working Paper 8061. National Bureau of Economic Research, Cambridge, MA.

Ellis, F, Devereux, S & White, P, 2009. Social Protection in Africa. Edward Elgar, Cheltenham.

European Report on Development, 2010. Social Protection for Inclusive Development. European Report on Development, Paris.

Midgley, J, 1984. Social Security, Inequality and the Third World. Wiley, London.

Midgley, J & Tang, K (Eds), 2009. Social Security, the Economy and Development. Palgrave Macmillan, Basingstoke.

Mkandawire, T (Ed.), 2004. Social Policy in a Development Context. Palgrave Macmillan, Basingstoke.

OECD (Organisation for Economic Co-operation and Development), 2009. Promoting Pro-poor Growth: Social Protection. OECD, Paris.

Ranis, G, Stewart, F & Ramirez, A, 2000. Economic growth and human development. World Development 28(2), 197–219.

Riddell, R, 1987. Foreign Aid Reconsidered. James Currey and Johns Hopkins University Press, London. & Baltimore, MD.

UNRISD (United Nations Research Institute for Social Development), 2010. Combating Poverty and Inequality: Structural Change, Social Policy and Politics. UNRISD, Geneva.

The politics of social protection expenditure and financing in southern Africa

Marianne Ulriksen[1]

Social protection is expanding in southern Africa, but consideration of its fiscal base is usually limited to affordability concerns. Little attention is paid to the different sources of revenue or how the interests of contributors to social protection may affect spending priorities. This article suggests there is a link between revenue source and social protection spending. Aid dependent countries' social protection policy is mostly determined by donors. The governments of countries that rely on natural resources or Southern African Customs Union revenue are relatively free to shape social protection policy. Only in countries that rely on domestic tax-based revenue, where the government must consider the interests of the taxpayer, is there something resembling a social contract for social protection, in which the citizens engage with their government through an exchange-based logic. This article concludes that a broad and diversified tax base is an important mechanism for creating a reciprocal relationship of this kind and thus increasing social spending.

1. Introduction

Since the mid-1990s many countries in southern Africa have introduced or extended social protection policies, be they safety nets, poverty targeted transfers or categorical provisions such as social pensions. Some of these programmes are supported by donor agencies while others are funded by governments using revenue from natural resources or general taxation of trade and consumption. Only in a few cases does direct taxation of the population constitute a relatively large share of governments' fiscal base for social (and other) spending.

Attention is increasingly being paid to the financing side of social protection policies. However, the issue of financing tends to focus on affordability and the importance of political commitment for social spending (Hickey, 2008; Taylor, 2008; Samson, 2009). Yet when discussing how to create political will and foster 'social contracts' for social spending, the literature on social protection has paid little attention to how the choice of social protection policies, and their possible expansion, may be determined both by who benefits from such policies and who pays for them.

This article explores the link between social protection expenditure and financing in southern Africa. Theoretically, it investigates how different sources of financing may affect spending priorities and discusses how the notion of a social contract for social protection expansion can best be understood as an exchange-based logic that includes both beneficiaries of and contributors to social protection policies. Empirically, it

---
[1] Post-doctoral fellow, Centre for Social Development in Africa, University of Johannesburg, South Africa.

examines the link between revenue source and priorities of social protection expenditure in southern Africa. The empirical section also compares four countries in the region (Zambia, Lesotho, Botswana and South Africa), exploring the extent of a social contract for social protection. The empirical analysis suggests that the revenue source tends to determine spending priorities for social protection and that social contracts between states and citizens are fairly rare in southern Africa.

2. Connecting the politics of spending and the politics of financing

The question of social protection expenditure is often considered separately from the challenges of domestic revenue generation. If the issue of financing is taken into account, the concern is usually how best to allocate a given amount of resources. However, if social protection is 'considered to be more than a residual category that merely compensates for market failures ... the financing side has to be treated as an integral part of the problem, and by extension, the solution' (Hujo & McClanahan, 2009:4). There is a need for more research that links financing, particularly taxation, and expenditure (DiJohn, 2010).

Connecting the spending and financing sides allows us to recognise that the source of revenue is closely connected with the type of expenditure: support for and choice of social protection policies is determined both by who benefits from such policies and who pays. In essence, policy making – whether fiscal or social – is not merely a technocratic exercise but the outcome of a political bargaining process where different social and economic groups will seek to promote their policy preferences.

Many studies have focused on 'the politics of social spending'; that is, how the interests and mobilisation of different groups and their political negotiations have affected the priority of specific social policies and the extent of social spending (see for instance Esping-Andersen, 1990; Castles, 1998; Huber & Stephens, 2001; Haggard & Kaufman, 2008). It is for instance well established that low income groups tend to support social protection spending whereas the well-to-do are more reluctant to support it – particularly if they do not benefit themselves (Esping-Andersen, 1990). In environments of perceived fiscal austerity, the threat of social spending cuts is always looming as governments have to decide which of many important areas of spending to prioritise. However, retrenchment of social protection policies may be difficult politically (Pierson, 1994), particularly when those policies provide broad coverage of the population. Beneficiaries of social protection policies become a constituency of which politicians need to be conscious – the wider the reach of social policies and the stronger and better organised the beneficiaries, the harder it will be to cut social spending (Skocpol, 1991; Pierson, 1994).

There has been less scholarly focus on the 'politics of social financing' (Steinmo, 1993; Kato, 2003; Hujo & McClanahan, 2009), which, interestingly, is quite contradictory to the politics of spending. This contradiction can largely be attributed to inconsistencies in public attitudes towards spending and financing (Steinmo, 1993). Citizens desire public spending, and everyone wants to benefit. Hence, social protection spending may be easy to introduce and will be politically popular among beneficiaries. On the other hand, as mentioned, once introduced such social benefits may be hard to cut. The situation with financing is the reverse. Citizens – though they want to benefit – are loath to pay. Tax cuts are politically popular and relatively easy, whereas it is politically difficult to introduce new taxes – particularly if no rewards are in sight for contributors. Hence, policy making is a political process, where policy choice is largely determined by the preferences and interests of beneficiaries as well as contributors. Crucially, as is elaborated in the next section, continued payment can only be assured in the long term if contributors get something in return.

The above discussion of social policy financing focuses on taxation, but it is likely that other revenue sources equally influence the priorities for social spending. The next section describes some types of revenue source salient in the southern African context and discusses how each is likely to affect social protection spending priorities.

2.1 Revenue sources and priorities of spending

Raising domestic revenue is critical to support sustainable social protection spending. In addition, the actual source of revenue is likely to affect the spending priorities. The first type of revenue source considered here is development aid, which provides substantial financing to the poorer countries in southern Africa. Aid makes important contributions to the budgets of low income countries with weak domestic revenue bases, but it also has drawbacks. For instance, social protection interventions are most effective in the medium to long term, which clashes with the short-term horizon of donors (Barrientos, 2008). Aid is also volatile and unpredictable and disturbs the relationship between the state and its citizens as the government must be accountable to donor agencies rather than the general population (Sindzingre, 2009:123–4).

Development aid may seem altruistic, but it is also motivated by the political and economic self-interests of donor countries (Lancaster, 2007). The revenue source of aid is ultimately taxpayers in donor countries. To ensure continued support, aid agencies must provide evaluation reports that demonstrate developmental impacts, efficient spending and sustainability. Even if they attempt to promote local ownership and sustainable development, donors tend to prioritise short-term projects with visible outputs (De Haan, 2009).

Revenue from natural resources appears to offer a convenient opportunity to minimise donor influence. Governments raising revenue from natural resources benefit from a more stable revenue source and are free to prioritise their own spending. However, countries reliant on natural resources often encounter substantial wastage on power preserving activities by the political elite and general misallocation (McGuirk, 2010). As with donor funds, the government gains revenue independently of the citizens, which renders citizens 'unable to exert leverage on the government for public service provision and responsible management' (Moss, 2011:5). There is in fact some indication that high reliance on natural resources causes political leaders to lower the tax burden on citizens, which in turn reduces citizens' demands for democratic accountability (Bornhorst et al., 2009; McGuirk, 2010). Thus, the spending of revenue from natural resources is likely to be determined by the political elites, and citizens may have limited leverage. However, as the political elite aim to ensure continued legitimacy in democratic elections, politicians may choose policies that have wide benefits and immediate and visible impact (Kjær & Therkildsen, 2011).

It has increasingly been noted that, unlike the effects of aid and resource rents, taxation improves democratic representation and state accountability as taxes on the population increase their incentives for public participation and raise their demands for prudent spending (Ross, 2004; Bräutigam et al., 2008; Gupta & Tareq, 2008). Given the recognition that taxation is a stable revenue base and that adequate tax policies can improve public revenue, it is surprising that taxation has received conspicuously little attention in research on social protection (Hujo & McClanahan, 2009; Lesage et al., 2010).

The literature on taxation and state-building follows an exchange-based logic, where the state and citizens establish a contract through which representation and accountability are granted in return for taxation (Timmons, 2005; Bräutigam et al., 2008). A few scholars link taxation directly to government spending. Ross (2004:234) points out that 'citizens ultimately care about the "price" they pay for the government services they receive'. Bates and Lien (1985) emphasise that a revenue-seeking government will find it to their advantage to strike bargains with the citizens they want to tax such that the state defers to citizens' policy preferences in order to induce a greater willingness to pay tax. In fact, it can be assumed that citizens want benefits and services from the state but that 'they would rather someone else pay' – the challenge then is to persuade them 'to see beyond narrow interests and to contribute to the collective welfare through tax' (Lieberman, 2002:93).

Consequently, states tend to provide more benefits and services to taxpayers who contribute more revenue. In a quantitative study of about 90 countries, Timmons (2005) finds that the state will provide the goods desired by the income group that contributes the bulk of revenue – mainly the protection of property rights in the case of the wealthy and basic public services and improved social welfare in the case of lower income groups. In a similar vein, the more tax-intensive welfare states in the West have a high reliance on taxes from labourers' wages, and in turn provide generous welfare spending in line with the preferences of such lower income groups (Cusack & Beramendi, 2006).

The question is not so much whether the tax system is progressive or regressive as from which social group the revenue is raised. For instance, steeply progressive and narrow taxation may cause government to target spending at the main contributors, i.e. high income groups. Conversely, a tax burden borne by all income groups can generate substantial revenues (potentially more so than from a narrow tax base), which in turn can be spent on generous and broad based social protection policies (Steinmo, 1993; Kato, 2003). Alternatively, as is common in many African countries, a state could have a regressive system in which neither upper nor lower income groups are taxed intensively, with subsequent low levels of public spending (Timmons, 2005).

It is also necessary to pay attention to the financing mix (Barrientos, 2008). If a state is able to diversify its tax base, it widens its engagement with different sectors in society and is less reliant on a narrow interest group (DiJohn, 2010). Furthermore, different types of taxes call for different types of bargaining logic. If a tax is easy to evade, the state will need to give a higher return to ensure compliance (Bates & Lien, 1985). If a tax is invisible (such as consumption tax), citizens are less likely to be aware of their contributions and hence less demanding. If, on the other hand, a tax is visible (such as income, profit and property tax), affected citizens are likely to demand substantial returns. Direct and visible taxation may require greater capacity to enforce, but such taxes also reflect greater levels of state–society relation and cooperation (Lieberman, 2002). In fact, direct taxation is a key mechanism in building a relationship based on reciprocity; it becomes an important element in a social contract between a government and its citizens – more so than other revenue sources, as the next section explains.

2.2 Social contract for social protection expansion

It has been suggested that the extension of social protection ultimately requires the development of a politically sustainable social contract (Barrientos & Hulme, 2008; Hickey, 2008; Devereux & White, 2010). The idea of a contract between the citizens and the state has intuitive appeal. However, the social protection literature remains unclear as to the content of such a contract and who participates in it.

Stemming from the works of Hobbes and Grotius, early ideas of a social contract were built on the principle of reciprocity. Basically a device for mutually gainful cooperation, where both parties gain advantages and fulfil obligations (Haddock, 2008; Sen, 2010), the social contract principle arguably corresponds well with the exchange-based logic discussed above, where a government and its citizens establish a contract through which privileges or benefits are provided in return for tax revenue or other contributions. Following this logic, contributors to and beneficiaries of social protection are equally important to the existence of a social contract. However, given that governments need not rely solely on domestic revenue sources, a social contract between a government and its citizens can in reality become meaningless – or one-sided at best. Take for instance development aid as reflected in Table 1, which is an externally controlled revenue source. Not only do donors have a strong influence on spending priorities, but the extent of a social contract is also limited as recipient governments need to be more accountable to donors than to their own citizens.

Revenue from natural resources as well as the SACU (Southern African Customs Union)[2] may improve the extent of a social contract in that governments need not be oriented towards external actors. Instead, this type of revenue is domestically controlled. Yet the relationship remains lopsided and based on an exchange that requires less commitment. As citizens do not contribute, politicians rely on the citizens merely for electoral support and not as a revenue base. Hence, citizens may receive benefits and strongly support the continued existence of such benefits, but they have limited leverage for determining the priority of spending and ensuring accountability.

Table 1: Relation between revenue source, spending and extent of social contract

Revenue source	Priority of spending	Extent of social contract
Externally controlled rents (development aid)	Donor set priorities: short-term spending, visible / developmental outputs e.g. pilots, pro-poor grants	Recipient government oriented towards / accountable to donor
Domestically controlled rents (natural resources / SACU)	Elite prioritise: the elite prefer minimal but broad-based spending to ensure legitimacy	Citizens are beneficiaries, but not contributors: they have limited leverage
Taxation	Citizens (taxpayers) have impact on spending priorities	Interdependent relationship between government and citizens

Note: Rents are understood as non-tax sources of revenue and include revenue from aid, natural resources, and (in southern Africa) the SACU (Southern African Customs Union).

---

[2] SACU is a revenue source specific to the southern African region, as is discussed further in Section 3.

Taxation is clearly the instrument where the citizen gains most leverage vis-à-vis the government. However, the character of the social contract will vary with the nature of the taxation system. As explained above, the larger tax contributors have a stronger influence on policy spending – particularly if such taxation is highly visible and hard to enforce. Quite simply, the 'tax-expenditure nexus signals the fundamental social values of society, the balance of social forces and the kind of "social contract" they have arrived at' (Mkandawire, 2010:1664).

Southern African countries rely on a number of different revenue sources. The nature of the revenue affects the priority of social protection spending and the extent to which there is a social contract for social protection expansion. This is the focus of the following sections.

3. Social protection programmes in southern Africa: An overview

This section describes social protection programmes and the various sources of financing in southern Africa. Supporting this account, Table 2 offers an overview of general national wealth per capita, social protection expenditure, and the share of income (personal and corporate) taxes, indirect (mostly value added) taxes, and rents of total revenue. Rents are non-tax sources of revenue and include revenue from natural resources, aid, and the SACU. Rents from the SACU are essentially revenue from customs and excise and therefore stem from trade and consumption by people (not only citizens) and companies in the union. However, as it is South Africa that collects the revenue and distributes it to the other member states in accordance with a specific formula, SACU funds to Botswana, Lesotho, Namibia and Swaziland are an indirect revenue source; some may even argue that these countries receive financial support from South Africa through this mechanism.

Table 2 lists the countries according to their main revenue sources. Malawi and Zambia are the poorest and the only ones largely reliant on donor funding. Both have very limited social protection legislation, and only a small fraction of the population is part of any formal social security schemes (Social Security Administration, 2009). In recent years, donors and governments have introduced various types of social transfer programmes aimed at the poor.

In Zambia donors have supported five pilot schemes of social cash transfers targeted at the neediest. These schemes were implemented by the Ministry of Community Development and Social Services, which is also responsible for other programmes such as the national government-financed Public Welfare Assistance Scheme. There is a stark contrast between these programmes and the pilot schemes, as the latter receive generous donor funding with ample technical support whereas the government-run means-tested social schemes are underfunded. In fact, despite only covering pilot projects the donors' contribution to the social assistance budget is double that of the government (ILO, 2008; Devereux & White, 2010).

Pro-poor food and cash transfer programmes in Malawi have also largely been externally driven and, despite their perceived significant impact, have remained outside the country's mainstream social protection discourse and without firm government partnership. The government itself has, despite donor antipathy, implemented a Farm Input Subsidy Programme to improve food security for the poor and vulnerable; the programme has been popular among the rural poor (Devereux & White, 2010; Chirwa & Dorward, 2010).

Table 2: Social protection expenditure and revenue sources in southern Africa

	GNI per capita (PPP 2008 US$)	Social protection expenditure (%)[a]	Income taxes, % total revenue	Indirect taxes, % total revenue	Rents,[b] % total revenue
Aid dependent					
Malawi	911	5	24	25	35
Zambia	1 359	6	32	22	25
SACU beneficiaries					
Lesotho	2 021	..	15	11	62
Swaziland	5 132	6	19	10	68
Namibia	6 323	8	23	16	54
Resource dependent					
Angola	4 941	..	6	5	80
Botswana	13 204	4	12	12	69
Domestic resource base					
South Africa	9 812	15	58	34	..
Mauritius	13 344	20	16	48	1

Sources: IMF country reports and statistical appendixes; UNDP Human Development Report (2010); South African Budget Review (2009); Zambia: Social Protection Expenditure and Performance Review and Social Budget, ILO (2008). Data for most recent year. Comparable data for Mozambique and Zimbabwe could not be obtained.

Notes: GNI = gross national income; PPP = purchasing power parity. [a]Expenditure on social security and welfare as a percentage of total government expenditure. [b]Rents include revenue from natural resources, SACU and/or aid.

In Lesotho, Swaziland and Namibia, domestic taxes (income and indirect) account for a relatively small share of total revenues, even proportionally less than in Zambia and Malawi. Unlike their poorer neighbours, these countries receive little aid; instead their governments' revenue comes mostly from the SACU. In Swaziland and Lesotho, incomes from the SACU account for more than 60% of total government revenue. These two southern African kingdoms have limited social protection legislation, though both introduced a non-contributory, universal and government-funded old age pension in 2005. There is little to indicate that the introduction of the pensions was due to any form of popular pressure. Nevertheless, once introduced the small rights-based pensions became popular amongst the electorate (Pelham, 2007; Social Security Administration, 2009; Devereux & White, 2010).

At independence in 1990 Namibia already had some social protection in place. This has subsequently been expanded: the old age and disability pensions have been extended, and the child maintenance grant has increased 10-fold since 2003. The pensions are not means-tested, and though the child grant is, the conditions do not appear to be strongly enforced (Levine, 2010). From 2007 until 2009 a coalition of civil society organisations funded and implemented a pilot project that provided a BIG (Basic Income Grant) to all residents below the age of 60 in Otjivero-Omitara, a typical Namibian town. Although it has been lauded as a great success in fighting poverty and fostering social development, the Namibian government has not been willing to adopt the programme and introduce BIG nationwide (Haarman et al., 2009; Van den Bosch, 2011). The Namibian government receives 37% of its revenue from SACU and 17% from natural resources. Revenue from income taxes is somewhat larger than in Swaziland and Lesotho, though the actual tax base is narrow – conservatively calculated, less than a quarter of the working population pays taxes (NPC, 2006; Weidlich, 2007).

Direct and indirect taxes also play a limited role in the resource dependent countries of Angola and Botswana. In Angola about 80% of government revenue comes from oil exploitation, whereas mineral wealth in Botswana accounts for about half of government revenue (with an additional 18% from the SACU). While limited institutional capacity may reflect inability to enforce taxation in Angola, this is hardly the case in well-administered Botswana. Instead, about two thirds of the Batswana households have such low incomes that they are exempt from paying income taxes (Ulriksen, 2010).

The extent of social protection in Angola is unclear, but it is assumed that the country has limited social programmes and focuses on building health and education services instead. Given Botswana's national wealth, stability, democracy and good governance, it is something of a surprise to find that of all southern African countries, this country spends the smallest percentage of its government revenue on social protection. Of course, a larger overall budget provides more actual money to spend. Even so, most of Botswana's social cash transfers are means-tested, and the universal non-contributory pension offers payments much smaller than those offered in Namibia, South Africa and Mauritius.[3] Botswana has prioritised spending on social services but has focused little on ensuring social protection. Only the well-paid and the formally employed receive social security, and the government offers minimal relief for the poor and vulnerable through various programmes (Nthomang, 2007; Ulriksen, 2010). This is in stark contrast to the only other two countries in the region – South Africa and Mauritius – that are economically and developmentally on a similar level to Botswana.

South Africa and Mauritius are exceptional in southern Africa as both countries have more diversified income bases and rely heavily on domestic taxes (incomes from individuals and companies as well as indirect taxes on goods and services). Though Mauritius traditionally relied heavily on progressive income taxes, the country has increasingly, and in line with international trends, shifted towards indirect taxes (Bräutigam, 2008; Ulriksen, 2010). In South Africa, on the other hand, income tax from individuals and companies still constitutes the largest share. Revenues from mining are included in corporate tax, of which minerals account for about 13%. Personal income tax amounts to 29% of total revenue. However, like Namibia, South Africa's tax base is narrow, with about five-and-a-half million taxpayers out of a population of 49 million (SARS, 2009).

Mauritius and South Africa are also remarkable for prioritising social protection. Mauritius has a long tradition of social welfare that combines social security schemes with social cash transfers across income groups. For instance, all citizens of 60 years or older receive a generous pension that can be complemented by a contributory

---

[3] Even allowing for some uncertainty in calculations due to exchange rates and annual changes to pension rates, Botswana's pension rate is closer to those of Lesotho and Swaziland. Monthly pensions in US$ are as follows: Botswana: 25, Lesotho: 28, Namibia: 42, Mauritius: 90, South Africa: 141 (maximum), and Swaziland: 14 (author's calculations).

pension. In addition, Mauritius is the only country that caters for the working age with a government-funded and strictly targeted unemployment benefit[4] (Bunwaree, 2007; Ulriksen, 2011). South Africa also has a long tradition of social protection – although under apartheid the level of benefits depended on race. Since the mid-1990s the South African government has dramatically extended social protection schemes. There are various types of grant, with the Child Support Grant, Old Age Pension and Disability Grant being most widely used. Though grants are means-tested, the income threshold is fairly high so that many South Africans qualify for a grant. The number of grants beneficiaries is close to 14.5 million (SASSA, 2010).

The southern African examples reflect a pro-poor focus on social protection and a trend of sparse domestic revenue generation, particularly from direct taxation. Many different factors may influence the priority of social protection spending, but it is evident from the southern African countries that differences in social protection spending are also related to the source of revenue. Hence, the aid dependent countries experience a split between donor preferences and national programmes, whereas countries reliant on domestically controlled 'rents' have more freedom to prioritise social protection spending. South Africa and Mauritius (and Namibia to some extent) are interesting in that both taxation and social protection spending are relatively comprehensive for the region.

4. The revenue–expenditure nexus and social contracts: Four case studies

Despite differences across the southern African countries, it is possible to discern some trends regarding the link between revenue source and priority of spending. In order to explore further how this revenue–expenditure nexus affects the extent of a social contract for social protection, I compare two low income countries with different revenue sources (Zambia and Lesotho) and two middle income countries with different revenue sources (Botswana and South Africa). These comparisons are based on the analytical framework shown in Table 1, and the findings suggest that social contracts vary depending on the dominant revenue source and related spending priorities.

4.1 Aid revenue compared with SACU-based revenue in low income countries

It has been argued that in aid dependent countries such as Zambia, the politics of social protection spending are donor driven, largely because most social programmes are financed through aid (Taylor, 2008; Niño-Zarazúa et al., 2010). As discussed earlier, donors in Zambia have promoted social protection pilot schemes targeted at vulnerable groups. Such schemes can be considered well-funded 'islands of excellence' where outputs are visible and the effectiveness of the schemes can be evaluated (by comparison with districts that are not part of a similar scheme).

Donor funded programmes in Zambia are unconnected to government programmes. However, given their resource dominance donors have substantial influence on social protection priorities and the actual implementation of programmes. Donors tend to

---

[4] South Africa has an unemployment insurance fund and Mauritius has recently introduced a workfare programme providing social security and training for the unemployed, but these two programmes are social insurance schemes and not government-funded social protection programmes, which are the focus here.

favour new initiatives rather than build on existing policies (Niño-Zarazúa et al., 2010); government-run social schemes in Zambia are underfunded and neglected. At the same time, donor-funded pilots tend not to take into account local politics and in fact hamper the potential for building a social contract between the government and its citizens. The Zambian government has been reluctant to scale up the projects to the national level (Devereux & White, 2010), for instance, and citizen influence on social protection priorities seems negligible. It is likely that beneficiaries of the pilot schemes would advocate for project continuity, but for the Zambian government it is easy to pass the responsibility to donors. The government itself does not appear to see the political benefit of extending donor projects and including them in government policy, thereby assuming the funding responsibility. As it stands, the future of social protection transfers in Zambia remains unclear (Devereux, 2010).

Despite being almost as poor as Zambia, the government of Lesotho has introduced its own non-contributory old-age pension scheme. The pensions are funded not by donors – who have remained sceptical about the introduction of this policy – but rather by domestically controlled resources (Devereux & White, 2010), which for the most part comprise revenue from SACU. In contrast to the cash transfer pilot projects in Zambia that are limited in scale, time-bound and discretionary, social pensions in Lesotho are rights-based, legally enforceable and permanent (Devereux & White, 2010).

From a social contract perspective, the citizens of Lesotho are not direct contributors to social protection, and it cannot be argued that the social pension was introduced as part of a contract where citizens receive a benefit in return for tax contributions. Instead, as in Swaziland, the decision to commence the social pension came from the political leadership (Devereux & White, 2010). Interestingly, however, and in line with my theoretical discussion, once introduced the pension scheme became a vehicle for social mobilisation. The pension was an important discussion point during the 2007 elections, and many voters revealed, in a post-election survey, that their electoral choice was based on parties' commitment to the pension (Devereux & White, 2010; Niño-Zarazúa et al., 2010). Compared to aid dependent countries, governments in countries reliant on SACU revenue, such as Lesotho, are more able to prioritise social spending. Pressure to expand social protection does not necessarily come from citizens, whose extent of influence and mobilisation relates to the continued existence of benefits.

4.2 Natural resources compared with domestic revenue in middle income countries

In many ways, the politics of social protection in Botswana are similar to those in Lesotho and not, as might be expected, to those in countries that are on a similar developmental and economic level, such as South Africa. Despite the extent of national wealth in Botswana, the overall spending on social protection is small. Policy making in Botswana has been dominated by the top political leadership. Over time, the government has introduced various means-tested social protection programmes targeted only at the very poor and vulnerable. In 1996, the government introduced a universal non-contributory old-age pension. As was the case in Lesotho, this pension was a government initiative introduced without much prior debate at a time when opposition parties were gaining ground in the rural areas that used to be the stronghold of the ruling party (Ulriksen, 2010).

As is the case in Lesotho, only a small proportion of the population actually pay any direct income tax in Botswana, so the social contract is limited. The divided and weak opposition in Botswana has since the 1980s advocated for the introduction of a comprehensive social protection scheme, but this has not been transformed into any substantial citizen demand. The extensive revenue from natural resources has given the Batswana government substantial freedom to prioritise spending, and the government has ensured continued legitimacy through social service spending. It is likely that the ruling party regained some popularity in the mid-1990s by introducing the pension scheme, though a clearer victory in the following elections can also be attributed to a split in the opposition party alliance (Ulriksen, 2010). Although civic mobilisation in Botswana is limited, a political attempt to reduce or means-test the pension could cause dissatisfaction and even protest.

Compared to Botswana, and indeed the southern African region as a whole, South Africa has – like Mauritius – quite an extensive social protection system with a long history. For instance, the old age pension was introduced in 1928 and was amended in 1944 to provide pensions for all South Africans of age 65 or older (subject to means-testing). However, rates differed according to race as it was argued that 'natives should receive lower benefits because they paid lower taxes and had a lower standard of living' (Devereux, 2007:542–3). In fact, there appear to have been strong links between revenue source and priorities of spending during the apartheid era. Modelled on European state welfare policies (Patel, 2005), South African social protection was originally introduced to prevent whites from falling into abject poverty. From a financing perspective, the strategy was to ensure that tax collected from whites also benefited this group. In the same way, spending in the so-called homelands relied on taxes collected by local governments in these areas – more than 90% of local government revenue in the homelands came from their own sources (Mkandawire, 2010).

The post-apartheid government has endeavoured to equalise rates of social protection so not to discriminate on the basis of race and yet still to redistribute across income groups. As illustrated by the old age pension, social protection is tax-funded and reaches almost exclusively the poor black majority (Devereux, 2007; Niño-Zarazúa et al., 2010). Like Namibia, South Africa saw a link between revenue source and spending priorities in the past, yet today there is a separation between those contributing to social protection and those benefiting from it. There may still be a social contract in South Africa in the sense that contributors accept generous social protection spending as a means to rectify past inequities (and this being the case, taxpayers may still feel that they get something in return for their contributions). However, in the long run, taxpayers may become loath to continued contributing if they are uncertain about the returns. In a recent report, the National Planning Commission supports this argument by arguing:

> South Africa has had an implicit compact in which the wealthy pay taxes and the government uses these taxes to deliver services and effect redistribution. This compact will be at risk if people believe that the tax revenues that they contribute are being spent inefficiently. (NPC, 2011:15)

In summary, it is evident from this brief comparison of four southern African countries that the revenue-expenditure nexus affects the extent of a social contract. In Lesotho and Botswana the governments are relatively free to introduce social protection policies as they deem fit, though once in place policies are more difficult to change. In Zambia, the priorities of the donor community prevail. South Africa comes the closest to having a social contract.

5. Conclusion

> While concerns have been raised about the fiscal sustainability of the social pension, its future as a social welfare programme in southern Africa and elsewhere depends mainly on political commitment from governments and taxpayers. (Devereux, 2007:539)

It is often acknowledged that political commitment is critical to ensure sustainable expansion of social protection policies. The role of those providing the fiscal base for spending – taxpayers for instance – is not acknowledged as often. In fact, the important links between the politics of spending and the politics of financing have received insufficient attention.

This is one of the first articles to examine the issues of revenue and expenditure for social protection in an integrated fashion. The above examination of southern African countries offers evidence that revenue source affects the priorities for social protection spending. Furthermore, it is clear that, when the concept of a social contract is based on an exchange-based logic, only a few countries in the region have something resembling a social contract for social protection. The main distinction should be drawn between tax-based revenue and non-tax-based revenue (also called rents). One can only talk about a reciprocal social contract in countries that mainly rely on domestic taxation; in these cases citizens receive benefits from government in return for contributions. In countries reliant on rents – whether aid, natural resources or SACU revenue – the citizens have much less leverage vis-à-vis the government.

The different types of rents affect the priority of spending in distinct ways. In the aid dependent countries of Malawi and Zambia where large parts of the revenue are externally controlled, social protection is divided between underfunded national programmes and donor funded pilot projects. As a recipient government is mostly oriented towards donor requirements, the social contract between the government and its citizens is limited. In Lesotho, Swaziland, Botswana and Angola, social protection spending is largely dependent on elite priorities. SACU revenue is a peculiarity of the region, but in many ways it has characteristics similar to natural resource revenue. These types of domestically controlled rents are not a direct contribution from citizens or donors. In this sense, the government is not bound to commitments made in an exchange agreement (where certain spending is promised in return for contributions), and it has more freedom to prioritise its spending. If there is a social contract in these countries, it is one-sided – citizens do not engage with the state in a relationship based on reciprocity but mostly as beneficiaries of social protection.

Compared to the countries discussed above, most of which rely on different types of rents, South Africa and Mauritius, where the domestic revenue source is also most significant, have more comprehensive social protection spending. Namibia is something of a mixed case as its revenue base has less dominant features (both rents and taxation are prominent).

In conclusion, a broad and diversified tax base is an important mechanism for creating a reciprocal relationship between citizens and the state that may build social contracts for increased social protection spending.

References

Barrientos, A, 2008. Financing social protection. In Barrientos, A & Hulme, D (Eds), Social Protection for the Poor and Poorest. Palgrave Macmillan, Basingstoke, pp. 300–12.

Barrientos, A & Hulme, D, 2008. Embedding social protection in the developing world. In Barrientos, A & Hulme, D (Eds), Social Protection for the Poor and Poorest. Palgrave Macmillan, Basingstoke, pp. 3–24.

Bates, RH & Lien, DH, 1985. A note on taxation, development, and representative government. Politics & Society 14(1), 53–70.

Bornhorst, F, Gupta, S & Thornton, J, 2009. Natural resource endowments and the domestic revenue effort. European Journal of Political Economy. 25(4), 439–46.

Bräutigam, D, 2008. Contingent capacity: Export taxation and state-building in Mauritius. In Bräutigam, D, Fjeldstad, O & Moore, M (Eds), Taxation and State-building in Developing Countries. Cambridge University Press, Cambridge.

Bräutigam, D, Fjeldstad, O & Moore, M (Eds), 2008. Taxation and State-building in Developing Countries. Cambridge University Press, Cambridge.

Bunwaree, S, 2007. The ballot box and social policy in Mauritius. In Bangura, Y (Ed.), Democracy and Social Policy. Palgrave Macmillan, Basingstoke.

Castles, F, 1998. Comparative Public Policy: Patterns of Post-war Transformation. Edward Elgar, Cheltenham.

Chirwa, E & Dorward, A, 2010. Addressing rural poverty in Malawi: The agricultural input subsidy programme. Poverty in Focus 22, 12–15.

Cusack, TR & Beramendi, P, 2006. Taxing work. European Journal of Political Research 45(1), 43–73.

De Haan, A, 2009. How the Aid Industry Works. Kumarian Press, Sterling.

Devereux, S, 2007. Social pensions in southern Africa in the twentieth century. Journal of Southern African Studies 33(3), 539–60.

Devereux, S, 2010. Building social protection systems in southern Africa. Paper prepared in the framework of the European Report on Development, Centre for Social Protection, Institute of Development Studies, Brighton, UK.

Devereux, S & White, P, 2010. Social protection in Africa: Evidence, politics, and rights. Poverty & Public Policy 2(3), 53–77.

DiJohn, J, 2010. Taxation, resource mobilisation and state performance. Crisis States Research Center, Working Paper No. 84, DESTIN (Development Studies Institute), London.

Esping-Andersen, G, 1990. Three Worlds of Welfare Capitalism. Polity Press, Cambridge.

Gupta, S & Tareq, S, 2008. Mobilizing revenue. Finance & Development 45(3), 44–7.

Haarman, C, Haarmann, D, Jauch, H, Shindondola-Mote, H, Nattrass, N, Van Niekerk, I & Samson, M, 2009. Making the Difference! The BIG in Namibia: Basic Income Grant Pilot Project, Assessment Report. Basic Income Grant Coalition, Windhoek.

Haddock, B, 2008. A History of Political Thought. Polity Press, Cambridge.

Haggard, S & Kaufman, R, 2008. Development, Democracy and Welfare States. Princeton University Press, Princeton, NJ.

Hickey, S, 2008. Conceptualising the politics of social protection in Africa. In Barrientos, A & Hulme, D (Eds), Social Protection for the Poor and Poorest. Palgrave Macmillan, Basingstoke, pp. 247–63.

Huber, E & Stephens, J, 2001. Development and Crisis of the Welfare State: Parties and Policies in Global Markets. University of Chicago Press, Chicago.

Hujo, K & McClanahan, S, 2009. Introduction and overview. In Hujo, K & McClanahan, S (Eds), Financing Social Policy: Mobilizing Resources for Social Development. Palgrave Macmillan, Basingstoke, pp. 1–23.

ILO (International Labour Office), 2008. Zambia: Social Protection Expenditure and Performance Review and Social Budget. Social Security Department and ILO, Geneva.

Kato, J, 2003. Regressive Taxation and the Welfare State: Path Dependence and Policy Diffusion. Cambridge University Press, Cambridge.

Kjær, M & Therkildsen, O, 2011. Elections in Africa: Mixed blessings for growth and poverty alleviation. DIIS Policy Brief, June. Danish Institute for International Studies, Copenhagen.

Lancaster, C, 2007. Foreign Aid: Diplomacy, Development, Domestic Politics. University of Chicago Press, Chicago.

Lesage, D, McNair, D & Vermeiren, M, 2010. From Monterrey to Doha: Taxation and financing for development. Development Policy Review 28(2), 155–72.

Levine, S, 2010. New challenges of cash transfers in Namibia. Poverty in Focus 22, 15–17.

Lieberman, ES, 2002. Taxation data as indicators of state–society relations: Possibilities and pitfalls in cross-national research. Studies in Comparative International Development 36(4), 89–115.

McGuirk, E, 2010. The illusory leader: Natural resources, taxation and accountability. Institute for International Integration Studies, Discussion Paper 327. Trinity College, Dublin.

Mkandawire, T, 2010. On tax efforts and colonial heritage in Africa. Journal of Development Studies 46(10), 1647–69.

Moss, T, 2011. Oil to cash: Fighting the resource curse through cash transfers. CGD Working Paper 237. Center for Global Development, Washington, DC.

Niño-Zarazúa, M, Barrientos, A, Hulme, D & Hickey, S, 2010. Social protection in sub-Saharan Africa: Will the green shoots blossom? Brooks World Poverty Institute Working Paper 116. University of Manchester Brooks World Poverty Institute, Manchester.

NPC (National Planning Commission), 2006. Namibia Inter-censal Demographic Survey. NPC, Windhoek.

NPC (National Planning Commission), 2011. Diagnostics Reports, Chapter 2: Nation Building. NPC, The Presidency, Pretoria.

Nthomang, K, 2007. Democracy and social policy in Botswana. In Bangura, Y (Ed.), Democracy and Social Policy. Palgrave Macmillan, Basingstoke, pp. 189–218.

Patel, L, 2005. Social Welfare and Social Development in South Africa. Oxford University Press, Oxford.

Pelham, L, 2007. The politics behind the non-contributory old age social pensions in Lesotho, Namibia and South Africa. Chronic Poverty Research Centre, Working Paper 83. University of Manchester.

Pierson, P, 1994. Dismantling the Welfare State? Reagan, Thatcher and the Politics of Retrenchment. Cambridge University Press, Cambridge.

Ross, M, 2004. Does taxation lead to representation? British Journal of Political Science 34(2), 229–49.

Samson, M, 2009. Social cash transfers and pro-poor growth. In OECD, Promoting Pro-poor Growth: Social Protection. pp. 43–59, Organisation for Economic Cooperation and Development, Paris.

SARS (South African Revenue Service), 2009. Annual Report, South African Revenue Service, 2008/09. SARS, Pretoria.

SASSA (South African Social Security Agency), 2010. Statistical Report on Social Grants, No. 35, October. Monitoring and Evaluation Department, Pretoria.

Sen, A, 2010. The Idea of Justice. Penguin, London.

Sindzingre, A, 2009. Financing developmental social policies in low-income countries: Conditions and constraints. In Hujo, K & McClanahan, S (Eds), Financing Social Policy: Mobilizing Resources for Social Development. Palgrave Macmillan, Basingstoke, pp. 115–40.

Skocpol, T, 1991. Universal appeal: Politically viable policies to combat poverty. The Brookings Review 9(3), 28–33.

Social Security Administration, 2009. Social Security Programs Throughout the World: Africa, 2009. Social Security Administration, Washington, DC.

Steinmo, S, 1993. Taxation and Democracy: Swedish, British and American Approaches to Financing the Modern State. Yale University Press, New Haven, CT.

Taylor, V, 2008. Social protection in Africa: An overview of the challenges. Report prepared for the African Union. Department of Social Development, University of Cape Town.

Timmons, JF, 2005. The fiscal contract: States, taxes, and public services. World Politics 57(4), 530–67.

Ulriksen, M, 2010. Politics, Policy, and Poverty in Botswana, Mauritius, and Other Developing Countries. Politica, Aarhus.

Ulriksen, M, 2011. Social policy development and global financial crisis in the open developing economies of Botswana and Mauritius. Global Social Policy 11(2–3), 195–214.

Van den Bosch, S, 2011. Basic Income Grant: Let others taste what we have tasted. IPS (Inter Press Service) News. http://ipsnews.net/news.asp?idnews=54503 Accessed 8 March 2011.

Weidlich, B, 2007. Only half of Namibia's taxpayers pay tax. The Namibian, 8 March. www.namibian.com.na/index.php?id=28&tx_ttnews%5Btt_news%5D=37409&no_cache=1 Accessed 8 March 2011.

'Growing' social protection in developing countries: Lessons from Brazil and South Africa

Armando Barrientos[1], Valerie Møller[2], João Saboia[3], Peter Lloyd-Sherlock[4] & Julia Mase[5]

The rapid expansion of social protection in the South provides a rich diversity of experiences and lessons on how best to reduce poverty and ultimately eradicate it. Knowledge on how best to 'grow' social assistance, understood as long-term institutions responsible for reducing and preventing poverty, is at a premium. This article examines the expansion of social assistance in Brazil and South Africa, two of the middle income countries widely perceived to have advanced furthest in 'growing' social protection. It examines three aspects: the primacy of politics in explaining the expansion of social protection and assistance, the tensions between path-dependence and innovation in terms of institutions and practices, and the poverty and inequality outcomes of social assistance expansion. The article concludes by drawing the main lessons for other developing countries.

1. Introduction

The rapid expansion of social protection in the South provides a rich diversity of experiences and lessons on how best to reduce poverty and ultimately eradicate it. In this article, social protection is taken to include three main components: contributory social insurance schemes covering life course and employment risks; non-contributory social assistance programmes addressing poverty and vulnerability; and labour market and employment policies, whether 'passive' or 'active'.[6] Rapid economic growth and improvements in basic services have contributed to the recent decline in global poverty, but direct assistance to the poorest households is increasingly acknowledged to be crucial in ensuring that these services reach them and that they can share in the growth. Knowledge on how best to 'grow' social assistance, understood as long-term institutions responsible for reducing and preventing poverty, is at a premium. A global debate on how best to design, focus and organise direct assistance, grounded on the diversity of country experiences, has been taking place among development researchers (Barrientos & Hulme, 2008; Grosh et al., 2008). This article discusses what lessons emerge from a comparative study of Brazil and South Africa, two of the

---

[1] Professor and Research Director, Brooks World Poverty Institute, University of Manchester, UK.
[2] Professor, Institute of Social and Economic Research (ISER), Rhodes University, Grahamstown, South Africa
[3] Professor and Director, Instituto de Economía, Universidade Federal do Rio de Janeiro, Brazil
[4] Professor, School of Development Studies, University of East Anglia, Norwich, UK
[5] Doctoral Candidate, Brooks World Poverty Institute, University of Manchester, UK
[6] Terminology varies across countries. In South Africa, the term 'social security' is used to cover social insurance, social assistance and public works programmes, and the term 'social welfare' to describe social assistance transfers.

middle income countries widely perceived to have advanced furthest in 'growing' social protection.

South Africa and Brazil provide an ideal context in which to examine the growth of social assistance. They are two middle income countries with persistent and high inequality, entrenched racial disparities and high poverty incidence. South Africa has a population of 50 million, a gross national income per capita of 10 360 US$ (PPP) and a life expectancy at birth of 52 years.[7] Brazil has a population of 195 million, gross national income per capita of 11 000 US$ (PPP) and a life expectancy at birth of 73 years.

Landmark political change in the two countries – in South Africa the fall of apartheid in 1990 and the rise to power of the African National Congress (ANC), and in Brazil the ending of 20 years of dictatorship in 1985 – led to renewed 'social contracts'. New constitutions, in 1996 in South Africa and 1988 in Brazil, opened the way to innovative social protection policies with an emphasis on social assistance. The term 'social contract' is open to a range of interpretations. Here we use it not in the classic sense of a compact between individuals and governments, as in Rousseau, Locke and Hobbes, but in the more restricted Rawlsian sense of an overlapping consensus, emerging in pluralistic societies with economic structures generating inequalities as to the equal distribution of primary goods and priority to the least advantaged (Rawls, 2001). This interpretation echoes European, but perhaps not Anglo-Saxon, definitions of the 'social' which include both institutions *and* political commitment to ensuring appropriate levels of well-being for the entire population (Leisering, 2003). Social protection systems in South Africa and Brazil have taken different trajectories. South Africa's has relied largely on social assistance, and especially transfers to vulnerable groups, and recent policy initiatives have extended this approach. Brazil's has traditionally relied on social insurance, but recent policy initiatives have given priority to the expansion of social assistance. As a consequence, the reform of social protection institutions and practices appears evolutionary in South Africa but more radical in Brazil. In this article we argue that key features of these reforms suggest the emergence of a new paradigm. A comparison of outcomes across the two countries brings to light an interesting set of issues. In both countries, studies suggest that poverty would be significantly higher in the absence of social assistance, but in Brazil social assistance also appears to have had a measurable impact on inequality.

We provide a comparative examination of these three key aspects: the primacy of politics in explaining the expansion of social protection and assistance, the tensions between path-dependence and innovation in terms of institutions and practices, and the outcomes of social protection expansion as regards poverty and inequality. This may seem an ambitious undertaking, but we aim to contribute substantially to the growing literature on comparative social policy in developing countries.

The article is organised as follows. Section 2 discusses the role of politics in the expansion of social protection in Brazil and South Africa, Section 3 examines institutional change and alternative paradigms, Section 4 assesses the outcomes of social protection policies for poverty and inequality in the two countries, and the final section discusses the main findings and draws out some lessons for other developing countries.

---

[7] PPP stands for purchasing power parity, and is a measure of the monetary value of a similar basket of goods in different countries in international US$.

2. The primacy of politics

The main stimulus to the growth of social assistance in Brazil and South Africa has come from political change and democratisation. It is perhaps a general rule that the emergence and reform of social assistance institutions reflects political processes, but the more specific hypothesis to be examined here is that the quality of these political processes has a bearing on the quality and reach of social assistance. After two decades of dictatorship, Brazil's new 1988 Constitution was intended to mark the beginning of an era of progressive and egalitarian policies (Jaccoud et al., 2009). In South Africa, the fall of apartheid and the rise to power of the ANC were also expected to lead to progressive and egalitarian policies, with the new 1996 Constitution embedding, as in Brazil, citizen rights to social security (Lund, 2008; Seekings, 2008). The renewal of social contracts in both countries led to policy activism in social protection, and particularly social assistance. The next section considers the institutional changes brought about by this political activism. We consider three ways in which the quality of political processes has shaped social assistance: reach and scale, productivism and a focus on poverty.

In a context of democratisation, unmet need and large differences in opportunity and outcomes across the population become a powerful drive for the expansion of social assistance. Growing social assistance by extending the reach of existing programmes is an obvious response. In Brazil the initial focus of policy activism was on strengthening existing non-contributory pension programmes. In South Africa a review of existing grants led to the introduction of the Child Support Grant. These initiatives aimed to extend support for groups perceived to be especially vulnerable. The expanded reach and scale of these programmes reflected political imperatives.

While political conditions were propitious to the growth of social assistance, economic conditions were not. In the last two decades of the 20th century economic growth rates in the two countries were disappointing. Annual GDP growth rates in South Africa and Brazil from 1993 to 2008 were similar at around 3%. Fiscal responsibility and economic growth and development were key political imperatives emphasising productivism in social policy, the requirement that all public policy contribute to economic inclusion and growth. In both countries these political imperatives encouraged discussion on the effectiveness of social assistance and its contribution to growth and development. In South Africa discussion consolidated around a notion of developmental welfare that informed the 1997 White Paper for Social Welfare. Lund describes 'developmental social welfare' as reflecting 'a commitment to overcoming inequity and racial discrimination', seeking 'to move away from curative services towards preventive programmes and towards linking welfare clients with opportunities for income generation' and to be 'inclusive of all citizens' (Lund, 2008:13). In Brazil, and in parallel to the expansion of non-contributory pension programmes, policy activism at the municipal level focused on linking transfers to households in extreme poverty with investment in the human capital of children, a perspective informing the development of Bolsa Escola, a social welfare programme of the Brazilian government. In both cases the quality of political processes pushed towards a more productivist approach to social assistance.

In Brazil, soft conditions attached to transfers for households in poverty are seen as a means of coordinating the work of different public agencies and ensuring investment in children. Public perceptions of the effectiveness of Bolsa Escola and broad political support rely, to an important extent, on the social investment quality of the transfers (Lindert & Vinscensini, 2008). In South Africa, grants are perceived to facilitate investment in health and education even in the absence of associated conditions. Research on the wider effects of the grants supports this (Woolard & Leibbrandt, 2010).

The same political imperatives were crucial in blocking proposals for a basic income in both countries (Matisonn & Seekings, 2003; Britto & Soares, 2010). Several factors explain why basic income proposals were rejected in both countries, but the fiscal implications (and the related implications for existing social assistance programmes), and an insufficiently productivist orientation, figured prominently in the associated policy debates. Proponents of basic income are often led to present it as a further extension ('universalisation') of social assistance transfers. They underplay the fundamental difference between basic income as a citizenship affirming intervention and social assistance as a poverty eradication intervention.

In sum, the impetus for the growth of social assistance in Brazil and South Africa has been the significant political change in both countries, leading to renewed social contracts. The quality of the political processes has been influential in determining the reach, orientation and objectives of social assistance. Our discussion now shifts to the social assistance institutions and the way they have evolved.

3. Institutional development

This section examines institutional developments, and especially the tension between path dependence and innovation.

3.1 Social protection systems in the 1990s

By the 1990s, South Africa had, perhaps uniquely among developing countries, well-developed social assistance programmes providing a range of means tested grants aimed at vulnerable groups. Social insurance provision, on the other hand, remained limited to employer retirement schemes. Among the social assistance grants, the Old Age Grant was dominant in terms of beneficiary numbers and budget (Van der Berg & Siebrits, 2010). Policy reforms in the early 1990s focused on eliminating discrimination in eligibility and benefit levels, both across racial groups and across provinces (especially in the former 'homelands' or Bantustans) (Lund, 2008).

In Brazil the most significant component of social protection was social insurance, providing earnings-related pensions and other benefits to workers in formal employment, especially in the public sector and for large employers in the private sector. The commitment to extending social security coverage in the 1988 Constitution led to the reform and expansion of two non-contributory pension schemes: the Previdência Social Rural, introduced in 1993, which provided social insurance benefits to workers in informal employment in agriculture, fishing and mining, and the Benefício de Prestação Continuada, introduced in 1996, a means tested social assistance transfer to older people or people living with disabilities in very low income households in urban and rural areas. The design of the Previdência Social Rural reflected efforts to include informal workers in the social insurance system. Brazilian researchers describe this scheme as 'partially contributory' because on paper there are contribution requirements applying to these benefits. In practice, contribution requirements have never been implemented. The cost of the scheme has been financed largely through public transfers to the social insurance fund covering private sector formal workers. These two programmes now reach more than

Table 1: Summary information on main social assistance programmes, Brazil and South Africa 2010

Country/programme	Target population	Number of transfers (million)	Value of transfers (US$) (% of median per capita income)	Budget (% GDP)
Brazil				
Bolsa Família	Households in poverty	12.8	If per capita household income is less than or equal to US$40, household transfer is US$23 plus US$18 for each child up to 3 and US$22 for 16/17 year olds up to 2. If per capita income is greater than US$40 and less than or equal to US$81, only child transfers apply. The range of transfers to a household has a minimum value of US$23 (5%) and a maximum value of US$178 (68%)	0.4
Benefício de Prestação Continuada	Older or disabled people in poverty	3.4	US$318 (122%)	0.6
Previdência Social Rural	Long-term rural informal workers	7.8	US$318 (122%)	1.4
South Africa				
Old Age Grant	Older people in poverty	2.5	US$230 (175%)	1.3
Disability Grant	Disabled people in poverty	1.3	US$230 (175%)	0.6
Child Support Grant	Children in poverty	9.4	US$53 (40%) per child	1.2
Other grants	Vulnerable groups	0.7	US$150 (115%) (Foster Care Grant only)	0.4

Sources: Woolard & Leibbrandt (2010), Barrientos (2011).

Notes: To enable comparison across the two countries, all monetary values are in purchasing power parity international US$. The conversion rates used are: 4.695 ZAR = 1 USD; 1.713 BRL= 1 USD. PPP conversion rates were accessed from EconStats. www.econstats.com/weo/V013.htm Accessed September 2011. The values are also given in brackets as a percentage of median per capita income.

10 million beneficiaries and provide a monthly transfer equivalent to a minimum wage (see Table 1 for current information on these programmes). At the turn of the century, non-contributory pension programmes dominated social assistance provision in both South Africa and Brazil.

3.2 Institutional reform and expansion in the 2000s

The 2000s saw rapid growth in the scale and scope of social assistance in the two countries. Table 1 provides summary information on the main social assistance programmes in Brazil and South Africa.

The introduction of a Child Support Grant in South Africa in 1998 was intended to address poverty and malnutrition in young children (initially those aged below seven) in low income households (Lund, 2008). In the following years the programme was gradually extended to older children (up to the age of 17). It now reaches over nine million children, who receive a monthly transfer equivalent to US$53, less than a quarter of the Old Age Grant. In Brazil the Bolsa Escola, introduced in a handful of municipalities in the mid-1990s and subsequently adopted as a federal programme in 2001, provided transfers to low income households conditional on children attending school. The effectiveness of Bolsa Escola encouraged a batch of direct income transfers to households in poverty. The Programme for the Eradication of Child Labour – introduced in some municipalities in the mid-1990s, at the same time as Bolsa Escola – was particularly effective. It provides direct income transfers conditional on children attending extended school hours. It was consolidated into Bolsa Família in 2004. In 2003 Bolsa Escola and four other social assistance programmes were integrated into Bolsa Família, which provides transfers to low income households conditional on schooling and health care utilisation. Bolsa Família reaches more than 12 million households in Brazil, providing transfers with values linked to household composition, a minimum of US$23 for households in moderate poverty, or in extreme poverty without children, and a maximum of US$178 for households with three or more children in extreme poverty.

From a mid-1990s baseline, both countries have expanded their social assistance significantly. Today, social assistance programmes reach over half of all households in South Africa and a quarter of all households in Brazil (Leibbrandt et al., 2010; Soares et al., 2010). The reach of the programmes exceeds the proportion of the population in extreme poverty. Old age transfers no longer dominate social assistance in either country, at least as far as beneficiary numbers are concerned. However, the different values of the transfers, with old age transfers being significantly larger than the Child Support Grant or Bolsa Família transfers, suggests that some age bias remains. (Examining the age bias in social assistance provision would require a separate article.) Before the recent expansion of social assistance, researchers in both countries raised this issue (Van der Berg, 2001; Camargo, 2004). Turra et al. (2007) note that in Brazil children were supported by private (intra-household) transfers whereas older people were supported through public transfers. The fact that transfers are shared within households suggests that in practice the situation was more complex. The expansion of assistance to children, albeit on a less generous basis, is likely to have reduced the age bias. In Brazil, the combined budget of the two non-contributory pension programmes is more than four times that of the Bolsa Família. In South Africa, the budget allocated to the Old Age Grant is approximately 10% higher than the budget for the Child Support Grant, with the latter reaching four times as many beneficiaries as the Old Age Grant (see Table 1).

3.3 Social assistance trajectories examined

The trajectories of Brazil and South Africa offer an excellent opportunity to study the dynamics of social assistance. Uniquely among developing countries, South Africa did not prioritise social insurance: medical aid and unemployment insurance have very limited coverage of the country's population. Brazil shows a very different trajectory, one that prioritised social insurance (Barreto de Oliveira & Iwakami Beltrao, 2001). Latin American policymakers expected that economic development would eventually lead to the formalisation of employment, enabling comprehensive social insurance coverage for the population. The perceived failure of social insurance institutions to reach workers in informal employment and groups in poverty has been the main driving force behind the expansion of social assistance. Equity considerations are also relevant as social insurance schemes are supported by large public subsidies that flow to better-off groups.

The orientation of social assistance in both countries was informed by a vulnerable-groups perspective. In line with traditional approaches, social assistance was intended to provide support to population groups facing significantly higher levels of vulnerability due to longer term factors, such as age or disability, which limited earnings capacity. The expansion of social assistance in Brazil and South Africa moves beyond that paradigm in at least three important respects: it focuses on households as opposed to individuals, it acknowledges that poverty and vulnerability are multidimensional, and it aims to progress towards more comprehensive, universalistic programmes.

As noted in the discussion above, social assistance grants in South Africa target specific categories of people facing deprivation and vulnerability, and old age grants dominate. To an extent the Child Support Grant can be interpreted as a linear extension of the grant system to another vulnerable group. Current proposals for the expansion of social assistance have also drawn attention to other groups that are currently left out, such as the unemployed who are unable to draw unemployment insurance, and the youth (Van der Berg, 2001; Møller, 2010). Research has amply demonstrated that transfers are not only shared within households but often lead to a re-arranging of households' labour resources (Ardington et al., 2009) and to changes in intra-household relations and decision making (Møller & Sotshongaye, 1996). Grants are therefore best understood as transfers to households in poverty that are channelled through particular individuals, for example the means tests used to establish eligibility also take account of other household members' income and assets. In Brazil, research has also established the fact that non-contributory pensions are shared within households, with implications for intra-household relations (Lloyd-Sherlock, 2006). A household focus is explicit in Bolsa Família. Whereas Bolsa Escola targeted families with children of school age and low incomes, Bolsa Família covers all households with per capita income below US$81 (about one fifth of the minimum wage in 2012). The focus on households is justified on the grounds that transfers are intended to facilitate exit from poverty by supporting agency, which is, by and large, located at the household level. The extent to which an implicit or explicit household focus on social assistance generates different outcomes is one area where further research is needed.

Linkages between transfers and service provision distinguish Bolsa Família from the grants in South Africa. Bolsa Família includes soft conditions on health utilisation and schooling but in fact institutional development in Brazil has gone further with the establishment of a Unified Social Assistance System combining a range of service provision and intermediation through reference centres. These centres are able to coordinate a range of public sector programmes and services and tailor them to the particular needs of individual households. There are two types: Centros de Referência em Assistência Social and Centros de Referência Especializada de Assistência Social, which deals with more complex cases. In South Africa, linkages between transfers and service provision are more limited and there is greater reliance on the income effect of grants and the availability of relevant services from other agencies. A normatively polarised debate about the desirability of adding conditions to existing grants has reduced the scope for assessing the potential gains from linking transfers with services and intermediation (Barrientos, 2011; Lund, 2011).

In both countries there has been a marked expansion in the reach of social assistance. There are grounds for arguing that this constitutes progress towards the development of social assistance programmes that are more inclusive and all encompassing of households in poverty. The term 'universalisation' is often over-used and mis-used in the social protection literature. In the context of social assistance, however, it appropriately describes the capacity of programmes to assist all households and individuals in poverty, regardless of personal characteristics. Bolsa Família constitutes a clear shift in paradigm towards universalising social assistance, as the only condition on eligibility is the household's income level. Reach is important for the effectiveness of social assistance. In both countries, social assistance reaches beyond households in extreme poverty and increasingly covers households that are not in poverty but are vulnerable to falling into poverty.

The legal institutionalisation of social assistance in the two countries merits a brief discussion. In Brazil, entitlement to non-contributory pensions is enshrined in the constitution, with the implication that provision is – at least on paper – not limited by the government's fiscal position. Bolsa Família, on the other hand, does not have the same legal position, and entitlements are subject to government discretion, including budgetary controls. In South Africa, the constitutional right to social assistance is dependent on budgetary conditions and the specific form of provision is at government discretion. Constitutional recognition of social assistance entitlements in Brazil can be advantageous in protecting non-contributory pension provision from government discretion, but it can also be disadvantageous if it prevents innovation and change in provision and also if it ensures different treatment of otherwise similar households in poverty depending on whether they include older persons. Acknowledging a general principle that is left to governments to implement, the constitutional approach in South Africa appears to achieve a better balance between the needs to protect rights, to enable innovation and to ensure fiscal sustainability. The use of the courts as an instrument for the expansion of social assistance is present in both countries, but to date it has been more successful in South Africa, for example making the age of entitlement to the Old Age Grant the same for men and women (Seekings, 2008). In Brazil the main issue considered by the courts is whether the government's interpretation of minimum benefit levels for non-contributory pensions, at the minimum wage, is appropriate in the case of beneficiaries living with severe disabilities.

To recap, this section focused on differences and similarities in the nature of institutional changes in social assistance expansion in South Africa and Brazil. Path dependence in social assistance is stronger in South Africa, because of the prominent role of grants and their income effects. In Brazil institutional innovation has been strongest in the expansion of Bolsa Família. A shift in the focus of social assistance – towards households, towards linking transfers and services and towards more comprehensive reach – can be observed in both countries. The shift is explicit in Brazil's Bolsa Família. Differences in legal institutionalisation across the two countries have implications for the future evolution of social assistance.

4. Poverty and inequality outcomes

This section discusses poverty and inequality trends in the two countries and assesses the contribution of social assistance.

4.1 National poverty and inequality outcomes

We begin by sketching aggregate trends in poverty and inequality. Figure 1 provides estimates of the poverty headcount rate and the Gini coefficient for the two countries. It shows a marginal drop in poverty incidence in South Africa between 1993 and 2008. Brazil, on the other hand, managed to make significant inroads into poverty incidence between 1993 and 2008 as the poverty headcount fell by half, with a

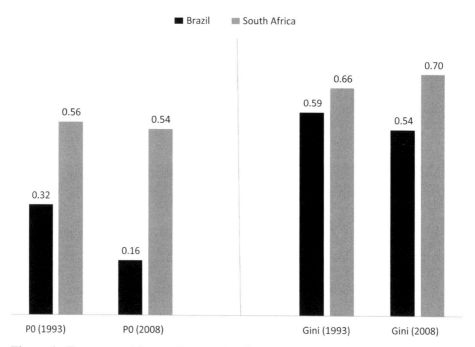

Figure 1: Poverty and inequality trends: South Africa and Brazil, 1993 to 2008
Sources: Leibbrandt et al. (2010) for South Africa; Ferreira & Leite (2009) and Soares et al. (2010) for Brazil.
Notes: Poverty lines are R515 (R2008) for South Africa and R100 (September 2004 reais) for Brazil; approximately US$96 PPP and US$68 PPP respectively.

sustained decline thereafter. Brazil and South Africa are among the countries with the highest inequality in the world. Estimates of the Gini coefficient for the two countries suggest divergent trends, as inequality increased in South Africa but fell in Brazil by as much as 10%, with most of the decline being between 2000 and 2008. The changes in inequality in the two countries are relatively small and from a very high base, but they do show divergent trajectories.

This raises the question of why Brazil has achieved large reductions in poverty and a significant reduction in inequality at the same time that South Africa has achieved only small reductions in poverty and experienced a marginal rise in inequality. In the context of this article, the interest is in whether the expansion of social assistance has played any part.

Research in both countries points to the *type* of growth process as the primary factor. Critics argue that in South Africa economic policy has emphasised growth in high-tech industries, perhaps at the expense of employment creation (Nattrass & Seekings, 2001), but others point to rigidities in the labour market. Persistently high unemployment has been a feature in South Africa, while in Brazil high commodity prices and generally favourable economic conditions have enabled a significant reduction in unemployment, from 12% in November 2003 to 5% in November 2011. Together with the expansion of social assistance, this has translated into strong income growth among the bottom 40% of Brazil's population. Assessing the types of growth in the two countries would need a longer and more detailed analysis than is possible in this article, but this brief discussion underlines the significance of the issue.

Redistribution, especially through the expansion of social assistance, is important too. Leibbrandt et al. (2010) simulate, for 2008, the potential impact on poverty of South Africa's grants by comparing the poverty headcount estimated from reported household income with a measure of household income excluding income from grants. This approach does not take account of behavioural responses to changes in income, for example labour supply responses. In the labour supply case, estimated poverty would have been around six percentage points higher (60% compared to the 54% shown in Figure 1). The impact of the grants on the Gini coefficient is marginal: in 2008 the Gini would have been 0.03 higher when estimated on a measure of household income excluding grants. In Brazil, researchers using a similar methodology compared the poverty headcount for household income with and without social assistance transfers and found a strong poverty reduction effect. Soares et al. (2010) find that Bolsa Família and its antecedent programmes are associated with around 40% of the reduction in the poverty headcount in the 2000s, and can be said to be solely responsible for the reduction in extreme poverty in the same period (from 10% to 5%). The same study estimates that Bolsa Família and non-contributory pensions are associated with around one third of the 10% reduction in the Gini coefficient in the same period. These estimates are based on a decomposition of the Gini coefficient by income source.

These figures need to be treated with caution, as the methods used to generate these estimates of the impact of social assistance on poverty and inequality do not take full account of the influence of complementary policies (Souza, 2011; Saboia, 2012). In Brazil, for example, non-contributory pensions, minimum pension guarantees in contributory schemes and wage bargaining in the informal sector are all benchmarked to the minimum wage, the value of which rose by around 50% in real terms from

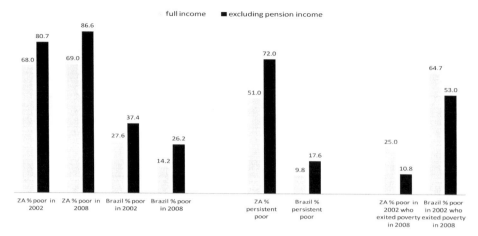

Figure 2: Estimates of poverty headcount with and without pension income for a panel sample of older households in selected locations in Brazil and South Africa, 2002 and 2008

Source: Study on ageing, well-being and development. Sample of households with older persons: 700 households in Brazil (metropolitan Rio and Ilhéus) and 615 in South Africa (ZA) (Eastern and Western Cape), visited in 2002 and 2008. www.sed.manchester.ac.uk/research/ageingandwellbeing/index.htm Accessed February 2012.

2002 to 2008 (Saboia, 2009). All in all, social assistance appears to have important effects on poverty in South Africa and larger effects on both poverty and inequality in Brazil.

4.2 Old age poverty and vulnerability

The poverty estimates discussed above represent snapshots of the population below the poverty line, but changes in households' poverty status over time are also important. It is of interest to consider how social assistance helps to facilitate exit from poverty. To look into the dynamics of poverty status, we make use of panel data from comparative surveys of older people and their households collected in 2002 and 2008 in the two countries.[8] The surveys focus on older people and their households and consider explicitly the role of pension provision. Figure 2 reports on changes in poverty status for survey respondents using reported income and a measure of income excluding pension income (Barrientos & Mase, 2012). The differences in poverty, estimated with and without pension income, provide an upper bound of the poverty reduction potential of pensions.

It is important to keep in mind that the panel samples are not nationally representative. The data were collected in the Eastern and Western Cape provinces of South Africa and in metropolitan Rio and Ilhéus in Brazil, and in low income locations in both countries. The interest here lies in the changes in poverty status for the older households sampled. The information in Figure 2 makes three points. First, and as noted in the discussion above, excluding non-contributory pension income from household income leads to higher headcount poverty in both samples. Although it is to be expected that lower

---

[8]See details of project at www.sed.manchester.ac.uk/research/ageingandwellbeing/index.htm

household income would worsen household welfare, the point is that non-contributory pension income is important enough to make a difference to the poverty headcount. Second, non-contributory pension income might not be sufficient to prevent persistent poverty, understood in this case as older households observed to be poor in 2002 and 2008. In the absence of social assistance for older people and their households, persistent poverty among them would be significantly greater. Persistent poverty in the sample would be close to 50% higher for the South African households and almost twice as large for the Brazilian households. Third, non-contributory pension income makes an important contribution in helping households to exit poverty. In the absence of pension income, the proportion of households in poverty in the South Africa sample in 2002 that would have exited poverty would have fallen from 25% to 10%. In the case of the Brazilian households, 65% of those in poverty in 2002 exited poverty, but this share would have been reduced to 53% if non-contributory pension income had been excluded. Social assistance support for older people is not as important for the Brazilian households sampled as it is for the South African households sampled.

This brief discussion of changes in the poverty status of older people and their households serves to underline the role of social assistance in explaining changes in poverty status over time. Furthermore, the comparison across the two countries also demonstrates the significance of complementary policies supporting exit from poverty. The effectiveness of social assistance in securing poverty reduction and equity is strengthened by complementary policies encouraging employment and basic service provision.

5. Conclusions

It is important to ensure that economic and social development reaches all. Countries in the South face significant challenges in achieving this goal, not least from globalisation, limited fiscal resources and accumulated social debt. As a means to achieve social justice and eradicate poverty, growing social protection is a global imperative. There is much to be learnt from the experiences of Brazil and South Africa, two middle income countries with considerable achievements in social protection. This article has provided a comparative perspective, and we conclude by underlining the main lessons learnt.

The first lesson concerns the primacy of politics. In the cases of Brazil and South Africa, landmark political change provided a renewed impetus for social protection and especially assistance. The growth of social assistance in the two countries has its roots in renewed social contracts, embedded in new constitutions redefining the right to social protection. As we have noted, the political processes had a significant effect on the extension of social assistance in the two countries, ensuring a focus on poverty reduction and equity. Research and policy discussions on social assistance have focused on design issues, but it is crucial to understand the political processes shaping the growth of social assistance. In the South, growing social assistance is part and parcel of democratisation processes shifting attention to poverty and equity. The quality of these processes shapes the reach and orientation of social assistance.

We next considered institutional changes. Tension between path dependence and innovation provided a focus for the discussion. In terms of their social protection system, South Africa and Brazil started off from entirely different points. Since the

1950s, Brazil's social insurance has been the dominant component of its social protection system, whereas in South Africa social assistance has played that role. This explains why the growth of social assistance in Brazil represents a more radical break with policy priorities, and why path dependence is stronger in South Africa. A key lesson for developing countries here is the need to pay attention to social assistance within social protection systems. For low income countries with weak social insurance institutions there are strong advantages in growing social assistance first. Recognising the difficulties in extending social insurance to workers in informal employment and groups in poverty, Brazil and Latin American countries in general are placing a stronger policy priority on the development of social assistance. In Brazil and South Africa, the reach of social assistance goes beyond the population in poverty to include groups vulnerable to falling into poverty. In developing countries with high poverty incidence, social assistance is a core policy area.

We noted the emergence of a paradigm shift as regards social assistance institutions. Three aspects are apparent: a growing focus on households as opposed to individuals, a productivist or developmental perspective that links transfers to human capital investment and economic inclusion, and a more inclusive perspective replacing the vulnerable groups approach that dominated developments in the previous century. This shift in perspective is 'work in progress', but Bolsa Família best represents the changes that are under way. The evolution of this paradigm shift is of great significance for other developing countries.

In both countries, social assistance makes a strong contribution to poverty reduction and equity. At the national level, overall trends diverge across the two countries. Poverty and inequality reduction trends are strong in Brazil, but in South Africa poverty reduction is marginal and inequality shows a rising trend. This suggests that the type of growth makes a difference to the impact of redistribution through social assistance on poverty and inequality. In Brazil a combination of factors is responsible for the strong gains in poverty reduction and equity: inclusive growth, the rise in real terms of the minimum wage, which affects social assistance and social insurance transfers and wage bargaining in the informal sector, and redistribution through social assistance. This finding is also supported by analysis of longitudinal data on older households. Old age social assistance transfers are associated with lower poverty and lower chronic poverty, but also exit from poverty. These effects are stronger for the Brazilian households sampled because of complementary policies. Perhaps the main lesson emerging from examining the poverty and inequality outcomes in the two countries is the need to combine redistribution through social assistance transfers with inclusive growth and employment policies.

The main lessons, in a nutshell, are as follows:

- In the South, renewal of social contracts and democratisation will shape the growth of social assistance as a means of reducing poverty and inequality.
- The growth in the reach of social assistance is important, but so is a shift in paradigm, with a stronger household focus, a productivist or developmental perspective and greater inclusion.
- In both countries social assistance has made a strong contribution to poverty reduction and equity. However, the stronger outcomes in Brazil emphasise the fact that social assistance is likely to be most effective when accompanied by, and embedded in, inclusive growth and employment policies.

References

Ardington, C, Case, A & Hosegood, V, 2009. Labour supply responses to large social transfers: Longitudinal evidence from South Africa. American Economic Journal: Applied Economics 1(1), 22–48.

Barreto de Oliveira, FE & Iwakami K, Beltrao, 2001. The Brazilian social security system. International Social Security Review 54(1), 101–12.

Barrientos, A, 2011. The rise of social assistance in Brazil. Mimeo, Brooks World Poverty Institute, Manchester.

Barrientos, A & Hulme, D, 2008. Social Protection for the Poor and Poorest: Concepts, Policies and Politics. Palgrave, London.

Barrientos, A & Mase, J, 2012. Poverty transitions among older households in South Africa and Brazil. European Journal of Development Research 24(4), 570–88.

Britto, T & Soares, FV, 2010. Bolsa família e renda de cidadania: Um passo en falso? Mimeo, IPEA (Instituto de Pesquisa Econômica Aplicada), Brasilia.

Camargo, JM, 2004. Política social no Brasil: Prioridades erradas, incentivos perversos. São Paulo em Perspectiva 18(2), 68–77.

Ferreira, FHG & Leite, PG, 2009. Halving Brazil's poverty, 1983–2006. In Von Braun, J, Vargas Hill, R & Pandya-Lock, R (Eds), The Poorest and the Hungry: Assessments, Analysis and Actions. IFPRI (International Food Policy Research Institute), Washington, DC, pp. 355–65.

Grosh, M, Del Ninno, C, Tesliuc, E & Ouerghi, A, 2008. For Protection and Promotion: The Design and Implementation of Effective Safety Nets. World Bank, Washington, DC.

Jaccoud, L, Hadjab, PDE-M & Chaibub, JR, 2009. Assistência social e segurança alimentar: Entre novas trajetórias, vehlas agendas e recentes desafíos (1988–2008). In Diretoría de Etudos e Políticas Sociais (Ed.), Políticas Sociais: Acompanhamento e Análise 17. IPEA (Instituto de Pesquisa Econômica Aplicada), Brasilia, pp. 175–250.

Leibbrandt, M, Woolard, I, Finn, A & Argent, J, 2010. Trends in South African income distribution and poverty since the fall of apartheid. OECD Social, Employment and Migration Working Papers 101, Organization for Economic Cooperation and Development, Paris.

Leisering, L, 2003. Nation state and welfare state: An intellectual and political history. Review essay. Journal of European Social Policy 13(2), 175–85.

Lindert, K & Vinscensini, V, 2008. Social policy, perceptions and the press: An analysis of the media's treatment of conditional cash transfers in Brazil. Discussion Paper, World Bank, Washington, DC.

Lloyd-Sherlock, P, 2006. Simple transfers, complex outcomes: The impacts of pensions on poor households in Brazil. Development and Change 37(5), 969–95.

Lund, F, 2008. Changing Social Policy: The Child Support Grant in South Africa. HSRC (Human Sciences Research Council) Press, Cape Town.

Lund, F, 2011. A step in the wrong direction: Linking the South Africa Child Support Grant to school attendance. Journal of Poverty and Social Justice 19(1), 5–14.

Matisonn, H & Seekings, J, 2003. The politics of a basic income grant in South Africa, 1996–2002. In Standing, G & Samson, M (Eds), A Basic Income Grant for South Africa. University of Cape Town, Cape Town, pp. 56–76.

Møller, V, 2010. Strengthening intergenerational solidarity in South Africa: Closing the gaps in the social security system for unemployed youth. A case study of the 'perverse incentive'. Journal of Intergenerational Relationships 8(2), 145–60.

Møller, V & Sotshongaye, A, 1996. 'My family eats this money too': Pension sharing and self-respect among Zulu grandmothers. Southern African Journal of Gerontology 5(2), 9–19.

Nattrass, N & Seekings, J, 2001. Democracy and distribution in highly unequal economies: The case of South Africa. Journal of Modern African Studies 39(3), 471–98.

Rawls, J, 2001. Justice as Fairness: A Restatement. Belknap Press of Harvard University Press, London.

Saboia, J, 2009. Efeitos do salário mínimo sobre a distribuição de renda no Brasil no período 1995/2005: Resultados de simulações. Economía 11(1), 51–77.

Saboia, J, 2012. Income Distribution in Brazil and the Role of the Minimum Wage. UFRJ (Universidade Federal do Rio de Janeiro), Instituto de Economía, Rio de Janeiro.

Seekings, J, 2008. Deserving individuals and groups: The post-apartheid state's justification of the shape of South Africa's system of social assistance. Transformation 68, 28–52.

Soares, S, Souza, PHGF de, Osório, RG & Silveira, FG, 2010. Os impactos do benefício do Programa Bolsa Família sobre a desigualdade e a pobreza. In de Castro, JA & Modesto, L (Eds), Bolsa Família 2003–2010: Avanços e Desafios (Vol. 1). IPEA (Instituto de Pesquisa Econômica Aplicada), Brasilia.

Souza, PHGF de, 2011. Poverty, inequality and social policies in Brazil, 1995–2005. Mimeo, IPEA (Instituto de Pesquisa Econômica Aplicada), Brasilia.

Turra, CM, Queiroz, BL & Rios-Neto, ELG, 2007. Idiosyncrasies of intergenerational transfers in Brazil. In Mason, A & Lee, R (Eds), Population Ageing and the Generational Economy: A Global Perspective. Edward Elgar, London, pp. 394–406.

Van der Berg, S, 2001. Social policy to address poverty. In Bhorat, H, Leibbrandt, M, Maziya, M, Van der Berg, S & Woolard, I (Eds), Fighting Poverty: Labour Markets and Inequality in South Africa. Zed Press, London, pp. 171–204.

Van der Berg, S & Siebrits, K, 2010. Social assistance reform during a period of fiscal stress. Stellenbosch Working Paper Series No. WP17/2010, Department of Economics, University of Stellenbosch.

Woolard, I & Leibbrandt, M, 2010. The evolution and impact of unconditional cash transfers in South Africa. SALDRU (Southern Africa Labour and Development Research Unit) Working Paper 51, University of Cape Town.

Gender and child sensitive social protection in South Africa

Leila Patel[1], Tessa Hochfeld[2] & Jacqueline Moodley[3]

Drawing from a 2010 study of women receiving the Child Support Grant in an urban area of South Africa, this article discusses the link between social protection, women's empowerment and the well-being of children. It appears that the Grant enhances women's power and control over household decision-making in financial matters, general household spending and child well-being. At the same time, the data show that women continue to bear the greatest burden of care in the household and that these responsibilities significantly heighten gender inequalities. Therefore, while the Grant has benefits for child well-being and women's empowerment, it cannot on its own transform unequal and unjust social relations of power. It should be working in concert with other public programmes not only to focus on children's needs but also to strive for gender equality for poor women.

1. Introduction

There is growing international interest in social protection policies as tools for social transformation, particularly for gender empowerment (ILO & UNDP, 2011; Sweetman, 2011) and child well-being (Handa et al., 2011). Economic and political crises have a significant and harmful effect on women and children, who are already disproportionately represented amongst the poor. Social protection measures could be an important tool to mitigate these disparate and negative impacts. Studies have been conducted to assess the gendered impact of cash transfers in places such as Latin America (Adato et al., 2000; Molyneux, 2006; Molyneux & Thomson, 2011), but research in Africa has been less extensive (see for example Patel & Hochfeld, 2011). There is scope for research of this nature to inform gender and child sensitive social policies locally, especially in South Africa, which has a well-developed social protection environment compared with other African countries.

The feminisation of social assistance is a new trend in post-apartheid South Africa. In this article we report on research in which a gender lens was used to gain insight into the impact of the Child Support Grant (CSG) and the ways in which gender influences and mediates development outcomes for women and children. Research on Old Age Pensions in South Africa indicates that money directed to women recipients of the grant has had a positive multiplier effect on women's status and the well-being of the children in their care (Ardington & Lund, 1995; Lund, 2006; Devereux et al., 2008). On the basis of these insights we hypothesised that the CSG is likely to give women

---

[1] Director and Professor, Centre for Social Development in Africa, Faculty of Humanities, University of Johannesburg, South Africa.
[2] Researcher, Centre for Social Development in Africa, Faculty of Humanities, University of Johannesburg, South Africa.
[3] Junior Researcher, Centre for Social Development in Africa, Faculty of Humanities, University of Johannesburg, South Africa

more power in the household over decisions that could improve their lives and those of their children. Increased power for women in the household may have other positive benefits for women: improving their agency, giving them access to resources and opportunities, reducing their vulnerability and the burden of care, enhancing their confidence and self-esteem, broadening their social and economic participation and increasing their autonomy. In this study we assumed that the empowerment of women due to the CSG leads to positive development outcomes for children in the form of improved health and nutritional status, better care and more regular school attendance.

The three-year study from which this article draws its data was a gendered impact analysis of the CSG with reference to intra-household relations and decision-making, access to services and support, care responsibilities and addressing the vulnerabilities of poor families in urban households (Patel et al., 2012). The focus of this article is on further understanding the link between social protection, women's empowerment and the achievement of well-being for children in an urban community.

The rest of the paper is structured as follows. Section 2 describes the CSG and the context of poverty for women in urban South Africa, Section 3 reviews the literature on the link between gender and the potential of the CSG to promote social transformation and child well-being, Section 4 sets out the method used, Section 5 discusses the findings and Section 6 concludes and offers recommendations.

2. The Child Support Grant

Social grants now reach close to 30% of South Africa's population and are one of the country's most important poverty reduction programmes, reaching 15.7 million beneficiaries in 2012 (SASSA, 2012). The decline in poverty levels, especially since 2000, irrespective of which poverty line is used, is attributed largely to the expansion of cash transfers (Van der Berg et al., 2008). Despite this progress, however, poverty, inequality and high unemployment levels remain the country's greatest challenges, with poverty continuing to be strongly associated with race, gender (Posel & Rogan, 2012), education and spatial dimensions. In particular, Africans, coloured and African women, children, youth and people in rural areas remain over-represented amongst the poor. New trends are emerging in the profile of the poor: rising urban poverty, an increasing proportion of the poor living in households with low educational levels, and an increase in the gendered nature of employment, including higher unemployment levels for women than for men (Leibbrandt et al., 2010). Two-thirds of children are living in income-poor households (Hall & Wright, 2011).

In a context of widespread poverty and inequality for both women and men, the differences in poverty rates by gender have increased over the last decade (Posel & Rogan, 2012), ensuring that poverty remains a gendered phenomenon in South Africa. Women are poorer than men (Casale & Posel, 2005; Posel & Rogan, 2012). Since women are predominantly the caregivers in this society, they bear a significant burden of mitigating the effects of poverty on their households and dependants. However, social grants (in particular the CSG and the Old Age Pension) have played an important role in redistribution and poverty reduction (Woolard, 2003; Van der Berg et al., 2008). In particular, the disproportionate level of poverty for women has meant that the 'receipt of social grant income may have been relatively more effective in reducing particularly the depth of poverty for females and female-headed households' (Posel & Rogan, 2012:111). There is evidence that the redistributive effect of social grants is significantly stronger when the grant goes to a female recipient (Duflo, 2003), and that households as a whole generally benefit from women's grant receipt irrespective of which household member receives the grant (Case & Menendez, 2007). Because the Old Age Pension is pooled with other household income, it produces significant benefits for children's development, especially in the areas of nutrition, health and education (Case & Menendez, 2007).

Of the three publicly funded social assistance programmes for older persons, people with disabilities and children, the CSG, introduced in 1998, is the largest and fastest growing social intervention in post-apartheid South Africa. The grant is paid to the primary caregiver of a child up to 18 years of age, and now reaches more than 11 million children (SASSA, 2012), which indicates the extensive reach of the programme. The grant is means-tested, but the criteria are relatively generous, resulting in a large number of children falling into the targeted group. The vast majority of grants go to female caregivers despite men being just as eligible to apply (Vorster & De Waal, 2008).

Although the CSG is crucial to reducing poverty, overall child poverty levels have declined only marginally since the introduction of this grant (Leibbrandt et al., 2010; Hall & Wright, 2011), possibly due to the modest amount of the grant, set at R280 per month in 2012. However, researchers have noted positive developmental outcomes in the reach of the CSG and its benefits in the form of improved school attendance and better nutritional status, and also longer-term benefits of mitigating the detrimental effects of poverty on children in the early years of life (Case et al., 2005; Agüero et al., 2006; Williams, 2007; Delany et al., 2008; Neves et al., 2009; Heinrich et al., 2012).

3. Gender, social protection and social transformation

A gender and development approach informed this study (Kabeer, 1994; Chant, 2010). This approach is based on two premises: firstly that gender is socially constructed and founded on socially acquired notions of appropriate expectations of and responsibilities for men and women, and secondly that socially patterned interactions between women and men are based on asymmetrical social positions that translate into inequality of access to resources, services and opportunities and impose constraints on women (Sabates-Wheeler & Kabeer, 2003). Finally, feminists argue that because poverty is a gendered experience researchers should take a gender perspective on poverty (Kabeer, 1994; Molyneux, 2006; Chant, 2010).

There is growing interest internationally and locally in how social protection might contribute to social transformation that tackles the multiple privations that cause gender inequality (Sabates-Wheeler & Devereux, 2008). The term 'social protection' is now widely used to refer to cash and in-kind support, including basic and social services that are of a public, private and informal nature to mitigate poverty, inequality, vulnerability and risks associated with social and economic changes in the society and globally (ILO & UNDP, 2011). Gender is rarely used as a lens to reveal the multifaceted social dynamics and impact of social protection, broadly incorporating labour markets and public, private, voluntary, individual, household and community support systems and networks. Anti-poverty measures to reduce vulnerability tend to be gender biased, focus on the breadwinner as the target of social policy, and take insufficient account of the gendered division of labour at household level and of the bargaining power of men in intra-household decision-making and in capturing household resources (Bertrand et al., 2003). In addition, complex intra-household relations and decisions about spending priorities and trade-offs about who seeks work, who cares for children and other dependants, and the dynamics of the care economy, are poorly understood.

We know from previous international research that there is an important relationship between a woman's empowerment and the well-being of her children (Adato et al., 2000). It is widely acknowledged that cash transfers are a relatively empowering form of social protection because they offer recipients a choice of how to use them (Ellis, 2007). Cash transfers are therefore a potentially significant pathway to achieve women's empowerment as benefits accrue from both the use of the cash itself and the opportunities for choice and control they present for women in gender unequal contexts (Adato et al., 2000; Case & Menendez, 2007; Kabeer et al., 2010).

Women's empowerment and increased access to resources have been shown to have a positive effect on children's well-being. For example, women use cash income that comes directly to them very differently from the way men do. Studies show that women's spending patterns benefit children and the family more than men's spending patterns, which tend to be focused on discretionary personal spending (Kabeer, 1994; Haddad, 1999). A local study also contends that women are 'more likely to use resources they control to promote the needs of children' (UNICEF, 2006:16). Other research has identified a positive correlation between higher literacy levels of mothers and improvements in children's health and education (Henshall Momsen, 2004).

While these studies point to important links between social protection, women's empowerment and children's well-being, these connections have not been substantively explored or empirically verified in South Africa, and their impact on social care in local households also remains largely unexplored (for research on this see Patel & Hochfeld, 2011; Patel et al., 2012).

To investigate the relationship between women's empowerment and children's well-being in households that receive a CSG, we used Kabeer's empowerment framework (1999) and indicators of empowerment developed by Adato et al. (2000). We drew indicators from the areas of decision-making and care responsibilities. Decision-making is a key intra-household process that is a proxy for bargaining power in relationships (Folbre, 1994; Kabeer, 1999). Specifically, decision-making about household expenditure (who spends what money on which household items) and about children (who makes financial, health, education and care decisions) are key indicators of women's status in the home (Adato et al., 2000). It would seem that women with partners or women living in homes where adult men reside are more gender empowered if they are the sole or most influential decision-maker regarding household and child related expenditure. Kabeer (1999) traces a direct link between cash resources controlled by women and their sense of agency (own goal achievement). These resources and the agency to use the money as they choose provide women with the freedom and opportunity to generate valuable outcomes that may enhance their capabilities (Sen, 1999). Other indicators of empowerment relevant to the study included women's self-belief and perceptions (individual empowerment), women's rights in the household, economic security and participation in the public domain (Adato et al., 2000).

The lack of public and private support for women's care responsibilities limits their access to employment and other opportunities that could improve life for them and their families. Care work is the unpaid labour in the home that is heavily gendered as women's work. Care involves the physical and emotional care of household members, both children and adults. Razavi (2007) argues that the care economy relies on the unpaid work of women, which remains largely invisible and unaccounted for in the calculation of gross national product. In particular, the goods and services that are crucial to satisfying human needs in the private sphere are not accounted for in economic analyses (Kabeer, 1994). Care work places a huge burden on women and this is exacerbated in South Africa by the need to care for sick household members. A household's care economy is important to the understanding of citizenship and women's disadvantage in the household in relation to income, time and freedom of movement, which is constrained if a woman is solely responsible for the supervision of children or dependent adults (Hassim, 2006; Folbre, 2008). In this study, in order to estimate the relative empowerment of women within households, we investigated who did household care tasks and how much of their time was spent on these.

Finally, child well-being was conceptualised in terms of impacts on children's health, education and access to care in line with other research of this nature locally (Agüero et al., 2006; Coetzee, 2011) and internationally (Adato et al., 2000).

4. Method
4.1 Population and research site

This study was conducted in 2010 in the urban area of Doornkop, Johannesburg. The target population was households with children aged 15 years and younger (the age of eligibility for the CSG at the time of the field work in 2010). The area of Doornkop was chosen because in a previous project, the Johannesburg Poverty and Livelihoods Study (De Wet et al., 2008), Doornkop was the area receiving the highest number of CSGs across eight of the poorest wards (municipal areas) in the City of Johannesburg. Ward 50, Doornkop, is the poorest ward of Region C and the tenth most deprived ward in Johannesburg. In this study, Doornkop had the largest number of CSG beneficiaries and the third-lowest score on the urban insecurity index measured in terms of multiple indicators of poverty, namely employment, health, food security, education, housing, access to services, overcrowding and social support (De Wet et al., 2008). Female-headed households are worse off than male-headed households across this deprived area of the city.

Despite its low urban insecurity score, the Doornkop community has access to a number of services such as free and accessible schools, primary health care clinics and free health services for pregnant women and children under six years, piped water and electrified homes (although only minimal usage is free, after which it is charged for), refuse removal and tarred streets and street lights. However, high levels of unemployment keep households very poor.

4.2 Sampling

We surveyed 343 households across Doornkop, which represents 10% of households with children in this ward. Households were sampled systematically, using a recent administrative map of Ward 50 to select municipal stands evenly across the ward. For each stand selected, we then selected one primary female caregiver of children 15 years or younger from the households on that stand. If more than one household had such a caregiver present, then the household to be interviewed was randomly selected on site using a pre-determined formula. The final sample included both CSG beneficiary and non-beneficiary households.

4.3 Data collection

To collect data we developed a questionnaire consisting of 14 sections of closed-ended questions broadly covering background household information, livelihood activities and income, food security, use of and views of the grant, partner relationships, household decision-making and care responsibilities, and dimensions of women's empowerment. The questionnaire was developed by the lead researcher in consultation with the research team and other experts and tested twice to ensure its appropriateness. The field work was conducted in July 2010 by 81 fourth-year social work students from the department of social work at the University of Johannesburg. This was integrated into their learning programme, and they were thoroughly trained to collect these data.

4.4 Limitations

Any research that includes investigating how income is used faces the problem of the fungibility of money. This means we can never be entirely certain what the CSG is used on as beneficiaries do generally have other sources of income. Since household income is pooled, separating out what the different income sources are spent on is often impossible.

The design of this study generated largely descriptive data and therefore does not permit conclusive direct causal links. However, the trends that were revealed suggest important relationships between the variables.

A further limitation is that the findings cannot be generalised to all CSG households nationally. Also, conducting the field work on weekdays excluded those with regular employment away from home, and as the questionnaire was lengthy some questions were unanswered, which left some gaps in the data. The results may, however, be generalised to other urban areas with similar social and demographic profiles. Finally, as this was a quantitative study, nuances and complexities that are best captured using a qualitative research design may have been missed.

5. Findings

5.1 Demographics of women CSG recipients

Of the 343 households surveyed, 281 were receiving one or more CSGs, covering a total of 421 children. Thus, 82% of the surveyed households with children 15 years and younger were receiving a CSG, which is a very high uptake of the grant. On average, a caregiver received 1.5 CSGs per household. Nearly half of the respondents were looking after very young children: 44% were under five years, which points to a large care burden. The demographics of the CSG recipients and their households were as follows.

Marital status: Just over a third (37%) were married or in a partner relationship and the rest (63%) had never been married, or were divorced or widowed.

Headship of households: Just over half (52%) were female headed, 38% were male headed and 10% had joint headship (self-identified).

Age of CSG recipients: Caregivers were fairly young, more than half falling between the ages of 21 and 40. The age ranges were as follows: 31% were aged 21 to 30, 26% were aged 31 to 40, 23% were aged 41 to 50 and 11% were aged 51 to 60. Caregivers who were particularly vulnerable because they were either very young or very old were a small minority: 5% were between 16 and 20 and 4% were 61 and above.

Level of education: CSG caregivers were on the whole fairly well educated. More than half (56%) had secondary school education, and 26% had a school leaving certificate. At the high end, 3% had a post-matric qualification, while at the low end 13% had only primary schooling and 2% had no schooling at all.

Source of income: Completing school does not guarantee income security: 71% of the households receiving the CSG earned R2500 or less per month, compared to only 10% of non-CSG households ($p = 0.000$). For 14% of the households the CSG was the only income. For the remaining 86% for whom the CSG supplemented household income, income was from multiple, diverse sources such as other grants, formal and informal employment and some support from outside their families, such as from their church or a non-governmental organisation. Regular income was most commonly from social grants, in the main the CSG and less so from other grants such as the Old Age Pension.

Figure 1 shows that only 13% of the respondents had regular wages, while 24% had occasional or irregular wages and a further 24% ran their own small businesses. More than 80% of respondents never received financial donations from outside their family. This shows that their income sources were varied and insecure with the exception of state cash transfers, which constitute regular income. The fact that 82% of all children in Doornkop were receiving a grant means the CSG contributes in an important way to reducing child poverty here, despite the small value of the grant (Patel, 2012). For all households receiving a CSG, on average the grant made up 31% (standard deviation 38) of the household's income. This means that when the income from the CSG was pooled with other household income it would almost certainly benefit all the

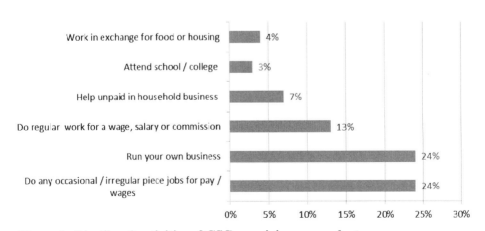

Figure 1: Livelihood activities of CSG–receiving respondents

children in the household, irrespective of whether they receive a grant or not (Case & Menendez, 2007; Delany et al., 2008).

5.2 Women's power in the household

Questions about how decisions are made in households revealed that the women receiving the grant were the primary decision-makers. First, as Figure 2 shows, women made the financial decisions in 81% of the households: 53% were the exclusive financial decision-makers in the household and 28% shared financial decision-making with partners or other adults. Women were consistently the main decision-makers when it came to specific areas of spending, for example, food and groceries (77%), health (77%), education (81%), children's clothes (84%) and transport (74%).

Second, the grant was being used largely to contribute to household or child needs, corroborating findings from other studies on how women use cash income in households (Kabeer, 1994; Haddad, 1999) and what CSG money is being used for (Delany et al., 2008; DSD, SASSA & UNICEF, 2012). The grant was mainly used to buy food (52% always used it for food and a further 23% often or sometimes did). It was also used to pay for school fees and uniforms (38% always used it for school costs and a further 27% often or sometimes did).

Third, decision-making related to children was even more strongly the responsibility of the woman, with 84% saying they were the sole decision-makers on children's health issues, 74% on discipline and 80% on education.

Women beneficiaries' views of the impact of the CSG on their lives were largely positive. Eighty-two per cent of recipients said that the grant had made their lives better. Sixty-five per cent said that they would not survive if it were stopped, which indicates how important the grant is for economic security for women and particularly

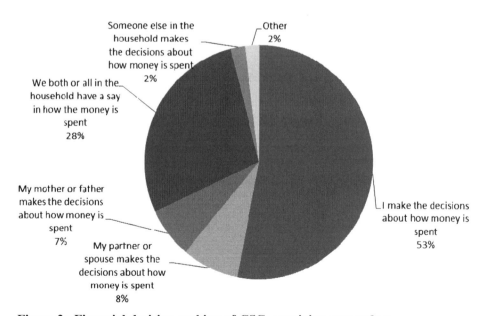

Figure 2: Financial decision-making of CSG–receiving respondents

for single women. A further 66% of respondents who were receiving the CSG believed that the grant gave them personal power and courage and 61% said it made them feel good about themselves. These are all significant indicators of personal empowerment and self-belief (Adato et al., 2000).

In summary, the women who were receiving one or more CSGs controlled the way the money was spent, were the key decision-makers in their homes, used the grant money largely for food and education, and believed the grant had benefited them and their households.

5.3 Gender and care

Eighty-six per cent of all the respondents interviewed said they spent most of their time at home on care and domestic responsibilities such as housework, shopping, care of children and care of other members of the family. Close to half of all respondents agreed that there are certain jobs that remain 'women's work', which indicates an acceptance of gendered roles. In addition, the CSG recipients were engaged in social care activities with their children either daily or often, such as help with homework (64%), accompanying children to school (35%) and playing with or reading to them (58%). Interestingly, CSG recipients were more likely to engage in these activities either daily or often than respondents who were not CSG recipients. The differences between CSG and non-CSG households that were statistically significant were in relation to watching television with their children ($p = 0.041$), providing help with school work ($p = 0.009$), and playing with or reading to the children ($p = 0.003$). We are therefore able to conclude that the caregivers who were receiving the CSG were more actively engaged in care activities with their children than non-CSG respondents, which is a positive indicator of parental involvement in promoting child well-being. There are emotional and social benefits to this, but also more clearly measurable advantages; for example, studies show that children whose caregivers are positively engaged in their education perform better at school (Desforges, 2003).

In addition, women respondents were also responsible for the care of other children who were not receiving the CSG. A total of 17% of respondents in CSG households cared for one or more non-CSG children. Seventy-four per cent of the respondents said they had not applied for grants for the other children in their care, for varying reasons, such as not having the correct documentation (46%), or not knowing how to apply for the grant (8%). The women in our sample were thus faced with additional care demands, with more dependants in households possibly in part because of the HIV/AIDS epidemic and in part because of economic and social stressors.

It is also evident from the data that the women were bearing the greatest responsibility for coping with poverty with limited resources and meeting the care needs of their families and households. Financial burdens are increased when fathers do not contribute to the maintenance of children. Sixty-one per cent of the total number of fathers ($n = 102$) who were not the current partners of all the women interviewed never paid private maintenance for their children. In addition, 30% of all the respondents receiving a CSG said that the fathers no longer provided support for their children now that they were receiving a CSG. This raises the question as to whether the CSG may be displacing private maintenance paid by the fathers. While no evidence prior to this exists of the CSG displacing remittances (Neves et al., 2009), remittance displacement is an unintended consequence of cash transfers in a range of other countries (Cox & Jimenez, 1995).

We were also interested in how access to basic services mediated women's domestic and care responsibilities. This picture was largely positive, with 95% of CSG households having access to electricity, 98% having running water in the house or yard and 76% having a flush toilet. About a third (34%) of the CSG recipients said that one or more of their children attended a crèche or was cared for by a child-minder.

Thus care activities were overwhelmingly the responsibility of women in these CSG households, leading to time poverty, a large domestic work burden and limited mobility (Folbre, 1994). This was somewhat eased by municipal services that alleviated the burden of domestic chores. For example, water piped directly to a household's stand relieves women from having to fetch and carry water for their homes.

5.4 Child well-being

We now turn to the question of child well-being. On the basis of CSG recipient perceptions, we considered four outcome indicators: food security, health status and immunisation, school attendance and pass rates, and family cohesion. These outcomes were not verified against administrative records or height-for-age measures of children to confirm their validity. However, the findings do provide an indication of how the caregivers perceived the well-being of the children in their care.

We used a validated Household Food Insecurity Access Scale (Coates et al., 2006) to measure household food security of respondent households. More than half (54%) of all CSG households said their households experienced severe food insecurity and a further 25% were moderately food insecure. This is despite the fact that 52% of women always spent the CSG on food. Therefore, without the CSG food insecurity would be more pronounced. The positive nutritional effects of the CSG were confirmed by Agüero et al. (2006), who found gains in child height-for-age. With respect to child health, 97% of CSG recipients said their children had been immunised, and the majority (92%) considered their children to be in good health.

All CSG children (100%) of school-going age were reported to be attending school regularly. Seventy-four per cent of school-going CSG children had not failed a grade. This was also confirmed by another study that concluded that children who received a grant were significantly more likely to be enrolled in school in the years following award of the grant (Case et al., 2005).

South Africa's history of migrant labour damaged family cohesion, resulting in large numbers of children being cared for apart from their biological parents (Lund, 2008; Hall & Wright, 2011). Acknowledging this, it was decided to make the grant payable to the 'primary caregiver' of the child, possibly in the extended family, but also by people outside the family. The policymakers also took account of the fact that the HIV/AIDS epidemic might worsen the situation. We were therefore interested in who cares for children and in their care arrangements. We found that all the CSG children in the sample were cared for within the family, living in households with relatives (made up of two or three generations), and 87% lived with either one or both biological parents, as Figure 3 shows. However, the dominance of women as primary caregivers and their consequent care burden is again revealed when Figure 3 is

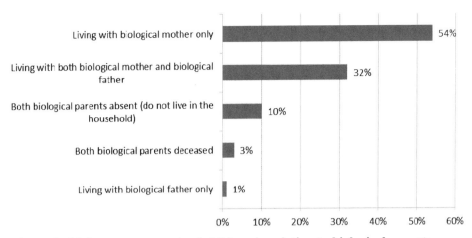

Figure 3: Living arrangements of children in relation to biological parents

examined, as it shows that 54% of the children in the sample lived with their mother only, while a small percentage (1%) of children lived with their biological father only. Sixty-two per cent of the CSG recipients said that the grant 'helped to keep their family together'.

In addition, 87% of all grants received by the caregivers were for children who actually lived in the household with the caregiver. This is contrary to the popular belief that CSG beneficiaries receive the grant but that the children do not actually live with them. Only 9% of the total number of children who received a CSG lived away from the household, and of this 9% the majority (70%) were between one and 10 years of age. The main reasons cited for children living away from home were a lack of accommodation (21%), school attendance (16%) and because the CSG recipient needed someone to care for the children while she worked (8%). Half the children (50%) who lived away from home were in a rural area, and in these cases their main caregiver was the grandmother (49%). The children who lived away from home were thus with close relatives. Of the children living away from home, 61% had been away for one to four years, 26% for five to eight years, 11% for nine to 10 years and 3% for more than 10 years.

In summary, the children in the sample who were in receipt of a CSG were generally healthy, lived with family, mostly with one or both biological parents, and had good school attendance and reasonable performance. Nevertheless, they lived in food-insecure households and we can therefore conclude that the grant is probably used largely to pay for food.

6. Conclusions

While this research cannot confirm direct causality between the key variables, the data are suggestive of trends and relationships between variables which could be explored in further research. Two important conclusions may be drawn from the findings. First, the evidence appears to support our contention that the CSG enhances women's power and control over household decision-making in financial matters and general household spending and promotes child well-being. The fact that the women in the sample could make decisions and exercise freedom of choice about how to spend the grant suggests that the grant enabled them to generate outcomes they considered important for the quality of their lives and their children's well-being (Sen, 1999). We conclude that the CSG may give female grant beneficiaries a sense of empowerment and that it therefore has some positive transformative effects. Indeed, Adato et al. (2000:51–2) also found that Mexico's cash transfer programme for children, which is paid to women, can contribute to empowerment by 'putting resources in women's hands' and thus 'directing the benefits toward expenditures that normally fall within the decision-making domain of women'. In contrast, we have limited knowledge of how the small numbers of men who receive the CSG spend the money, what the gender dynamics are in these households, and how the grant affects both gender relations and child well-being. More research is needed in these areas.

Second, the data clearly show that South African women bear greater responsibility than men for the care of children, given the entrenched gender-based patterns of care and past historical factors, such as the impact of the migrant labour system on family life. This unequal distribution of care burdens between men and women in the private domain (family and household) increases gender inequality and curtails the ability of CSG beneficiaries to engage in activities (such as earning income) outside the home. The enormous domestic and care responsibilities of CSG beneficiaries remain largely unacknowledged and invisible to policymakers. Public discourse about how grants create dependency seldom takes into account the gendered nature of care and how it affects women's quality of life. Helping to lessen the care burden on women should be viewed positively and not because we merely assume that 'things are good for women because they are good for children' (for a critique of this approach, see Budlender in Patel, 2009:52). Molyneux (2006) correctly cautions against positioning motherhood as the key to the successful outcome of poverty reduction programmes and viewing women merely as conduits to reach children in order to promote child well-being. Instead the empowerment of women should be supported as an end goal in itself (Kabeer et al., 2010). Thus, improving the status and position of women and overcoming unequal gender relations are important policy outcomes that need to be incorporated into social protection programmes (Jones & Holmes, 2010), even those that focus primarily on children. However, social protection programmes by themselves cannot achieve all these outcomes: they need to work in concert with other public policies and social programmes to promote both social transformation and child well-being.

Acknowledgements

The authors wish to thank Reem Mutwali for assistance with the statistical analysis for the study and the reference group, Nhlanhla Jordan and Professors Francie Lund, Shireen Hassim, Vivienne Bozalek and Trudie Knijn for their input at both the conceptualisation and analysis phase of this research. This research was funded by the South Africa Netherlands research Programme on Alternatives to Development (SANPAD), and the University Research Committee at the University of Johannesburg.

References

Adato, M, De la Brière, B, Mindek, D & Quisumbing, A, 2000. The Impact of PROGRESA on Women's Status and Intrahousehold Relations. IFPRI (International Food Policy Research Institute, Washington, DC.

Agüero, JM, Carter, MR & Woolard, I, 2006. The Impact of Unconditional Cash Transfers on Nutrition: The South African Child Support Grant. SALDRU (Southern Africa Labour and Development Research Unit), University of Cape Town.

Ardington, E & Lund, F, 1995. Pensions and development: Social security as complementary to programmes of reconstruction and development. Development Southern Africa 12(4), 557–77.

Bertrand, M, Mullainathan, S & Miller, D, 2003. Public policy and extended families: Evidence from pensions in South Africa. The World Bank Economic Review 17(1), 27–50.

Casale, D & Posel, D, 2005. Women and the economy: How far have we come? Agenda 19(64), 21–9.

Case, A & Menendez, A, 2007. Does money empower the elderly? Evidence from the Agincourt Demographic Surveillance Site, South Africa. Scandinavian Journal of Public Health 35(Suppl 69), 157–64.

Case, A, Hosegood, V & Lund, F, 2005. The reach and impact of Child Support Grants: Evidence from KwaZulu-Natal. Development Southern Africa 22(4), 467–82.

Chant, S (Ed.), 2010. The International Handbook of Gender and Poverty: Concepts, Research and Policy. Edward Elgar, Cheltenham.

Coates, J, Swindale, A & Bilinsky, P, 2006. Household Food Insecurity Access Scale (HFIAS) for Measurement of Food Access: Indicator Guide. FANTA (Food and Nutrition Technical Assistance Project, Washington, DC.

Coetzee, M, 2011. Finding the benefits: Estimating the impact of the South African Child Support Grant. Stellenbosch Working Paper Series No. WP16/2011, Department of Economics and Bureau for Economic Research, University of Stellenbosch.

Cox, D & Jimenez, E, 1995. Private transfers and the effectiveness of public income distribution in the Philippines. In Van de Walle, D & Nead, K (Eds), Public Spending and the Poor: Theory and Evidence. Johns Hopkins University Press, Baltimore, MD.

De Wet, T, Patel, L, Korth, M & Forrester, C, 2008. Johannesburg Poverty and Livelihoods Study. Centre for Social Development in Africa, University of Johannesburg.

Delany, A, Ismail, Z, Graham, L & Ramkisson, Y, 2008. Review of the Child Support Grant: Uses, Implementation and Obstacles. Department of Social Development. CASE, SASSA & UNICEF (Community Agency for Social Enquiry, South African Social Security Agency & United Nations Children's Fund), Johannesburg.

Desforges, C, 2003. The impact of parental involvement, parental support and family education on pupil achievement and adjustment. Research Report 433, Department for Education and Skills. London.

Devereux, S, Ellis, F & White, P, 2008. Social Pensions. Regional Hunger and Vulnerability Programme, Johannesburg.

DSD, SASSA & UNICEF (Department of Social Development, South African Social Security Agency & United Nations Children's Fund), 2012. The South African Child Support Grant Impact Assessment: Evidence from a Survey of Children, Adolescents and their Households. UNICEF South Africa, Pretoria.

Duflo, E, 2003. Grandmothers and granddaughters: Old-age pensions and intrahousehold allocation in South Africa. The World Bank Economic Review 17(1), 1–25.

Ellis, F, 2007. Regional lesson learning from the case studies. REBA (Regional Evidence Building Agenda) Case Study Brief Series, Regional Hunger and Vulnerability Programme, Johannesburg. www.cashlearning.org/downloads/resources/casestudies/reba_case_study_brief_lessons.pdf Accessed 15 November 2012.

Folbre, N, 1994. Who Pays for the Kids? Gender and Structures of Constraint. Oxford University Press, London.

Folbre, N, 2008. Reforming care. Politics and Society 36(3), 373–87.

Haddad, L, 1999. The income earned by women: Impact and welfare outcomes. Agricultural Economics 20, 135–41.

Hall, K & Wright, G, 2011. A profile of children living in South Africa in 2008. Studies in Economics and Econometrics 34(3), 45–68.

Handa, S, Devereux, S & Webb, D (Eds), 2011. Social Protection for Africa's Children. Routledge Studies in Development Economics, New York.

Hassim, S, 2006. Gender equality and developmental social welfare in South Africa. In Razavi, S & Hassim, S (Eds), Gender and Social Policy in a Global Context: Uncovering the Gendered Structure of the 'Social'. Palgrave, Basingstoke, pp. 109–29.

Heinrich, C, Hoddinott, J, Samson, M, Mac Quene, K, Van Niekerk, I & Renaud, B, 2012. The South African Child Support Grant Impact Assessment. UNICEF, SASSA & DSD (United Nations Children's Fund, South African Social Security Agency & Department of Social Development), Pretoria.

Henshall Momsen, J, 2004. Gender and Development. Routledge, London.

ILO & UNDP (International Labour Organization & United Nations Development Programme), 2011. Sharing Innovative Experiences: Successful Social Protection Floor Experiences. ILO & UNDP, New York.

Jones, N & Holmes, R, 2010. Gender, Politics and Social Protection. Why Social Protection is 'Gender Bling'. ODI (Overseas Development Institute), London.

Kabeer, N, 1994. Reversed Realities: Gender Hierarchies in Development Thought. Verso, London.

Kabeer, N, 1999. Resources, agency, achievements: Reflections on the measurement of women's empowerment. Development and Change 30(3), 435–64.

Kabeer, N, Mumtaz, K & Sayeed, A, 2010. Beyond risk management: Vulnerability, social protection and citizenship in Pakistan. Journal of International Development 22, 1–19.

Leibbrandt, M, Finn, A, Argent, J & Woolard, I, 2010. Changes in income poverty over the post-apartheid period: An analysis based on data from the 1993 Project for Statistics on Living Standards and Development and the 2008 base wave of the National Income Dynamics Study. Studies in Economics and Econometrics 34(3), 25–43.

Lund, F, 2006. Gender and social security in South Africa. In Padayachee, V (Ed.), The Development Decade? Economic and Social Change in South Africa, 1994–2004. HSRC (Human Sciences Research Council) Press, Pretoria.

Lund, F, 2008. Changing Social Policy: The Child Support Grant in South Africa. HSRC (Human Sciences Research Council) Press, Cape Town.

Molyneux, M, 2006. Mothers at the service of the new poverty agenda: Progresa/Opportunidades, Mexico's conditional transfer programme. Social Policy & Administration 40(4), 425–49.

Molyneux, M & Thomson, M, 2011. Cash transfers, gender equity and women's empowerment in Peru, Ecuador and Bolivia. Gender and Development 19(2), 195–212.

Neves, D, Samson, M, Van Niekerk, I, Hlatshwayo, S & Du Toit, A, 2009. The Use and Effectiveness of Social Grants in South Africa. FinMark Trust, Institute for Poverty, Land and Agrarian Studies, and Economic Policy Research Institute, Cape Town.

Patel, L, 2009. The Gendered Character of Social Care in the Non-profit Sector in South Africa: Thematic Paper. Centre for Social Development in Africa, University of Johannesburg and UNRISD (United Nations Research Institute for Social Development), Geneva.

Patel, L, 2012. Poverty, gender and social protection: Child Support Grants in Soweto, South Africa. Journal of Policy Practice 11(1–2), 106–20.

Patel, L & Hochfeld, T, 2011. It buys food but does it change gender relations? Child Support Grants in Soweto, South Africa. Gender and Development 19(2), 229–40.

Patel, L, Hochfeld, T, Moodley, J & Mutwali, R, 2012. The gender dynamics and impact of the child support grant in Doornkop, Soweto. Report. University of Johannesburg.

Posel, D & Rogan, M, 2012. Gendered trends in poverty in the post-apartheid period, 1997–2006. Development Southern Africa 29(1), 96–113.

Razavi, S, 2007. The political and social economy of care in a development context: Conceptual issues, research questions and policy options. Gender and Development Programme Paper No. 3, UNRISD (United Nations Research Institute for Social Development), Geneva.

Sabates-Wheeler, R & Devereux, S, 2008. Transformative social protection: The currency of social justice. In Barrientos, A & Hulme, D (Eds), Social Protection for the Poor and Poorest: Concepts, Policies and Politics. Palgrave MacMillan, London, pp. 64–84.

Sabates-Wheeler, R & Kabeer, N, 2003. Gender Equality and the Extension of Social Protection. International Labour Office, Geneva.

SASSA (South African Social Security Agency), 2012. Fact Sheet no. 4 of 2012: Summary of Social Grants Distribution in South Africa as at 30 April 2012. SASSA, Pretoria.

Sen, A, 1999. Development as Freedom. Oxford University Press, Oxford.

Sweetman, C, 2011. Introduction: Social protection. Gender and Development 19(2), 169–77.

UNICEF, 2006. State of the World's Children 2007: Women and Children – The Double Dividend of Gender Equality. UNICEF (United Nations Children's Fund), New York.

Van der Berg, S, Louw, M & Yu, D, 2008. Post-transition poverty trends based on an alternative data source. South African Journal of Economics 76(1), 59–76.

Vorster, J & De Waal, L, 2008. Beneficiaries of the Child Support Grant: Findings from a national survey. The Social Work Practitioner-Researcher 20(2), 233–48.

Williams, MJ, 2007. The Social and Economic Impacts of South Africa's Child Support Grant. Economic Policy Research Institute, Cape Town.

Woolard, I, 2003. Impact of government programmes using administrative data sets: Social assistance grants. Project 6.2. of the Ten Year Review Research Programme. www.sarpn.org/documents/d0000946/P1041-Woolard_10year_June2003.pdf Accessed 25 July 2012.

The contribution of non-formal social protection to social development in Botswana

Rodreck Mupedziswa[1] & Dolly Ntseane[2]

This article documents the non-formal system of social protection in Botswana, identifies opportunities for synergies between the non-formal and formal systems, and considers the challenges of integrating the two. Non-formal initiatives depend on traditional forms of social protection such as self-help, self-organisation, membership of a social group and cultural norms of community solidarity, reciprocity and obligations; whereas the formal social protection system is undergirded by statutes and laws, institutionalised in policy and legislation, publicly funded and delivered within national norms and eligibility criteria. The article argues that integrating the two could produce a complementary and responsive system of social protection that takes account of indigenous and other non-formal systems of support and enhances the delivery of social protection services, and that other countries in the region might derive lessons from Botswana's experience.

1. Introduction

At just over two million, Botswana has a relatively small population. At independence in 1966, the country was ranked among the poorest in the world, but its position improved in the 1970s when diamonds were discovered. In recent times, Botswana has set an example of socioeconomic and political stability in the sub-region. Among the 15 members of the SADC (Southern African Development Community), the country's HDI (human development index) compares quite favourably at 0.694, being inferior only to that of the Seychelles (0.845) and Mauritius (8.04) and superior to all the rest, including South Africa (0.683) (NDSD, 2010). This incontrovertibly depicts a vibrant economy. Even so, up to a third of the population may be living below the national poverty datum line (Statistics Botswana, 2011). In addition, Botswana is among the countries in the sub-region hardest hit by HIV and AIDS. As at 2009, 331 432 citizens aged 15 and above were living with AIDS and 61 840 citizens aged 0 to 17 had lost their parents to AIDS (NACA, 2009). Those largely affected by poverty and disease are older people, children, youth and female-headed households. The government of Botswana has therefore opted to provide a fairly comprehensive formal social protection system. Non-formal social protection initiatives have played a critical role in promoting welfare and there is now debate about whether or not to integrate the two systems. Many commentators appear to support integration. For instance, the SADC Protocol has called for integration, but without spelling out the concomitant issues and challenges.

---

[1] Professor and Head of Department of Social Work, University of Botswana, Gaborone, Botswana.
[2] Senior Lecturer, Department of Social Work, University of Botswana, Gaborone, Botswana

Since there is a dearth of documentary evidence on the role of the non-formal system of social protection in Botswana, this article aims to help fill the gap by examining how the non-formal system affects social development in Botswana. The Batswana government has recently indicated that it intends to develop a more holistic and integrated social development policy (Ministry of Local Government, 2010a). Documenting the contribution of the non-formal system will be useful for planning purposes. The non-formal system is important since the formal social protection initiatives currently in place in Botswana may not be sustainable given the country's narrow economic base and the current global economic crisis (RHVP, 2011). Successful integration of the two systems would undoubtedly strengthen the provision of social protection in the country, and such integration might serve as a model for the rest of southern Africa, where governments struggle to meet their social protection obligations.

Non-formal initiatives are locally arranged social protection measures that are predicated on people's cultural beliefs, norms and values. Olivier et al. (2008) note that the core values of the non-formal system include, among others, self-help, inherent solidarity, reciprocity, and contribution obligation and entitlement. These values are socially and culturally determined. In other words, non-formal social protection consists of self-organised safety nets based on membership of a particular social group or community that includes family, kinship, age group, neighbourhood or ethnic group. Olivier & Dekker (2003:562) state that non-formal social protection is the 'counterpart' of formal initiatives, 'covering social protection mechanisms outside the formal social security paradigm'. The non-formal mechanisms are self-regulating, involve local community members in the provision of care and support, and are culturally motivated. They deliver a variety of benefits, including income and psychosocial and emotional support. In Botswana, the non-formal system complements the formal to an enormous extent, so it is important to explore the role it plays.

Formal social protection initiatives, on the other hand, are based on statutory arrangements provided by the state through policies and legislation. The World Bank defines (formal) social protection as public measures to provide income security for individuals (Kaseke, 2004). The International Labour Organization explains that the goal of (formal) social protection is not mere survival, but social inclusion and the preservation of human dignity (Kaseke, 2004). The term 'formal social protection' means public intervention to provide support to the critically poor and to help individuals, households and communities to manage risk (Holzmann & Jorgensen, 1990). Various African Union documents describe formal social protection as a 'package' of policies and programmes to reduce the poverty and vulnerability of large segments of the population and their exposure to risks, promote efficient labour markets, and enhance people's capacity to protect themselves against lack or loss of adequate income and basic social services (Partnership for African Social & Governance Research, 2011).

Before independence in 1966, the majority of the Batswana relied on the subsistence economy and non-formal social protection. With time, urbanisation began to undermine the non-formal social protection system as people migrated from rural villages to urban areas, abandoning vulnerable people such as the elderly and the frail. Social ills mushroomed. In response, the government launched the National Development Plan (1970–1975), in which it articulated for the first time the need to promote formal social protection based on the principles of social justice and equality of opportunity (GoB, 1970). To this end, the government mandated the then Social

Welfare Unit to develop a social protection regime that would address the problems of poverty and destitution. The foundation was laid for the establishment of a minimum level of social protection, which is discussed below. However, the shortcomings of the formal system persisted, hence the continued role played by non-formal social protection. It is therefore pertinent that the nature and role of the non-formal system be documented.

Despite the growth of the formal social protection system, the people of Botswana cling to the non-formal system for many reasons. The formal system has disadvantages of programme gaps and inadequate reach of programmes for poor and vulnerable persons (Ellis et al., 2009; RHVP, 2011), and it lacks the comprehensive and inclusive policies that would contribute to long-term human security and enable people to get out of the quagmire of poverty. Various factors have eroded traditional cultural practices and systems of support – changes in economic conditions bringing poverty and vulnerability, changes in social and family structures, migration, HIV/AIDS – yet despite these negative impacts on non-formal social support, many people continue to rely on it, as documented below.

Globally, views differ on how the formal system of social protection should relate to the non-formal system. Some authors (e.g. RHVP, 2011) argue that formal social protection systems should be integrated with and build on rather than substitute for non-formal social support systems. Others, however, argue that although the non-formal system should continue while the formal system is being established, once it is established the formal system can replace the non-formal (Nhabinde & Schoeman, n.d.). Proponents of the latter school of thought thus see the non-formal system as transitory. This article argues that the former view, which calls for integration of the two systems, is more realistic for Botswana. Yet in Botswana today there is limited recognition of this view given that insufficient attention has been paid to what actually exists and how the two systems might work together. The reality is that developing countries such as Botswana, with their limited resources, cannot afford to discard the non-formal system that is still the mainstay of the majority of ordinary people.

The rest of this article is structured as follows. Section 2 presents the theoretical framework, Section 3 describes the non-formal systems of social protection in Botswana and Section 4 the formal systems, Section 5 considers possibilities for integrating the two and the various challenges, and Section 6 concludes and offers suggestions for the way forward. Note that we use the term 'non-formal' to mean organised but happening outside the formal system that is guided by laws, rather than 'informal', which would simply mean occurring in a manner that is not organised.

2. Social development and social protection

'Social development' is a relatively new concept that originated in the Global South and is associated with efforts by governments and non-government actors to improve the living conditions of millions of poor people the world over. Midgley (1995:250) sees it as 'a process of planned change designed to promote the well-being of the population in conjunction with a dynamic process of economic development'. Patel (2005) argues that social programmes that enable people to participate in the productive economy are the most effective way to enhance their welfare and achieve economic development. Midgley & Tang (2001) say that social development requires purposeful intervention from state and non-state actors and the creation of organisational and institutional arrangements at national level that harmonise economic and social policies within a comprehensive commitment to people-centred development, and that to this end government action through protective policy and legislation is indicated. Gray (1996) points out that social development discourages dependency, promotes the active involvement of people in their own development, employs a multi-faceted, multi-sectoral approach, and encourages partnership between the state and other stakeholders. Proponents therefore argue that well-being is about development of people, and that social investment in key social services actually contributes to economic development.

Patel (2005) observes that South Africa has adopted a social development approach to social welfare that includes social protection and developmental welfare services based on a rights-based approach, active citizenship, participation in development, and empowerment of the socially excluded and marginalised. She envisages a leading role for the state in social development in partnership with individuals, families, communities, civil society organisations and the private sector. She points out that post-apartheid social development policies have attempted to integrate the formal and the non-formal systems of support through a partnership approach to welfare service delivery, but that many institutional challenges remain (Patel, 2008). She considers social development programmes to be investments with significant economic and social benefits to society and not a drain on societal resources (Patel, 2005:85).

Social development is thus about opportunities for participation and for vulnerable groups to pursue a sustainable livelihood. It addresses the socioeconomic and political concerns of individuals and communities about critical challenges associated with pervasive threats to their livelihoods and dignity, and their very lives. In developing countries such as Botswana, primary threats to social development are poverty, unemployment and disease, including HIV/AIDS. Consequently, any meaningful definition of social development must encompass social protection, since this is the heart of the matter.

The term 'social protection' covers, broadly, public and private measures, or a combination of the two, designed to protect individuals against life-cycle crises that curtail their capacity to meet their needs (Kaseke & Dhemba, 2007; Mpedi, 2008; Midgley, 2013). Social protection transcends the market focus of the social policy approach and includes the contribution of the state and other actors in development and innovations at household, neighbourhood and community levels. Considerable attention has been focused on formal systems of social protection at the expense of the non-formal systems. Yet the need to account for activities outside the formal sphere cannot be over-emphasised. Non-formal arrangements such as indigenous forms of social provision and efforts by CBOs (community-based organisations), FBOs (faith-based organisations) and NGOs (non-governmental organisations) play a critical role in assisting individual households and communities (Midgley, 1994; Maes, 2003; Olivier & Dekker, 2003; Foster, 2004; Patel, 2005, 2008; Mpedi, 2008). The formal system on its own has not been able to cater sufficiently to the needs of ordinary people in developing countries such as Botswana. Poverty, unemployment, war, famine, harvest failures, floods, chronic illness and loss of assets continue to cripple many developing economies, leaving people without any meaningful form of support. Further, the HIV/AIDS pandemic has forced many communities to rely more on the non-formal social support system, putting this system under severe pressure.

The non-formal system includes what Patel et al. (2012) refer to as indigenous practices: essentially community-based welfare practices that historically have promoted social welfare. The Regional Hunger and Vulnerability Programme (RHVP, 2010) refers to the non-formal system as 'informal insurance', explaining that it comprises two main features, social reciprocity and household asset building, and argues that formal and non-formal systems can co-exist to provide more comprehensive social protection.

Donors, NGOs and governments in a number of countries have built on indigenous practices to support poor and vulnerable persons. Examples of these practices include the sharing of produce from the chief's fields in Swaziland, small livestock transfers in Zimbabwe, burial societies in Lesotho and farm input support in Mozambique and Malawi. These are examples of social protection strategies built on traditional ways of providing support; they are innovative new initiatives designed to suit contemporary conditions (RHVP, 2007).

As this brief literature review shows, attempts are being made to mainstream the discourse on the non-formal social protection system by placing it firmly in the public domain. According to the RHVP (2010), non-formal approaches on the African continent have been eroded in recent decades, for reasons such as urbanisation, industrialisation and regionalisation. But the non-formal social protection system has not ceased to exist. Indigenous welfare practices continue to play a significant role in social development although they are seldom recognised. For this reason their contribution needs to be noted and documented.

The RHVP (2011) argues that because of its long-standing commitment to state-led social protection, its solid governance and its economic potential, Botswana of all African countries has the best chance of expanding its social protection system. However, the RHVP (2011) discusses only the formal social protection system in Botswana and does not appreciate the role of the non-formal system.

3. Non-formal social protection in Botswana

Three types of non-formal support are common in Botswana: family and kin, community support networks and mutual aid associations. Although research has shown that rural–urban migration, and famine, HIV/AIDS and other shocks, have weakened the effectiveness of such support (Apt, 2002; Emmanuel et al., 2011), indigenous welfare practices still operate in many African countries, Botswana included, and will continue to provide support to the poor and vulnerable (Shaibu & Wallhagen, 2002; Maes, 2003; Foster, 2007; Ntseane & Solo, 2007; Mpedi, 2008; Patel et al., 2012).

3.1 The extended family and kin support systems

In sub-Saharan Africa the extended family system, defined by Schapera (1970) as a group of families closely united by blood or marriage, is the most effective support for a household facing a crisis (Foster, 2007). Members of extended families assist each other socially, economically, psychologically and financially. Such assistance may take the form of regular urban–rural and inter-household income transfers. When crops fail, family members in town will send food and cash to needy relatives in rural areas. A relative in town who becomes unemployed will receive food from the rural areas or be received back into the rural homestead. Households experiencing income stress due to HIV and AIDS may send their children to live with relatives, who become responsible for feeding the children in their care (Foster, 2004, 2007; Miller et al., 2006; USAID, 2010).

The extended family also fosters children orphaned by AIDS. Fostering of children by aunts, uncles, grandparents and other relatives is common in Africa. In sub-Saharan Africa, an estimated 90% of orphaned children live with extended family members (Miller et al., 2006). Working or income earning households provide support in the form of food, access to education, shelter, clothing, psychosocial support and other basic needs (Foster, 2004; Miller et al., 2006).

In Botswana the extended family, driven by principles of solidarity and reciprocity, continues to provide a safety net in times of crisis. Members come together to carry out important domestic and economic activities: building or thatching huts, clearing the fields, weeding, harvesting, helping one another with gifts, livestock and other commodities. Well-to-do families foster or formally adopt relatives' children. The concept of *motlhoki* ('destitution') has always existed in the Setswana vocabulary, but the extended family has always been there to provide support and care.

3.2 Community support networks

Community support networks also continue to play an important role in meeting critical needs, be they spiritual, social or economic. In the pre-colonial era, this assistance was provided by the village chiefs, neighbours and other community members. Prior to independence, the chief occupied a position of privilege and power over his people (Wass, 1969; Schapera, 1970), and it was under his auspices that non-formal social protection was arranged. Two main non-formal social protection schemes were regulated by the chiefs: *masotla* (large tribal pastures) and *kgamelo* (milk cattle). The *masotla* belonged to the chief, and crops grown on these pastures were stored in tribal granaries (*difalana*) and then distributed to the community in times of starvation and to disadvantaged individuals from time to time. The chief sometimes gave *kgamelo* to the poorer members of the community to supplement their livelihood, but these animals were more often entrusted to prominent commoners for herding (Schapera, 1970; Denbow & Phenyo, 2006); milk from these animals would often be given to vulnerable groups in the community (Schapera, 1970).

Other support systems, such as *mafisa*, *majako*, *go tshwara teu* or *bodisa* and *letsema* or *molaletsa*, were provided by neighbours or the community. The *mafisa* system (lending cattle to the poor) was a special contract according to which destitute people were given cattle by wealthy relatives (Schapera, 1970). The *majako* system allowed poor people to work in the fields of the rich in return for a share of the harvest. *Go tshwara teu* or *bodisa* gave able-bodied poor people the opportunity to break the cycle of poverty by looking after cattle and receiving a cow each year in return (BIDPA, 1997). *Letsema* or *molaletsa* allowed members of the community to perform voluntary work on behalf of a deserving family. Although this type of support is diminishing, it still exists in some rural areas.

Community-based initiatives tend to focus on responding to poverty and unemployment and mitigating the impact of HIV/AIDS. Some attempts have been made to integrate the formal and the non-formal systems. Below, we review three such initiatives.

Introduced by the government in 1995, the CHBC (community home-based care) model provides comprehensive care services at home and at community levels in order to meet the physical, psychological, social and spiritual needs of terminally ill patients, including people living with AIDS and their families (Department of Social Services & Ministry of Local Government, 2005). Volunteers from the community are trained to work with family members to provide support such as bathing the patient, cleaning the homestead, cooking and assisting the patient to adhere to medication. NGOs and CBOs are also involved (NACA, 2010). Assistance is also provided in the form of a monthly food basket, transport, relocation, counselling, rehabilitation and burial.

In 2009 the number of registered patients was 3242, compared to 5745 in 2002. The decline in the number of beneficiaries reflects the transformation that free anti-retroviral treatment has achieved in the lives of individuals living with HIV (Ministry of Local Government, 2010b). The CHBC programme has helped the majority of the beneficiaries to return to an economically active life. Further, the CHBC model demonstrates how government programmes (formal social protection) can be integrated into non-formal initiatives spearheaded by community organisations and NGOs.

The FSP (Family Strengthening Programme) is an initiative that fosters community involvement. It has been run since 2008 by SOS Children's Villages, an independent NGO that takes care of orphans and abandoned, destitute and traumatised children. The FSP is a community-based child care programme aimed at strengthening the capacity of families and communities to take care of children (SOS Botswana, 2011). The programme supports disadvantaged families faced with adverse external circumstances within their communities. Beneficiaries include single parents and households headed by siblings or grandparents. The programme complements government efforts by targeting vulnerable children who do not qualify for the orphan care programme but are very poor and needy. By 2010 the programme had reached an estimated 1526 children. The programme works in close partnership with social workers, community leaders and community volunteers.

Finally, there is BOCAIP (Botswana Christian AIDS Intervention Programme), a national level FBO that operates a network of 11 Christian HIV/AIDS counselling centres in 11 districts across the country. The organisation works in close partnership with local churches, religious leaders, FBOs and other HIV/AIDS service networks. With approximately 130 employees spread across the country, BOCAIP's primary goal is to mobilise and coordinate the Christian community to implement HIV-related behavioural change interventions, products and services (BOCAIP, 2008). In 2010, BOCAIP provided a total of 39 555 counselling sessions in locations across Botswana. These included pre-test, post-test and ongoing supportive sessions as well as marital or relationship and spiritual counselling. A further 5527 home visits were made to provide psychosocial support. An estimated 23 000 people were reached in clinics, workplaces, churches and schools (BOCAIP, 2010). Notably, these interventions help people by providing services, not cash, and are designed to improve human capabilities.

3.3 Mutual aid associations

Responding to specific member-defined contingencies, mutual aid associations embrace the principles of *botho* (i.e. *ubuntu*)[3] reciprocity and solidarity (Ntseane & Solo, 2007). These aid associations include burial societies and savings and credit enterprises, the three most dominant forms of non-formal social support initiative in southern Africa (Foster, 2007).

---

[3] For a definition of this concept, see Whitworth & Wilkinson (2013).

3.3.1 Burial societies

Burial societies (*diswaeti*) are self-reliant institutions found in many villages and urban settings in Botswana (Ngwenya, 2003). They fall into three categories: work-based societies that draw memberships from workplaces in urban settings, ethnic-oriented burial societies that are predominantly defined along ethnic lines, and communal burial societies whose memberships cuts across social and physical boundaries.

Social networks within kin relations often determine membership of a burial society (Ngwenya, 2003). The primary role of the society is to provide emergency relief to members and their relatives during bereavement. The support rendered may be in the form of financial contributions as well as physical labour during funerals, and psychosocial support and other essential services to allow the family time to grieve with dignity for their loved one. Burial societies receive no external financial support (Ngwenya, 2003). Members collectively pay an agreed subscription fee that ranges from P5 to P30 (less than US$1 to about US$4.5).[4] Older and destitute members of these societies often use their monthly cash transfers, such as pensions and destitute cash allowance, to pay for these subscriptions (Seleka et al., 2007). These societies all have member-nominated management committees who oversee the financial assets, facilitate fund-raising activities and maintain contact with key stakeholders.

3.3.2 Savings and credit associations

The financial sector in Botswana comprises both the formal and non-formal sub-sectors. Commercial and merchant banks are regulated by the Banking Act of 1995. Included in the non-formal sector are self-regulated financial transactions, including those overseen by rotating savings and credit associations, pawn shops and landlords, and financial transactions between friends and relatives. Available data show that non-formal financial activities continue to grow in urban and semi-urban areas and major villages (Mosene, 2002). This sector is apparently dominated by women (Okurut & Thuto, 2010). These activities play a key role in meeting financial needs, particularly for those who have limited access to the formal financial market. Commercial banks in Botswana lend money to individuals who have secure and permanent jobs or are able to offer collateral security for loans. Such conditions tend to drive many low income earners to non-formal financial sources.

Okurut & Thuto (2010) have established that medium and low income earners are the target clientele for non-formal institutions. The SACCOS (savings and credit co-operative society) at the University of Botswana, which has a membership of 300, is an example of a workplace-based initiative. Member benefits include investment and credit facilities, low income loans, high interest income on savings and a share of the SACCOS's profits (Kealeboga, 2011).

4. Formal social protection in Botswana

In Botswana, national planning principles of democracy, development, self-reliance and unity have been emphasised since independence, and it is these same principles that have guided formal social protection in the country (GoB, 1970). Below, we briefly review each of the formal social protection schemes.

---

[4] 1 USD = 7 to 7.5 BWP at the time of writing.

4.1 Programme for Destitute Persons

The rationale for this programme is 'to ensure that government provides minimum assistance to the genuine destitute persons to ensure their good health and welfare' (GoB, 2002). The programme targets individuals without assets, people with mental and physical disabilities, minor children without family support, and victims of natural disasters or temporary hardships. Destitute persons who are able-bodied are provided with rehabilitation activities that enable them to become self-sufficient and hence exit the programme. Benefits for this means-tested programme include a food basket, shelter, medical care, transport, funeral expenses, exemption from service levies and other necessary services. Children under the age of 18 are eligible to receive school uniforms, toiletries, transport, protective clothing, boarding requisites, tuition fees and street clothes (Ntseane & Solo, 2007). The monthly food basket is worth between P450 and P750, and there is also a cash component of P81. Currently, 40 865 individuals are registered on this programme (Ministry of Local Government, 2010a).

4.2 The Orphan Care Programme

A social allowance programme, this programme is not means-tested. It is open to children under the age of 18 who do not have parents and lack access to basic necessities. The programme has done much to respond to the immediate needs of orphans. Benefits for orphans include a nutritionally balanced monthly food basket worth P216 developed by the Ministry of Local Government and Lands in partnership with the Ministry of Health, clothing, toiletries, assistance with educational needs and psychosocial support. In 2002, 39 571 children were on the government's register, while by 2004 the figure had increased to 47 964. By 2008/9 the figure had risen to 48 119 (RHVP, 2011).

4.3 Vulnerable Group and School Feeding Programmes

These twin programmes distribute meals and nutritional supplements to people who are vulnerable to malnutrition. Beneficiaries include pregnant and lactating mothers, nutritionally at risk under-fives and tuberculosis patients. Supplementary feeding is provided to all under-fives, while food rations are distributed to lactating mothers. The School Feeding Programme targets all school children in government schools. Students receive at least one meal per day. In 2009/10 the figure for registered primary school beneficiaries stood at 261 513 and for secondary school beneficiaries at 165 097. The Vulnerable Group Feeding Programme, which targets adults and preschool children at nutritional risk, has been quite popular: in 2009/10 there were 239 985 beneficiaries (RHVP, 2011).

4.4 Universal Old Age Pension scheme

This scheme was introduced to arrest the increasing vulnerability of older people, a result of the rural-to-urban migration which is severely weakening the extended family structure. All older people are eligible, irrespective of their socioeconomic backgrounds. Those registered under other schemes such as the Programme for Destitute Persons are still eligible to receive their pension benefits if they qualify on account of age. The cash transfer is made through beneficiaries' bank accounts or at the post offices (Ministry of Local Government, 2010b). The number of beneficiaries steadily increased from 84 577 in 2003 to 86 859 in 2006. In 2010, 91 446 beneficiaries received P220 per month each.

4.5 Remote Area Development Programme

This programme is rolled out in designated settlements through the Department of Social Services. It targets over 90% of remote area dwellers in 64 settlements in seven districts (BIDPA, 1997). Virtually all remote area dwellers are eligible to receive rations and allowances based on their destitution. The government has also established the Economic Promotion Fund to create employment opportunities for remote area dwellers. The Fund provides seed money for business-oriented activities, including game ranching, handicrafts and agricultural activities such as poultry rearing and livestock production and related activities such as tannery (Seleka et al., 2007). An estimated 43 070 beneficiaries are currently enrolled in this programme (Ministry of Local Government, 2010a; GoB & UNDP, 2010).

4.6 Ipelegeng Programme

Ipelegeng is a nationwide government sponsored programme that targets unskilled and semi-skilled labour, and it is envisaged as a source of supplementary income. It involves carrying out essential development activities across the country with the objective of providing short-term employment support and relief. Local authorities assign public works tasks to beneficiaries, such as collecting litter, minor construction, clearing of fields, maintenance of buildings and secondary roads. Current wage rates are pegged at P18/day for casual labourers and P24/day for their supervisors. An estimated 19 431 people benefited from the programme in 2010, compared to 14 363 in 2008 (Ministry of Local Government, 2010a).

5. Synergies, opportunities and challenges

It is evident from the above discussion that the formal and non-formal social protection systems have the same goal – that of providing various forms of support to a variety of social groups. The relevant focus areas are generally similar: they include food and basic needs for various categories of people including the extremely poor, destitute and older persons. There is therefore a need to build synergies between the two systems. Four points suggested by Olivier et al. (2008) for consideration when integrating formal and non-formal social safety net systems in Africa can usefully be adapted to help find the best way to do this in Botswana:

- *Properly understand social protection arrangements:* It is pertinent to understand the reasons for the existence of the non-formal forms of social protection, the different types, their role and the nature of the current relationship between the formal and the non-formal social safety nets in Botswana before attempting integration.
- *Preserve the cultural basis of traditional social protection arrangements:* It is important to ensure that integrative measures do not destroy the cultural basis of non-formal social protection. If integrative measures are seen to disrupt the cultural basis, ordinary people are likely to resist them.
- *Appreciate that non-formal initiatives are not a substitute for formal measures:* Traditional arrangements should not be seen as the ultimate medium serving the social protection needs of the people in any given country. Formal safety nets

continue to play a critical role, and they ought to be revamped with a view to increasing their clientele base.

- *Consider issues of compatibility:* Start with initiatives that lend themselves more easily to integration. An example would be to consider seriously the relationship between burial societies and savings clubs (non-formal) in relation to modern social insurance schemes (formal).

While the integration of the formal and non-formal systems has been advocated by many, the purpose of integration should be to enhance the efficiency and effectiveness of the social protection regime. The greatest benefit of successful integration, where the two systems truly complement each other, is the extension of sufficient levels of social protection to those in need (Olivier et al., 2008).

There are a number of challenges to the integration of formal and non-formal systems in Botswana: the apparent lack of acknowledgement of the non-formal system and how it complements the formal system; a lack of clear understanding of the different types of non-formal initiatives and their role; and the fact that indigenous welfare systems tend to lack organisational capacity and resources, both human and material. Hence, mechanisms are needed to recognise the strengths and limitations of both systems and to create a new system that builds on the strengths of each in order to progressively build a national social protection regime for all citizens. Government and international partners need to provide assistance such as capacity building and financial and technical expertise.

Further, Olivier et al. (2008) argue that in instances where the formal and the non-formal co-exist, the non-formal systems tend to get over-burdened, sometimes even entirely substituting for the formal. For Botswana this is particularly true in the context of the high HIV prevalence and declining social and economic conditions. The challenge therefore is to ensure that integrative measures do not destroy the spirit of solidarity and reciprocity that is embedded in the indigenous welfare system.

Finally, as other countries in the southern African region attempt to develop and grow their social protection systems, account needs to be taken of non-formal provisions and how these might be integrated into the overall system of social protection based on country-specific conditions.

6. Conclusion and the way forward

This article has considered the nature of social protection in Botswana. It noted that, unlike in other African countries, the formal system in Botswana has fairly wide coverage, yet gaps still do exist. These have been filled by the non-formal system, which continues to play a critical role in social protection today. From the analysis, it can be concluded that the non-formal social protection system is an integral part of Botswana's welfare regime, despite the fact that its contribution has not been officially appreciated.

In regard to the way forward, we call for the integration of the formal and non-formal systems as this would aid the development of a comprehensive social protection regime in Botswana. Such a development would, without doubt, enhance service delivery, particularly among vulnerable groups, and address the needs of the poor and the vulnerable more effectively. If the government of Botswana takes this route, the country could offer a lesson to other sub-Saharan African countries on how to develop a social protection floor that is more responsive to the local context.

References

Apt, NA, 2002. Aging and changing role of the family and community: An African perspective. International Social Security Review 55(1), 39–47.

BIDPA (Botswana Institute for Development Policy Analysis), 1997. Study of Poverty and Poverty Alleviation in Botswana. BIPDA, Gaborone.

BOCAIP (Botswana Christian AIDS Intervention Programme), 2008. Strategic Plan 2008–2013. BOCAIP, Gaborone.

BOCAIP (Botswana Christian AIDS Intervention Programme), 2010. Bocaip Annual Report. BOCAIP, Gaborone

Denbow, J & Phenyo, C, 2006. Culture and Customs of Botswana. Greenwood, London.

Department of Social Services & Ministry of Local Government, 2005. Guidelines for Provision of Social Safety Net for Community Home-based Care Patients. Department of Social Services and Ministry of Local Government, Gaborone.

Ellis, F, Devereux, S & White, P, 2009. Social Protection in Africa. Edward Elgar, Cheltenham.

Emmanuel, J, Maundeni, T & Letshwiti-Macheng, P, 2011. Child Protection Issues in HIV and AIDS Burdened Countries: The Case of Botswana. Thari ya Bana, University of Botswana & UNICEF, Gaborone.

Foster, G, 2004. Safety nets for children affected by HIV/AIDS in southern Africa. In Pharoah, R (Ed.), A Generation at Risk? HIV/AIDS, Vulnerable Children and Security in Southern Africa. Institute of Security Studies, Pretoria & Cape Town, pp. 65–92.

Foster, G, 2007. Under the radar: Community safety nets for AIDS-affected household in sub-Saharan Africa. AIDS Care 19(Suppl 1), S54–63.

GoB (Government of Botswana), 1970. National Development Plan 1970–1975. Government Printer, Gaborone.

GoB (Government of Botswana), 2002. Revised National Policy on Destitute Persons. Government Printer, Gaborone.

GoB & UNDP (Government of Botswana & United Nations Development Programme), 2010. Millennium Development Goals Status Report: Botswana. Government Printer, Gaborone.

Gray, M, 1996. Towards understanding of developmental social work. Social Work Practice 1(96), 9–12.

Holzmann, R & Jorgensen, S, 1990. Social risk management: A new conceptual framework for social protection, and beyond. International Tax and Public Finance 8, 529–56.

Kaseke, E, 2004. Social protection in SADC: Developing an integrated and inclusive framework-social policy perspective. In Olivier, MP & Kalula, ER (Eds), Social Protection in SADC: Developing an Integrated and Inclusive Framework. University of Cape Town, CICLASS (Centre for International and Comparative Labour and Social Security Law), RAU (Rand Afrikaans University, now University of Johannesburg) & Institute of Development and Labour Law, Cape Town, pp. 1–11.

Kaseke, E & Dhemba, J, 2007. Community mobilization and the fight against HIV/AIDS in Zimbabwe. In Patel, L & Mupedziswa, R (Eds), Research Partnerships Build the Service Field in Africa: Civic Service in the SADC. Social Work Practitioner-Researcher and Journal of Social Development in Africa (joint publication). VOSESA (Volunteer and Service Enquiry Southern Africa), Johannesburg, pp. 85–99.

Kealeboga, C, 2011. Mmadikolo SACCOS information brief. Cooperative of staff members. University of Botswana, Gaborone.

Maes, A, 2003. Informal economic and social security in sub-Saharan Africa. International Social Security Review 56(3–4), 39–58.

Midgley, J, 1994. Social security policy in developing countries: Integrating state and traditional systems. Focaal 2(22/34), 219–30.

Midgley, J, 1995. Social Development: The Developmental Perspective in Social Welfare. SAGE, London.

Midgley, J, 2013. Social development and social protection: New opportunities and challenges. Development Southern Africa 30(1), 2–12.

Midgley, J & Tang, K, 2001. Introduction: Social policy, economic growth and developmental welfare. International Journal of Social Welfare 10(4), 244–52.

Miller, C, Gruskin, S, Subramanian, S, Rajaraman, D & Heymann, J, 2006. Orphan care in Botswana's working households: Growing responsibilities in the absence of adequate support. American Journal of Public Health 96(8), 1429–35.

Ministry of Local Government, 2010a. Unpublished handout, data obtained from Department of Social Services, Botswana.

Ministry of Local Government, 2010b. Preparation of a Social Development Policy: Phase 1: Situation Analysis. Government Printer, Gaborone.

Mosene, O, 2002. Informal credit demand in Botswana: Micro lending industry in Gaborone. MA thesis, Faculty of Business, University of Botswana, Gaborone.

Mpedi, LG, 2008. The role of religious values in extending social protection: A South African perspective. Acta Theologica 1, 105–25.

NACA (National AIDS Coordinating Agency), 2009. The Second Botswana National Strategic Framework for HIV and AIDS, 2010–2016. NACA, Gaborone.

NACA (National AIDS Coordinating Agency), 2010. Community home based care programme. www.naca.gov.bw%node%26 Accessed 9 February 2012.

NDSD (National Department of Social Development), 2010. Evaluation of Retirement: Systems of Countries within SADC. Government Printer, Pretoria.

Ngwenya, BN, 2003. Redefining kin: Burial societies in Botswana. Journal of Social Development in Africa 18(1), 85–110.

Nhabinde, VC & Schoeman, NJ, n.d. Does social security enhance growth in SADC countries? Unpublished paper, Department of Economics, University of Pretoria.

Ntseane, D & Solo, K, 2007. Social Security and Social Protection in Botswana. Bay Publishing, Gaborone.

Okurut, N & Thuto, B, 2010. Informal financial markets in Botswana: A case of Gaborone City.www.bidpa.bw%documents%InformalFinancialMarkets.pdf Accessed 11 October 2011.

Olivier, M & Dekker, AH, 2003. Informal social security. In Olivier, M (Ed.), Social Security: A Legal Analysis. LexisNexis Butterworths, Durban.

Olivier, M, Kaseke, E & Mpedi, LG, 2008. Informal social security in Africa: Developing a framework for policy intervention. Paper presented at the International Conference on Social Security, 10–14 March, Cape Town.

Partnership for African Social & Governance Research, 2011. Scoping study on social protection in Africa. Unpublished handout, Nairobi.

Patel, L, 2005. Social Welfare and Social Development in South Africa. Oxford University Press of Southern Africa, Cape Town.

Patel, L, 2008. Getting it right and wrong: An overview of a decade of post-apartheid social welfare. Practice: Social Work in Action 20(2), 71–81.

Patel, L, Kaseke, E & Midgley, J, 2012. Indigenous welfare and community based social development: Lessons from African innovations. Journal of Community Practice 20(1–2), 12–31.

RHVP (Regional Hunger and Vulnerability Programme), 2007. Social Transfers: Experiences and Evidence from Southern Africa. Vol. 1, Case Studies 3, 16, 18. RHVP, Johannesburg.

RHVP (Regional Hunger and Vulnerability Programme), 2010. Social Protection in Africa: Where Are We, and How Did We Get There? RHVP, Johannesburg.

RHVP (Regional Hunger and Vulnerability Programme), 2011. Social Protection in Botswana – A Model for Africa? RHVP, Johannesburg.

Schapera, I, 1970. A Handbook of Tswana Law and Custom. Frank Cass, London.

Shaibu, S & Wallhagen, M, 2002. Family caregiving of the elderly in Botswana: Boundaries of culturally acceptable options and resources. Journal of Cross-Cultural Gerontology 17, 139–54.

Seleka, T, Siphambe, H, Ntseane, D, Mbere, N, Kerapeletswe, C & Sharp, C, 2007. Social Safety Nets in Botswana: Administration, Targeting and Sustainability. Lentswe La Lesedi, Gaborone.

SOS Botswana, 2011. SOS Children's Villages in Botswana. Facts and Figures 2010/11. SOS Children's Villages, Gaborone.

Statistics Botswana, 2011. Preliminary Results of the Botswana Core Welfare Indicators (Poverty) Survey 2009/10 No 2011/15, 2011. Statistics Botswana, Gaborone.

USAID (United States Agency for International Development), 2010. Assessing the Implementation of Botswana's Program for Orphans and Vulnerable Children. USAID, Washington, DC.

Wass, P, 1969. A case history: Community development gets established in Botswana. International Review of Community Development 2(21/22), 181–98.

Whitworth, A & Wilkinson, K, 2013. Tackling child poverty in South Africa: Implications of *ubuntu* for the system of social grants. Development Southern Africa 30(1), 122–35.

Social protection in Lesotho: Innovations and reform challenges

Marius Olivier[1]

Given its current socioeconomic conditions and fiscal ability, Lesotho has achieved an impressive record in creating a basic social assistance and social protection system, informed by political commitment and through budget reprioritisation. It has set up and administered near universal schemes operating at scale with fairly low transaction costs, addressing core areas and serving vulnerable constituencies – including the aged, orphaned and vulnerable children and children of school-going age. A contribution-based comprehensive national social security scheme to provide coverage for Lesotho workers and their families is also planned. Nevertheless, the task of providing adequate social protection coverage faces systems and delivery challenges; several human development indicators have worsened, and most of the Millennium Development Goals are far from being achieved. There is scope for creating greater fiscal space by establishing a compulsory national contributory scheme, and donor support in the short to medium term is inevitable.

1. Introduction

Bearing in mind the prevailing socioeconomic conditions and its fiscal ability, Lesotho has already achieved an impressive record in incrementally building a basic assistance system and a social protection floor. It has made substantial progress along the road to developing social protection initiatives to provide minimum levels of protection to everyone – even before this has become an official UN initiative – and introducing social assistance measures targeting the indigent and vulnerable. In addition, some acceleration has taken place in recent years. The programmes that have been introduced include, among others, a universal OAP (Old Age Pension) for those aged 70 and above, free primary health care and subsidised health services at public facilities, indigent support, orphans and vulnerable children support, free primary education and food security measures.

At the same time Lesotho is contemplating the establishment of a contribution-based comprehensive national social security scheme, to provide coverage for Lesotho workers and their families. This development is prompted partly by the insufficient protection available in the event of maternity, sickness, unemployment, occupational injuries and diseases, retirement, disability and survivorship (i.e. dependency).

In this paper I trace the socioeconomic context and current scope of these interventions, with particular reference to core areas of social assistance, social protection floor[2] and

---
[1]Extraordinary Professor: Faculty of Law, North-West University, Potchefstroom, South Africa, and Adjunct-Professor, Faculty of Law, University of Western Australia, Perth, Australia.
[2]The term 'social protection floor' refers to access to essential services (such as health, education, housing, water and sanitation, and others, as defined nationally) and social transfers, in cash or in kind, to guarantee income security, food security, adequate nutrition and access to essential services (ILO–UN, 2010).

social insurance-oriented initiatives and interventions. I highlight critical success indicators and identify deficiencies and shortcomings. I reflect on reform challenges facing policymakers, the legislature and service delivery institutions, and on how they can be meaningfully addressed. In conclusion I note that while impact evaluation studies of the various programmes have not yet been undertaken in Lesotho, it is evident that there is scope for improvement and synergy. In particular, I argue that there is scope for creating greater fiscal space to undertake further required reforms: international technical and financial support, at least in the short and medium term, remains imperative.

2. Contextual framework[3]

Lesotho is a small landlocked country, with a population of approximately 1.9 million people. Poverty, deprivation and extreme vulnerability largely characterise Lesotho and the conditions in which Basotho live. The United Nations Development Programme (UNDP, 2012:para. 2) noted recently:

> While, since its earlier years of political turmoil and conflict, Lesotho has made great progress in consolidating democracy following the successful 2002 general elections and local government elections of April 2005, the country still faces considerable development challenges, driven primarily by the effects of the high prevalence of HIV (estimated at 23 percent of the adult population, the third highest prevalence rate in the world). Lesotho's human development indicators have worsened rapidly over the last decade because of the increased mortality associated with HIV and resulting AIDS-related deaths since the 1990s. Life expectancy has been steadily declining over the past decade, dropping from 56 years in 1997 ... to 35.2 in 2004 ... Average incomes have also been falling during this period. As a result, Lesotho's overall position in the UNDP human development index (HDI) ranking fell steadily from 127 out of 174 countries in 1998 to 137 in 2003, then to 149 out of 177 countries in 2006.

Poverty and HIV/AIDS are endemic: 56% of Basotho are believed to live below the national poverty line, and 23.2% of the population are said to be suffering from HIV/AIDS. Food insecurity is prevalent, with the poor spending almost half of their income on food: 25% of the population are malnourished, and the severe 2007/08 drought affected 352 000 people (especially children) and required emergency interventions, involving in particular international agencies. There has, however, been a discernible improvement at national level in access to safe drinking water (UNDP, 2007, 2011a, 2011b, 2012). While there has been some improvement in the overall poverty rate, the poor have high dependency ratios. Due to the impact of HIV/AIDS, households headed by those aged 70 years or more have the highest dependency ratios, highlighting the need for social protection measures targeting both the elderly and the (orphaned) young (TWG, 2011).

While there has been a slight decrease in child mortality for children under five, infant mortality has in fact increased. In addition, maternal mortality is rising and is, according to the UNDP, among the highest in southern Africa (UNDP, 2011a, 2011b). Children in particular have been affected: 10% of all new HIV cases are children

---

[3] Section 2 of this paper has been adapted from Olivier (2010:para. 4).

below four years of age (UNDP, 2007). The number of orphaned and other vulnerable children has been rising and was reported to be 220 000 in 2006, significantly up from 180 000 in 2004 (TWG, 2011; UNDP, 2011a).

From an overall perspective, both HDI (Human Development Index) and HPI (Human Poverty Index) trends have worsened (UNDP, 2007); by 2011 Lesotho's position had fallen to 160 out of 187 countries and territories in the UNDP human development ranking (UNDP, 2011a). Added to this is Lesotho's extreme vulnerability to shocks, which appear to be compounded by the weak economy and high levels of poverty. And further, while inequality may have decreased outside rural areas, and despite a much higher percentage of women working in the public sector, gender inequality and disparities remain, especially in the labour market (UNDP, 2007, 2011a). It is increasingly clear that Lesotho will not be able to meet most of the MDGs (Millennium Development Goals); in fact, only two are said to be on track in Lesotho: achieving universal primary education and promoting gender equality and empowering women (UNDP, 2011a).

Economic activity is generally low and often marginal. According to the 2008 Integrated Labour Force Survey, the overall labour force participation rate is 42.3% (MFDP, 2011). In 2008 the unemployment rate was 25.3% – this reportedly rose to more than 29% in 2009 (UNDP 2011a, 2011b). Almost 72% of the total employed population is only informally employed (MFDP, 2011). Of particular importance is the figure for those involved in subsistence farming, indicating the deep geographical segmentation in Lesotho – of the 617 000 people who are actively employed in Lesotho, 238 000 are engaged in subsistence farming (93.5% in rural areas and 6.5% in urban areas) (MFDP, 2011).

The labour market position described above is exacerbated not only by the impact of the current economic crisis on small underdeveloped countries such as Lesotho in particular but also by the economic impact of certain negative developments, especially in the regional context. Three issues need to be mentioned in particular. First, SACU (Southern African Customs Union) revenues, which constituted 60% of Lesotho's GDP in 2008, declined by nearly 60% in 2010/11 (UNDP 2011a, 2011b). A limited projected recovery is foreseen for the 2012/13 and 2013/14 periods. Second, for some years now Lesotho has experienced the impact of competition in textile manufacturing and the phasing out, in 2005, of the Multi-Fibre Agreement (UNDP, 2012). Third, Lesotho has also been at the receiving end of changes in the South African migration policy, which saw a drastic decline in the number of Lesotho mineworkers in South Africa. This has had a direct bearing on remittances paid over to Lesotho – for example, in 2001 remittances in Lesotho were estimated to contribute as much as 26.5% of GDP (Crush et al., 2005).

3. The building of a social protection edifice in Lesotho

The situation described above requires serious intervention. The government of Lesotho has embarked on several initiatives to address this. However, given the magnitude of what it has to deal with, comprehensive international support, emanating in particular from the UN and the EU, has to be relied on. This is evident from, among others, the various steps taken under the current UN Development Assistance Framework (2008–2012), the support given to disaster management by the UN, and the activities of UN agencies such as the UNDP, the UN World Food Programme and UNICEF (the UN Children's Fund) (UNDP, 2011b, 2012). In addition, extensive support is provided by the ILO

(International Labour Organization) in establishing a comprehensive contribution-based social security (i.e. social insurance) system that will provide short-term and long-term benefits (retirement, disability, survivors, occupational injuries and diseases, sickness, maternity and, later, unemployment benefits) – essentially for those who are formally employed within the framework of an employment relationship, but to be extended to own-account workers and those who work informally (ILO, 2011a).

To inform the creation of a social protection floor, with particular emphasis on those categories of persons who operate on the margins of society and who are generally poor, a policy agenda supported by a regulatory framework has been incrementally developed. Overall, this process has been guided by the adoption of Lesotho's National Vision 2020 (GoL, 2003), a 2005 poverty reduction strategy paper and several NSDPs (national strategic development plans) – the NSDP for 2012/13 to 2016/2017 is currently being developed, while an interim national development framework 2009/10 to 2010/11 covers the period leading to the new NSDP (GoL, 2005, 2009). A national social security policy was formulated in 2002 (TWG, 2011). These policies – as is the case with a host of sectoral policies in areas such as health, education, and OVCs (orphaned and vulnerable children) – were mostly developed with the support of international organisations and donor agencies. The regulatory framework covers parts of the state-provided social assistance, social protection floor support and contribution-based social insurance interventions. These laws include:

- as far as social assistance is concerned, the OAP Act, 2005, the Education Act, 2010, and the Children's Protection and Welfare Act, 2011; and
- as far as contribution-based social insurance measures are concerned, the Workmen's Compensation Act, 1977,[4] the Pensions Proclamation, 1964, and the Public Officers' Defined Contribution Pension Fund Act, 2008.

However, as is discussed later in this paper, both the policy and regulatory frameworks are in many respects incomplete and often do not reflect a rights-based approach.

3.1 Social assistance and social protection floor initiatives

A key social assistance programme of the Lesotho government is the OAP. Introduced in 2004, this is payable to Lesotho citizens (other than an ex-civil servant who draws a government pension of a higher value) aged 70 years and above. Since the pension is not subject to a means or income test, it is therefore in principle a universal pension from the perspective of Lesotho citizens. The current value of the pension is 300 maloti (US$33) per month – incrementally increased from 150 maloti (US$16.5) in 2004 to 200 maloti (US$22) in 2007, and to 300 maloti (US$33) in 2009. The legislative basis for the payment of the pension is informed by the OAP Act, 2005, and the OAP Regulations, 2007. The pension is administered by the Ministry of

---

[4]The 1977 law covers in some detail the circumstances under which an injury or disease would constitute an occupational injury or disease; the range of benefits available, in particular in the event of partial and total incapacity, as well as medical benefits; benefits payable to dependants; the rate at which benefits are calculated; applicable procedures; employer and employee obligations; and appeals. Determining who is covered by a particular workmen's compensation legal instrument could be complicated, if not confusing: different legal regimes, provided for in a range of laws, are applicable to different categories of workers. Provisions in relation to workmen's compensation are contained in at least six legal instruments, namely the Labour Code of 1992, the Public Service Regulations, 2008, the Workmen's Compensation Act, 1977, the Pensions Proclamation of 1964 and the Regulations made in terms of the Proclamation, and the Public Officers' Defined Contribution Pension Fund Act, 2008.

Finance and Development Planning. Approximately 83 000 Basotho (4.5% of the population) are entitled to the pension, which for demographic reasons reaches more females than males. The number of pensioners covered by the scheme increased by 30% from 2004 to 2011, while the expenditure (288 million maloti – US31.8 million – for the year 2010/11) has risen five-fold over the same period, constituting 3.6% of recurrent expenditure (TWG, 2011).

The OAP is a truly national programme, fully funded from government's expenditure. Introduced in the face of initial donor opposition (EC, 2010) as a measure to bring about a more egalitarian society, and not merely to address poverty, the programme reflects strong government commitment and enjoys considerable political and societal support (EC, 2010). To enable government to shoulder the burden of expenditure, a fiscal reprioritisation took place. The OAP is largely funded from SACU revenues received by Lesotho, which indicates government's willingness to find and increase fiscal space despite the global economic crisis (EC, 2010; ILO, 2011b). It is, however, doubtful whether a scaling-up of the programme to include pensioners above age 60 would be financially sustainable given the current economic climate (EC, 2010). This large-scale programme is operated relatively inexpensively, as administrative costs account for only 2% of the organisational costs per unit of transfer (EC, 2010) – partly due to the use of post offices in Lesotho as the primary payment mechanism. However, a proper impact assessment of the programme has not yet been undertaken, although the African Peer Review Mechanism Lesotho Report of 2010 noted the perceived positive impact of the grant (APRM, 2010). Also, there has not yet been a concerted attempt to consider the OAP in the light of the rest of the social assistance programmes and social protection floor initiatives in Lesotho, and to link it in appropriate fashion to the social insurance framework. I suggest that this lack of a concerted attempt flows partly from the fragmented and disjointed nature of social security policy-making, provisioning and service delivery in Lesotho.

Cash transfers play a major role in alleviating conditions of poverty and vulnerability in Lesotho. The UN and implementing partners have been involved in a full roll-out of the Harmonised Approach to Cash Transfers since 2009 (UNDP, 2009, 2011b). In this regard, the Lesotho government launched a child grants programme (CGP) in 2009 that would reportedly provide a regular and unconditional quarterly cash payment of about $15.9 million between 2007 and 2011, with EU support channelled via UNICEF. The aim of the programme is to have financial resources available within households to ensure that vulnerable children can gain access to essential services (UNICEF, 2009). The CGP, for which the Ministry of Health and Social Welfare takes responsibility, pays out 120 maloti (US$13.25) per beneficiary (i.e. 360 maloti (US$39.75) per average three-member household) each quarter. This is intended to reach 50 000 children. The CGP has low transaction costs (5.6%) and is said to have a positive impact on food consumption, as was found in a recent rapid assessment of the programme (TWG, 2011).

Furthermore, in 2005 the Lesotho government adopted a policy framework to deal with the plight of OVCs (MHSW, 2005). In accordance with the provisions of the national policy, both cash and non-cash benefits, and services and facilities are provided to these children and their families. These include a regular stipend, free primary education (as is also the case with other non-vulnerable children) and related benefits, and payment of fees for post-primary studies and access (like anybody else) to the Loan Bursary from the Manpower Development Secretariat for the purpose of tertiary study (Bitso, 2009; TWG, 2011). In the meantime, a dedicated legislative framework that affects OVCs has been introduced in the form of the Children's Protection and Welfare Act, 2011. While this law does not specifically regulate the social transfers, it provides for a rights basis for the protection of children's rights, as aligned with international instruments and standards, in particular the UN Convention on the Rights of the Child and the Africa Charter on the Rights and the Welfare of the Child. Despite its shortcomings, it is evident that, given the nature and magnitude of the problems facing OVCs and the households in which they live, support to OVCs is a major programme of huge importance within the social assistance and social protection constellation provided by the Lesotho government.

Since there is an obvious overlap between the CGP and other social protection floor initiatives, such as food security programmes and cash transfers, care should be taken to ensure that an integrated approach aimed at maximum impact but avoiding unnecessary duplication is followed. Also, there is a need to ensure inter-governmental synergy and links with other (potential) service providers. Different ministries – including for example the ministries of Education, Health and Social Welfare, and Finance and Development Planning – are responsible for different parts of the support rolled out to OVCs. It is important that steps be taken to deal with the fragmentation in policy-making and service delivery and to develop integrated approaches and mechanisms for a coordinated roll-out of support to OVCs. Furthermore, it might be prudent and cost effective to develop closer links with government institutions at a lower level and with a range of NGOs that could be of assistance in rendering the range of services. Finally, as is the case with several other social assistance and social protection floor programmes, there is clearly a need to undertake a proper and overall evaluation of the forms and level of support rolled out to OVCs, as well as the supporting strategy and mode of roll-out (Olivier, 2010).

It has to be acknowledged that some of the programmes initiated by the Lesotho government have thus far achieved impressive results. One of these programmes, in addition to the above, is the Free Primary Education programme, which provides universal primary education to children of school-going age on a no-fee basis. This programme, which commenced in 2000, has already achieved a net enrolment of close to 84%, one of the highest in sub-Saharan Africa; it also encompasses other elements of support, such as school feeding schemes (UNDP, 2011a).

There is, of course, room for further policy development in order to address poverty and vulnerability. Apart from the need for integrated and coordinated programmes that include a holistic approach to the needs, circumstances and conditions of beneficiaries, it also appears necessary to adopt well-targeted issue-specific policies. One such issue is food insecurity. The 2008 Annual Report of the UNDP Resident Coordinator noted that there was not yet a clear, well-resourced government strategy to tackle food insecurity in the long term (UNDP, 2009). In fact, the need for appropriate interventions is emphasised by the increasing prevalence of malnourishment (said to have affected 25% of the population by 2009) and stunting, which has increased from about 30% in 2002 to 39% in 2009. Clearly, Lesotho is not on track to achieve the target for part of the first MDG, the eradication of extreme hunger (UNDP, 2011b). This is an area where an evident need exists for the adoption of a dedicated integrated policy framework and legislative basis, which should together ensure the rolling out of an appropriate programme aimed at addressing food insecurity in the short, medium and long term. Ideally, the policy and accompanying legislation should be aligned with international standards relating to adequate food and the right to be free from hunger – standards as embedded in article 11(2) of the International Covenant on Economic, Social and Cultural Rights to which Lesotho formally ascribed.

3.2 Social insurance framework

The contributory dimension of social security is extremely weak in Lesotho. One would expect that coverage should be extended to workers (and their dependants) on the basis of payment of contributions. That being the case, the assumption is that there would be a reasonable relationship between contributions paid and benefits made available, and that the benefits would provide a sufficient level of income maintenance to beneficiaries, rather than minimum income protection.

To this general picture there are, in the case of Lesotho, two important exceptions. The first is that in certain cases – in particular relating to the position of parliamentarians, politicians, judges and public servants still covered by the Pensions Proclamation of 1964 – social security benefits, and especially retirement benefits, are non-contributory, as these are paid out of the Consolidated Fund. The implication is that social security benefits for these categories of persons are effectively a public purse liability (Olivier, 2010). The second exception is that in the absence of a comprehensive national social security scheme, the burden of providing certain social security benefits is placed on the employer. This applies in particular to maternity benefits, sickness benefits, redundancy pay (in principle payable also in the event of retirement of a worker) and workmen's compensation, where the principle of employer liability, for which the employer must take out compulsory insurance, applies. This raises, among others, the question of affordability, in particular in an environment of general socioeconomic deprivation, where many employers, especially small and medium-sized employers, face severe financial constraints (Olivier, 2010).

Furthermore, placing the burden for paying benefits solely on the employer is (in certain cases) prone to disadvantage women and thus distort gender representation in the labour market. This applies in particular to maternity benefits and, to some extent, severance benefits. For example, in the case of maternity benefits, the ILO is of the opinion that these benefits should be provided through a mandatory social insurance system or public fund. The rationale for this provision is that employer liability acts as a 'disincentive for the employment of women of a child-bearing age', as it is likely to influence employer hiring policies (ILO, 2000:172). Similarly, burdening the employer with the sole responsibility for paying sickness benefits and individual liability for workmen's compensation may encourage discrimination against incapacitated employees, and hence be a source of disability discrimination.

Three of the core contingencies, besides occupational injuries and diseases, affected by insufficient provision and regulation in Lesotho are maternity, sickness and retirement. As far as maternity is concerned, the position in the private sector in Lesotho appears to be as follows – with specific reference to the provisions of the Labour Code of 1992 and the Labour Code Wages (Amendment) Order, 2009:

- female workers are entitled to a total of 12 weeks' paid maternity leave – payment of maternity benefits is an individual employer liability (restricted to two confinements per employee);
- however, in the textile, clothing and leather manufacturing industry the period of paid maternity benefits is two weeks; and

- the dismissal of a female employee during the period of statutory maternity leave automatically constitutes an unfair dismissal.

Full details of maternity protection available to public servants have not been gazetted, although the period of maternity leave is reportedly determined to be two months (Regulation 81 of the Public Service Regulations, 2008, provides for ministerial determination). It needs to be noted that the payment of maternity benefits in Lesotho is an employer liability. In the case of public servants, this implies a fiscal liability, to be provided for from the annual budget.

While some provision is made for maternity protection in the Lesotho legal framework and practice, it is evident that the current scope and level of protection disadvantages working women, is insufficient and inconsistent, and that consideration should be given to making the payment of maternity benefits a public scheme, rather than an individual employer liability. The main shortcomings appear to be the following (Olivier, 2010:24–5):

- The failure to regulate the adjustment of working conditions of women who are or have recently been pregnant.
- The absence of appropriate medical care arrangements. Ante-natal and post-natal facilities are apparently available at government clinics at subsidised rates, while public medical aid, special medical care or health insurance coverage for expectant and nursing mothers is not available (Bitso, 2009).
- The general failure to regulate the various forms of maternity protection available to women in the public service.
- The insufficiency of the period of paid maternity leave and the inconsistent treatment of this matter in the private and public sector.
- The restricted period of paid maternity benefits available to workers in the textile, clothing and leather manufacturing industry and the inconsistent treatment of their position vis-à-vis workers in other industries.
- The failure to include maternity as a specific non-discrimination ground in the Labour Code – the current provision is of a general nature and merely includes prohibition on the basis of the sex of a person.
- Potential negative employer hiring practices are not sufficiently covered by the current dismissal and anti-discrimination provisions of the Labour Code. For example, it would be possible for an employer not to hire a woman because she is pregnant or may have the intention, or potential, to become pregnant.
- Increased family care responsibilities flowing from the absence of appropriate paternity leave provisions.

In the light of the above, there is need to align maternity protection in Lesotho to appropriate international and regional standards – embedded in the provisions of the ILO Maternity Protection Convention 183 of 2000 and the Code on Social Security in the SADC (Southern African Development Community) of 2007. In particular, consideration should be given to including the payment of maternity benefits in a public scheme framework, to which both employees and employers contribute. In the event that the public service were to be included in a public scheme framework indicated above, the liability for paying maternity benefits would require the state as employer to pay regular contributions towards the scheme, instead of the state paying the benefits in full. Given the fact that public servants would also contribute to the scheme, and in view of the insurance principles applicable to the operation of a public scheme, it might well be that this will result in a saving for the public purse.

An analysis of the payment of sickness benefits in Lesotho leaves one with the following impressions (Olivier, 2010:27–8):

- The period during which sickness benefits have to be paid is wholly inadequate, from the perspective of international (see ILO Social Security (Minimum Standards) Convention 102 of 1952) and regional standards, in particular in the private sector in Lesotho.
- The Labour Code does not regulate the provision of leave for purposes of family responsibilities. Since the Labour Code is silent on the issue, the Labour Court of Lesotho relied on the provisions of Section 4(c) of the Code to invoke the application of ILO Convention 156 of 1981 concerning Workers with Family Responsibilities and ILO Recommendation 165 of 1981 concerning Workers with Family Responsibilities to find that a worker has an entitlement to obtain leave of absence in the case of illness of a dependent child (*Palesa Peko v The National University of Lesotho* Case no. LC/33/95 –judgment of 1 August 1995).
- There seems to be insufficient justification for the inconsistent treatment of sickness benefits in the private and public sector, in particular concerning the period of sick leave and entitlement to paid benefits.
- The practice, in terms of the current legal framework, of providing cash sickness benefit under labour law only and in line with the principle of employer liability is unduly burdensome on employers and may even promote discrimination against workers with poor health. Therefore, consideration should be given to including the payment of sickness benefits in a public scheme framework, to which both employees and employers contribute. Alternatively, employers might provide benefits for the initial period of sickness, in terms of the provisions of the relevant labour laws and/or collective agreements; the envisaged public scheme would then be responsible for paying a cash sickness benefit for the subsequent period of sickness.

The area of retirement and related benefits is complex, confusing and fragmented. Different arrangements exist in the public and private sector in Lesotho. Private and occupation-based schemes cover some private sector employees, but by far the minority. Different laws provide for various categories of employees in the public sector. Recently, through the establishment of a contributory retirement (pension) scheme for all public officers, some of the applicable arrangements were consolidated.

There are about 250 private retirement schemes in Lesotho. Some of them operate as employer-initiated (i.e. occupational) schemes. There is no universally applicable framework of conditions, contributory arrangements, qualification or eligibility criteria and benefit regimes as far as these schemes are concerned. In essence, unlike the public sector framework discussed below, there is no general legal obligation to belong to a private or occupational scheme, nor is an employer legally obliged to establish a new scheme or to affiliate with an existing one. As a result, the position is that private and occupational schemes are effectively restricted to middle-income and high-income earning employees in certain companies. The bulk of the workforce in Lesotho, including those working for most small and medium-sized enterprises, is therefore not covered by a contributory retirement scheme.

Retirement schemes for public servants are provided for in a range of laws in Lesotho, some of which overlap. The general framework is provided for in the Pensions Proclamation of 1964. In terms of Section 4 of the Proclamation, benefits are paid on a DB (defined benefit) and non-contributory basis; they constitute a charge against

Lesotho's public revenue. In terms of legislation adopted in 2008, i.e. the Public Officers' Defined Contribution Pension Fund Act, all public officers or public servants employed on pensionable and permanent terms who are 45 years of age and below (including new entrants to the public service), are covered by a new DC (defined contribution) scheme to which both government and public servants contribute and which pays out an extensive range of benefits; older public servants could continue in the existing DB scheme described above. Separate legislation still regulates other aspects, not covered by this Act, of the retirement of particular categories of public servants, in differing fashion. These different laws lack a uniform approach, for example in the area of retirement age. The generally prescribed retirement age for those employed in the armed forces is 55, for those in local government it is 60, for those in the public service it is 60, and for those in the public teaching profession it is 65 (Olivier, 2010).

The area of retirement, including benefits available under the various retirement regimes, displays a number of deficiencies and shortcomings in addition to those mentioned above (Olivier, 2010:40–4):

- In a country like Lesotho it may not be possible or appropriate to require small and medium-sized employers who struggle in weak economic conditions to establish retirement schemes. Inclusion of such enterprises in a suitable national or public retirement framework, situated within a more comprehensive contributory social security scheme, may be more appropriate.
- Similarly, it may be necessary to consider including small employers in a public or national retirement framework, as they are not likely to be able to arrange for or otherwise contribute to their own retirement provision.
- There is no legal or policy framework requiring mandatory preservation of the contributions (employee's fund credit) of members who resign, retire early, or are retrenched. In fact, premature labour market exit will entitle a public servant, for example, to access their fund credit in the form of a withdrawal benefit. There is scope for introducing the principle of mandatory preservation in Lesotho, as this will help to protect the employee's retirement benefit until they are due to retire.
- Similarly, there is no legal or policy framework requiring or regulating inter-scheme and/or cross-border transfer of contributions or fund credits, should the employee:
  o move between one formal sector job to another, or
  o from a private sector job to a public service job or vice versa, or
  o from working in Lesotho to working outside the borders of the country given the prevalence of cross-border employment in South Africa of many Basotho, or
  o be a foreign worker who commences working in Lesotho after having been a member of a retirement scheme in another country, such as South Africa.
- There is need to provide specifically for breaks in employment for family-related reasons such as in the case of temporary labour market exit caused by maternity and childrearing responsibilities. In the absence of specific provision in this regard, which would at least guarantee the continued membership of a scheme, women in particular may be negatively affected, as they would not be able to build up a sufficient retirement benefit.
- With some exception (e.g. in the event of a retirement benefit payable under the new DC contributory pension scheme for public servants), almost no provision is made in the legislative and policy framework for the payment of a regular pension. Lump sum payments have the obvious disadvantage that beneficiaries and dependants would soon exhaust such benefits, and thereafter become reliant on state support.

The above deficiencies and shortcomings can be dealt with within the framework of an appropriate comprehensive national or public contribution-based social security scheme, which also provides for retirement benefits. In this way economies of scale can be achieved and disparities in treatment addressed. There will of course be a need to make transitional arrangements and to address the fears of the private pension industry in the event that a national scheme is established.

4. Strengthening and reforming social protection in Lesotho: Some conclusions and recommendations

Internationally, Lesotho has been hailed as a true example of what an LDC (least developed country) can achieve in terms of developing a social protection floor (EC, 2010; ILO 2011b). The record is indeed impressive and the lessons instructive. As an LDC Lesotho has been able to set up and administer near universal schemes operating at scale with fairly low transaction costs, addressing core areas and serving highly vulnerable constituencies in need of social protection – in particular, the aged, OVCs and children of school-going age. This has been made possible through relatively effective institutional and operational arrangements, including an effective system of revenue and tax collection, centralised payment modalities (especially via the post office) and appropriate central registry and programme monitoring systems (EC, 2010; ILO, 2011b). What has made the achievement even more significant is the fact that some of these programmes, in particular the OAP, are self-funded, and not dependent on donor support. Government's commitment to upholding social protection as a key area of social and human investment through deliberate budget reorientation and reprioritisation is further indicated by a 7% increase of total social benefit payments in 2011/12 (TWG, 2011), during a period of constricted economic performance due to the global economic crisis and reduced revenue income from, among others, SACU payments. Widely appropriated by the Basotho, these governmental initiatives can indeed be regarded as constituting a social contract, 'with the state expected to deliver on its end of the contract by providing a minimum level of protection to its citizens' (EC, 2010:82).

And yet the task of transforming social protection to provide adequate coverage to everybody, whether employed or not and irrespective of the life-cycle contingency involved, remains formidable. The reform challenges are daunting, including:

- Extending the personal sphere of coverage, as several vulnerable categories of persons are either legally or factually excluded from access to social assistance and social protection floor interventions and the employee benefits regime, while inconsistent treatment, also of different categories of workers, is evident. There is a clear need to extend coverage incrementally and innovatively to, among others, persons with disabilities, old persons in the 60 to 70 age bracket, and those who work outside the context of a formal employment relationship.
- Improving the adequacy of cash and non-cash transfers, for example by providing regular income instead of lump-sum payments in the contributory part of the system.
- Streamlining conflicting and unequal provisioning to different categories of persons, also in the employee benefits regime, and building a social protection structure that logically links provisioning via the non-contributory and contributory parts of the system to address particular life-cycle contingencies effectively – for example, an integrated retirement benefits model should incorporate and combine the OAP and contributory arrangements, both of a mandatory and voluntary nature.

- Undertaking an impact assessment of current cash and non-cash transfers to evaluate their effect and to adjust these to achieve the desired policy outcomes.
- Creating exit and graduation modalities as far as possible for those dependent on social transfers.
- Aligning the non-compliant different elements of the social protection system to core international (UN, ILO, African Union) and regional (SADC) standards.
- Strengthening the policy basis (including the development of an overarching national social protection policy that encapsulates the different parts of the system, contributory and non-contributory) and introducing a rights-based framework to ensure consistency and clarity of treatment and entitlement.
- Simplifying, coordinating and consolidating policy-making, institutional, organisational and service delivery components in view of the large-scale present fragmentation.
- Building institutional, human, systems and organisational capacity to cope with the expanding social protection edifice, in particular when a national social security (insurance) scheme is introduced.

The current social and macroeconomic context raises legitimate questions about Lesotho's ability to address the various social protection challenges. As I have pointed out, despite discernible improvements in certain areas, several human development indicators have worsened, while achieving the MDGs is for the most part not on track. In fact, this has prompted Lesotho's adoption in 2011, with UN assistance, of the MDG Accelerated Framework, which is designed to provide a 'systematic way of identifying bottlenecks and solutions to address them' and to enhance efforts to 'focus and coordinate efforts and resources of the Government and other stakeholders in bringing the MDGs back on track' (UNDP, 2011a:1). Significant donor support and involvement in the provisioning of social protection, at least in the short to medium term, appears inevitable. And yet it is also evident that there is scope for creating greater fiscal space to enable government to undertake crucial social protection interventions. This can be achieved by accelerating coordination, streamlining and linking at the different levels indicated above, as well as enhancing the efficacy of the programmes and strengthening the capacity to deliver them. In particular, significant fiscal space could be created by establishing a compulsory national contributory scheme, designed so as to reduce the burden on the fiscus.

References

APRM (African Peer Review Mechanism), 2010. Country Report: Kingdom of Lesotho. African Union, Addis Ababa.

Bitso, B, 2009. Access to Social Services for Non-citizens and the Portability of Social Benefits within the Southern African Development Community: Lesotho Country Report. Southern Africa Trust, Maseru.

EC (European Commission), 2010. European Report for Development (ERD) 2010: Social Protection for Inclusive Development: A New Perspective in EU Co-operation with Africa. European University Institute, San Domenico di Fiesole. http://erd.eui.eu/media/2010/Social_Protection_for_Inclusive_Development.pdf Accessed 10 May 2012.

Crush, J, Williams, V & Peberdy, S, 2005. Migration in southern Africa. Paper prepared for the Policy Analysis and Research Programme of the Global Commission on International Migration. Global Commission on International Migration, Geneva.

GoL (Government of Lesotho), 2003. National Vision 2020. www.gov.ls/documents/National_Vision_Document_Final.pdf Accessed 10 May 2012.

GoL (Government of Lesotho), 2005. Poverty Strategy Reduction Paper 2004/2005–2006/2007. www.gov.ls/documents/PRSP_Final.pdf Accessed 10 May 2012.

GoL (Government of Lesotho), 2009. Interim National Development Framework 2009/10–2010/11. www.finance.gov.ls/news/INDF.pdf Accessed 10 May 2012.
ILO (International Labour Organization), 2000. World Labour Report 2000. ILO, Geneva.
ILO (International Labour Organization), 2011a. Position Paper on the Establishment of Lesotho Social Security Law and the Creation of the Lesotho Social Insurance Scheme. ILO, Pretoria.
ILO (International Labour Organization), 2011b. Social protection floor for a fair and inclusive globalization. Report of the Advisory Group chaired by Michele Bachelot, convened by the ILO with the collaboration of the World Health Organization. ILO, Geneva.
ILO-UN (International Labour Organization-United Nations), 2010. Social Protection Floor Initiative: The Role of Social Security in Crisis Response and Recovery, and Beyond. ILO, Geneva.
MFDP (Ministry of Finance and Development Planning), 2011. Lesotho Integrated Labour Force Survey. Ministry of Finance and Development Planning, Maseru.
MHSW (Ministry of Health and Social Welfare), 2005. National Policy on Orphans and Vulnerable Children. Ministry of Health and Social Welfare, Department of Social Welfare, Maseru.
Olivier, M, 2010. Social security in Lesotho: A situation analysis report. Report prepared for the International Labour Organization. Pretoria.
TWG (Sub-Technical Working Group on Social Protection), 2011. Draft Social Protection Issues Paper: National Strategic Development Plan (NSDP) 2012/13–2016/17. TWG, Maseru.
UNICEF (United Nations Children's Fund), 2009. New programme provides grants for orphans and vulnerable children in Lesotho. www.unicef.org/infobycountry/lesotho_49498.html Accessed 11 May 2012.
UNDP (United Nations Development Programme), 2007. National Human Development Report 2006. http://hdr.undp.org/en/reports/national/africa/lesotho/lesothoNHDR2006.pdf Accessed 10 May 2012.
UNDP (United Nations Development Programme), 2009. Resident Coordinator's Annual Report 2012. www.undp.org.ls/practice/Resident_Coordinator_Annual_Report_2008.php Accessed 10 May 2012.
UNDP (United Nations Development Programme), 2011a. Millennium Development Goals in Lesotho. www.undp.org.ls/millennium/Millenium%20Development%20Goal%201.pdf Accessed 10 May 2012.
UNDP (United Nations Development Programme), 2011b. Resident Coordinator's Annual Report 2012. www.undp.org.ls/practice/RCAR_2010.pdf Accessed 10 May 2012.
UNDP (United Nations Development Programme), 2012. Lesotho Country Programme Document (CPD) 2008–2012. www.undp.org.ls/practice/cdp.php Accessed 10 May 2012).

Legislation

Children's Protection and Welfare Act, 2011.
Education Act, 2010.
Labour Code Order No. 24 of 1992.
Labour Code Wages (Amendment) Order, 2009.
Old Age Pension Act, 2005.
Old Age Pension Regulations, 2007.
Pensions Proclamation, 1964.
Public Officers' Defined Contribution Pension Fund Act, 2008.
Workmen's Compensation Act, 1977.

Case law

Palesa Peko v The National University of Lesotho Case no. LC/33/95 (judgment of 1 August 1995).

Are social protection programmes child-sensitive?

Scelo Zibagwe[1], Themba Nduna[2] & Gift Dafuleya[3]

There is no doubt that child focus in the social protection agenda makes development and economic sense, yet child-sensitive social protection still remains elusive in some African country programmes. The case study of the Productive Safety Net Programme in Ethiopia discussed in this paper shows that the child-conditioned component in both the design and the implementation of this huge social protection programme is largely absent. Child-sensitive social programming, which discretely improves children's schooling and access to basic health care services and protects them from child labour, is recommended, with prioritisation of child labour saving assets as one of the key interventions.

1. Introduction

This research note demonstrates the negative and unintended outcomes of a well-intended social protection programme in Ethiopia, the Productive Safety Net Programme (PSNP), which was started by the government and its development partners in 2005 to graduate poor households out of poverty. A close scrutiny of the programme shows that it lacks child focus and sensitivity in its design and implementation. This is clearly observable in the larger labour-based conditional transfers and discretionary quotas on unconditional transfers embedded in the programme, which provides no guidelines on protecting children and ensuring they derive the most opportune benefit from the programme. We argue that the PSNP has had a number of indirect adverse effects on child labour and schooling. We also provide a conceptual background on child-sensitive social programming (CSSP). This is followed by a description and critique of Ethiopia's PSNP as a case study and concludes with policy recommendations.

2. Child-sensitive social protection

Social protection is increasingly being viewed as part of the response to child poverty and vulnerability (Shaffer, 2003). In policy, however, it has 'tended to focus on vulnerable groups other than children' (Handa et al., 2010:3). Research indicates links between poverty prevalence and a disproportionately large incidence of child poverty (Lanjouw et al., 1998). 'Child-sensitive social programming' is the catch-phrase used to summarise a wide range of policies and programmes (Roelen & Sabates-Wheeler, 2011) in the social protection landscape. In most of these programmes, social transfers

---

[1] PhD Student, Sociology & Social Anthropology, Stellenbosch University, South Africa.
[2] PhD Student, Public Health Nutrition Research Group, School of Medicine and Dentistry, Division of Applied Health Sciences, University of Aberdeen, UK
[3] Lecturer, Department of Economics, University of Venda, South Africa

are widely used as instruments to tackle child poverty and associated vulnerabilities discretely (Adato & Basset, 2008).

Before the CSSP phrase was coined, Crawford (2001) challenged governments to prioritise its future citizens – children and young people – in health, education and early childhood development. Later, 'child-conditioned' income transfers, support for maternal employment, and early childhood programmes became key apparatuses for both reducing child poverty and enhancing child development (Kamerman et al., 2003). Investment in children is linked to long-term poverty reduction, particularly in 'critical areas of child protection such as health, education, early childhood development' (Crawford, 2001:503). More discrete CSSP will especially prevent, manage and overcome child-related risks and vulnerabilities as they change throughout childhood (Jones & Holmes, 2010).

This discreteness has led to some UNICEF-supported diagnostic studies, for example, Bailey et al. (2011) in the Democratic Republic of Congo (DRC) and Roelen et al. (2011) in nine countries.[4] Bailey et al. show that CSSP measures in the DRC are still limited mainly to formulating legislation and national child protection plans, while Roelen et al. map out lessons built around children affected by HIV/AIDS and scaling them up. These lessons include the need for government to be the leading actor and bearer of responsibility without undermining the role of non-formal modes, and reaching those children who cannot be supported through families. Roelen et al. (2011:23) observe that although this CSSP-HIV/AIDS programming in east and southern African countries is being piloted, it is still plagued by the problems of 'translating policy and strategic rhetoric' and putting into practice the 'theoretical conceptualisation' contained in the programming guidelines and policy documents and declarations by several international organisations and agencies.

There have been claims that most child-specific guidelines fail to guide practice in social protection programmes. For example, a statement issued jointly by the United Nations Children's Fund and other development partners, which spells out seven CSSP guidelines, does not provide sufficient guidance for programme planners, designers and implementers of child-friendly social programming interventions (Roelen & Sabates-Wheeler, 2011). Jones & Holmes (2010) call for the Millennium Development Goals to be revised, because they believe that in their current design they do not adequately tackle the complexity of childhood poverty and vulnerability. The literature reviewed above suggests that the lack of clear guidelines may be part of the reason why CSSP remains elusive in some country programmes. The following Ethiopian case study is used to further explore this assertion.

3. PSNP public works and direct support programmes in Ethiopia

South Africa is generally acknowledged as having the most comprehensive state-led system of cash transfer-based social protection in sub-Saharan Africa, followed by Ethiopia's PSNP (Devereux, 2001). In 2009, the Ethiopian Ministry of Agriculture and Rural Development (MoARD, 2009) reported that the PSNP annual budget stood at US$347 million (1.2% of Ethiopia's GDP). This programme covered 7 574 480 beneficiaries, with the budget for 2010–2014 exceeding US$2 billion.

---

[4] Angola, Botswana, Lesotho, Swaziland, South Africa, Malawi, Mozambique, Namibia and Tanzania.

The PSNP seeks to address food insecurity by smoothing consumption patterns and preventing asset depletion for food insecure households totalling 14 million people, of which more than six million are children in chronically food insecure areas (MoARD, 2006). This is to be achieved via appropriate, timely and predictable transfers of food or cash, or both, either through a public works programme (PWP) (food or cash for work) or direct transfers through a direct support programme (DSP) component. The former entails the provision of counter-cyclical employment on rural infrastructure projects such as road construction and maintenance, small-scale irrigation and reforestation, while the latter constitutes direct unconditional transfers of cash or food to vulnerable households with no able-bodied members who can participate in PWPs. In addition, the PSNP is expected to enhance child welfare by increasing household income and smoothing consumption, potentially improving education and reducing child labour. Through a third component of the PSNP, called 'other food security programmes', some households benefit through access to credit, agricultural extension services and technology transfers in areas such food crop production, cash cropping, livestock production, and soil and water conservation as well as irrigation and water harvesting schemes (Hoddinott et al., 2010). However, this supplementary programme is not the subject of this paper.

The PWP is the larger component of the PSNP. It constitutes approximately 85% of the PSNP budget (MoFED, 2007) and it paid eligible beneficiaries 10 birr (US$0.81) per day as at 2009/10. By design, each adult household member is to work a maximum of five days per month up to a maximum of 20 days (Gilligan et al., 2007). In cases where the labour input exceeds the maximum number of working days, the outstanding transfers have to be given to the household through a DSP. This limit on time spent on PWP activities is intended to avoid the problem of the PSNP shifting households from their usual livelihoods activities, i.e. to avoid dependence on the PSNP (an outcome to which the government is sensitive).

As this is a food security programme, PWP wages were originally calculated to equal a shopping basket containing the equivalent of 15 kg of grain, 1.5 kg of pulses and 0.5 litres of oil. Eligible households are those with a three-year continuous dependence on relief (prior to the programme) and able-bodied members who are above 18 years of age. PWP planning engages the communities to identify and prioritise work to be done. The work includes projects such as construction of roads and schools, soil and water conservation, and water development, among others.

The DSP, which is distributed in the form of unconditional cash or food transfers, is provided to labour-poor households who do not have support from their adult children or remittances from other relatives. DSP beneficiaries include, but are not limited to, orphans, pregnant and lactating mothers, the elderly, households with sick individuals and female-headed households. Though DSP transfers are unconditional, Save the Children (UK) Ethiopia piloted attendance at health and nutrition education sessions as conditions for transfer. This pilot study explored synergies between the PSNP and the health sector to produce the maximum benefits for children. The results from this study were encouraging: for instance, there were improvements in care for infants and young children and health seeking practices (Fenn, 2009).

4. Child focus of PSNP: A critique

The proportion of children who started Grade 1 at the expected official age (seven years) used to be just above 20% (World Bank, 2005). While this rate has risen to 60%, an estimated 25% drop out before finishing Grade 1, and 50% do not finish Grade 5 (Woldehanna et al., 2011). According to Ethiopia's Central Statistical Authority, 27% of school dropouts cite the need to work as the main reason for dropping out (CSA, 2005). In a survey of 3043 Ethiopian children aged between four and 15, Admassie & Singh (2001) found that 75% were engaged in different forms of work (59% paid and approximately 41% without fixed payment). The CSA's 2003 national child labour survey indicated that 62% of rural 10- to 14-year-olds were involved in economic activity (CSA & ILO, 2003). It has been observed that households under-invest in the human capital of their children during exposure to shocks (Jacoby & Skoufias, 1997). Furthermore, children who work are more likely to fail at school, and their educational attainment is reduced by almost two years (Psacharopoulos, 1997).

But how well does the PSNP address this problem? Arguably, not so well. For one thing, the PWPs ignore the circumstances of the parents or guardians and the children themselves. PSNP beneficiaries generally have a relatively lower labour capacity, so it was to be expected that DSPs, which do not require labour capacity, would occupy the greatest part of the PSNP. Yet, PWPs, which require labour, occupy the greatest part of the PSNP. Furthermore, the PSNP imposes a ceiling on the DSPs and this reduces both paid and unpaid child labour activities. This occurs despite the fact that the DSP has a strong impact on improving child education in Ethiopia (Hoddinott et al., 2010).

We also ask: what strategies do households adopt to obtain their entitlements from the PSNP? And what strategies do they use to supplement these entitlements? Empirical work conducted by Nigussa & Mberengwa (2009) in the Kuyu *woreda* (district) confirms general claims that PSNP entitlements are too low to support typical household consumption. Households therefore supplement these entitlements with income earned by the children in the households in both PSNP (PWP) and non-PSNP activities (during planting and weeding time).

Devereux et al.'s research (2008) could not conclude that the PSNP has resulted in fewer children being withdrawn from schools. There are other factors that may account for this outcome, such as the government's campaign urging that 'every school-age child should go to school' and promoting 'expansion of schools' initiatives carried out prior to and during the same period as its promotion of schooling. Further secondary data analysis also shows that 2% of children of households supported by the PSNP and 1% of children from non-PSNP households were withdrawn from schools during 2005/06 (Devereux et al., 2008). This effect on schooling (and the child work effect highlighted in the next paragraph) is based on a difference-in-difference regression and nearest neighbour matching method used by Devereux et al. (2008), Woldehanna (2010) and Hoddinott et al. (2010). In this method, a comparison group of non-PSNP beneficiaries with statistically average observable characteristics was selected so as to generate robust comparisons. While the difference is small, the question still remains: why were more children from PSNP-supported households (that receive additional income) withdrawn from school than children from non-PSNP households? Since primary school education is free in rural areas, it could be argued that children were withdrawn not for financial reasons but to add to the household labour pool and thus increase household income through paid work.

Woldehanna (2010) uses data from the Young Lives study of 12-year-old schoolchildren in rural and urban Ethiopia to assess the effects of the PSNP on children's work division between work and school, and how the split affects attainment of education. The analysis reveals that in rural areas PWPs increase paid child labour 'due to direct involvement of children in public work or substitution of children for adults when adults go to public work' (Woldehanna, 2010:183).

A further question would be: where and how did the design of the PSNP miss the mark? We argue it missed the mark because of its timetabling errors, which unintentionally supplement adult labour with child labour, and its lack of child labour-saving assets (see Section 4.3 below). We consider these situations separately below.

4.1 Timetabling errors

PWP activities are generally scheduled for the post-harvest period of April to September when food is generally in short supply. The expectation was for the PSNP to supplement income during this period. PWP activities generally come to an end once the planting season starts so that household members can return to the fields where they traditionally earn their livelihood.

The timing of the PSNP does not take into account strategies that favour childhood development. Before the programme was introduced, children generally worked only during the farming season. Once the PSNP was introduced, children started working all year round – in the fields or in PWP activities – dropping out of school if needed to contribute to household income. This would not have been the case had there been a preference for DSPs instead of PWPs.

Woldehanna's research (2010) shows that some children in rural areas missed classes for entire weeks, mainly from October to January when agricultural work (such as harvesting) is very intensive (see Figure 1). The main reasons for this were that children had to do paid work or were required for domestic and agricultural work.

4.2 Substitutability of adult labour with child labour

The PSNP adopted what is called the 80:20 principle, where 80% of the beneficiaries receive transfers in exchange for labour, while 20% are eligible to receive transfers

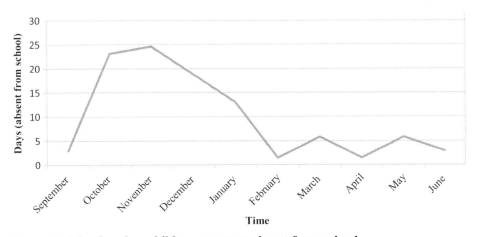

Figure 1: Months when children are most absent from school
Source: Adapted from Woldehanna (2010).

gratuitously or unconditionally. Put simply, this principle assumes that 80% of food insecure households have the labour capacity to meet the requirements for full transfer entitlement, as it is pre-determined by the budget. But it is practically impossible that 80% of any population can be available to work since children under 18 years generally constitute approximately 50%, and nursing and pregnant women, the elderly and people living with physical and mental disabilities constitute another 25% (Adams & Kebede, 2005). This ultimately reverses the 80:20 principle to a 20:80 principle. Given that the transfer did not consider the nature or form of labour contributed, it was inevitable that child labour would be contributed in order to receive the full entitlement.

4.3 Lack of child labour-saving asset creation

Output-based PWPs can have positive external effects if the physical assets accumulated are strategically aligned to reduce child work. This strategic alignment stems from a recognition that increased household income withdraws children from work and puts them into schools, but the opposite scenario exists where there is a wider portfolio of productive assets. Greater access to productive assets in turn increases the productivity of, and demand for, child labour – and children are pulled out of school to work the assets (Cockburn & Dostie, 2007:560). What has been overlooked in linking child labour with income is that some assets can augment child labour, to the extent that households are encouraged to withdraw their children from school so as to exploit the increased returns from these assets (Cockburn & Dostie, 2007). Cockburn (2001:2) observes that

> In rural Ethiopia, the principal activities of children are fetching wood or water and herding, whereas adult males are primarily involved in farming and adult females in domestic work. It therefore seems likely that the effects on child work will vary considerably depending on the types of physical assets targeted in poverty alleviation policies. In particular, targeting assets used in activities commonly performed only by adults may make it possible to avoid increased child work and reduced schooling. Furthermore, child labour-saving assets such as a nearby well or a wheelbarrow can be expected to directly reduce child work and poverty.

We argue that the PSNP did not make a 'judicious choice of assets targeted' (Cockburn & Dostie 2007:560) in respect of the problematic issues of child labour and school participation. The key intervention here is access to water and fuel, because the likelihood of children attending school falls significantly as the distance to the nearest water and fuel source increases. A water intervention has also shown positive spillover effects such as improvement in children's health (Fenn et al., 2012). An overview of the achievements of PWPs (Table 1) shows extensive community asset building that is said to have brought about 'environmental transformation' (Del Ninno et al., 2009). A relevant issue is that of increased groundwater recharge as some dry springs have started flowing again (Fenn et al., 2012). Flowing springs that are closer to home reduce the time children spend fetching water and create time for mothers to spend caring for young children, among other benefits that can lead to health improvements observed in the PSNP-Nutrition pilot project (Fenn et al., 2012).

As mentioned earlier, the construction of community assets did not directly reduce child labour or improve school participation, regardless of the fact that classrooms were

Table 1: Sample of public works programmes supported under the PSNP, Ethiopia 2007

Activity	Result
Soil embankment construction (kilometres)	482 542
Stone embankment construction (kilometres)	443 148
Pond construction and maintenance (number)	88 936
Spring development (number)	598
Hang-dug well construction (number)	491
Land rehabilitation through area enclosure (hectares)	530
Small-scale irrigation canals (kilometres)	2 679
Tree nursery site establishment (number)	285
Seedlings produced (number)	301 778 607
Seedling planted (number)	12 883 657
Rural road construction (kilometres)	8 323
Rural road maintenance (kilometres)	20 458
School classroom construction (number)	340
Animal health post construction (number)	71
Farmer training centre construction (number)	119

Source: Food Security Coordination Bureau in Del Ninno et al. (2009:12).

renovated. Indirectly, a study by Nigussa & Mberengwa (2009) shows that despite a community in one of the PSNP districts saying that the shortage of potable water was its major problem, this priority was not only ignored by the authorities, the PWP sites were also located far away from participants' homes, which weakened the positive contribution of these assets to the problems of child labour and schooling.

5. Conclusion

This paper challenges a general view in the discourse of social protection – that social protection programmes are child-sensitive. The case of Ethiopia's PSNP was presented to demonstrate how concealed fundamentals in the design of social protection programmes may result in unintended outcomes in an otherwise well-intended programme. In the case of the PSNP, we identify the basic flaws as bad timetabling of its PWP component, the inevitable need to supplement adult labour with child labour, and the lack of child labour-savings assets. While these flaws may have been difficult to identify ex ante, there is now an urgent need to revise the PSNP, add provisions to enhance education and protect children from child labour, and prioritise child labour-saving assets as one of the key interventions. Lessons may be drawn from Latin American social protection programmes, where it has been noted that income effects protect children from child labour and improve their education (ILO, 2007). Child-sensitive programmes should take guidance from Article 6 of the United Nations Convention on the Rights of the Child and focus on 'the circumstances of the child' and 'persons having responsibility for the maintenance of the child'. At policy and operations level the PSNP implementation manual (2006 version) prohibits children under 16 years from working on PWP activities. Child research and advocacy has made calls for upward revisions that will align the limit with the UN Convention on the Rights of the Child to 18 years.

However, even if this revision is made, everyday practice in PWP sites holds sway and supervisors perpetuate the same output-based perspective and ignore the child work issues. For instance, one supervisor quoted by Tafere & Woldehanna (2012:12) openly said 'We do not care whether [parents] send their children or [whether they] come themselves because what we need is the job done. [Children] work better than the adults because they have the capability'.

We recommend an increase in the size of the cash transfer so that the income effect offsets the current strong substitution effect. In terms of research, there is need to find how the problem – of parents sending children to work and the PWP supervisor allowing this – can be addressed if these critical actors at community level ignore the effects of child work on schooling. One possible way is to cascade the child protection screening and oversight downwards from policy level so that PWP supervisors will enforce the age restrictions and employ only those who are eligible to provide labour.

Programme planners and policymakers need to explore of the possibility of integrating social protection programmes with other child survival interventions for complementarity and strengthening of intervention impact. The ongoing initiatives to link the PSNP with the National Nutrition Program (NNP) in Ethiopia offer an opportunity for synergy between the two programmes for better health and nutrition outcomes for children, especially when also combined with the exemption of pregnant and lactating mothers from PWP. Good performance at school is, among other things, a function of the good health and nutrition status of children (Victora et al., 2008). Baseline studies for labour based social protection programmes should consider households' labour capacity in future designs so as to eliminate the temptation to use children as sources of labour Attaching a conditional clause linking the receipt of transfers with certain child care practices and behaviours (e.g. school attendance) in a facilitated way could be a solution, given its success in some PSNP-linked projects (Fenn, 2009; Fenn et al. 2012) in Brazil, Mexico and other countries (Lindert et al., 2007). Such 'facilitation', i.e. including benevolent conditions, would help overcome the much criticised 'aid conditionality' which has adverse effects on beneficiaries.

Referring again to the diagnostic studies reviewed above that attempted to trace discrete CSSP outcomes, we recommend an intensive advocacy and oversight at implementation stage to promote appropriate child-sensitive management of PWP activities (so as to keep children at school), increased size of transfers (so as to augment the income effect) and integrating child labour-saving assets into the household and community asset creation processes. This, however, needs to rely on built-in monitoring and evaluation as part of programme implementation, with a focus on outcome and impact indicators that will reveal whether the programme or intervention is producing undesirable outcomes or is likely to do so in the long run.

References

Adams, L & Kebede, E, 2005. Breaking the Poverty Cycle: A Case Study of Cash Interventions in Ethiopia. ODI (Overseas Development Institute), Brighton.

Adato, M & Bassett, L, 2008. What is the Potential of Cash Transfers to Strengthen Families Affected by HIV and AIDS? A Review of the Evidence on Impacts and Key Policy Debates, JLICA (Joint Learning Initiative on Children and HIV/AIDS). IFPRI (International Food Policy Research Institute), Washington, DC.

Admassie, A & Singh, A, 2001. Attending school: Two 'Rs' and child work in rural Ethiopia. Unpublished manuscript, Department of Economics, University of Addis Ababa.

Bailey, S, Pereznieto, P & Jones, N, 2011. Child-sensitive Social Protection in DRC: A Diagnostic Study. Overseas Development Institute, London. www.odi.org.uk/sites/odi.org.uk/files/odi-assets/publications-opinion-files/7620.pdf Accessed 5 November 2012.

Cockburn, J, 2001. Child Labour versus Education: Poverty Constraints or Income Opportunities? Centre for the Study of African Economies, University of Oxford.

Cockburn, J & Dostie, B, 2007. Child work and schooling: The role of household asset profiles and poverty in rural Ethiopia. Journal of African Economies 16(4), 519–63.

Crawford, PJ, 2001. Child protection: Theoretical background. In Ortiz, I (Ed.), Social Protection in Asia and the Pacific. Asian Development Bank, Manila, pp. 137–56.

CSA (Central Statistical Authority), 2005. Welfare Monitoring Survey 2004: Statistical Report Indicators on Living Standard, Accessibility, Household Asset, Food Security and HIV/AIDS. CSA, Addis Ababa.

CSA & ILO (Central Statistical Authority & International Labour Organization), 2003. Ethiopia Child Labour Survey: Statistical Bulletin 262. CSA & ILO, Addis Ababa.

Del Ninno, C, Subbarao, K & Millazo, A, 2009. How to make public works work: A review of the experiences. Social Protection Discussion Paper Series, World Bank, Washington, DC.

Devereux, S, 2001. Social pensions in Namibia and South Africa. IDS Discussion Paper 379. Institute of Development Studies, Brighton.

Devereux, S, Sabates-Wheeler, R, Slater, R, Tefera, M, Brown, T & Teshome, A, 2008. Ethiopia's Productive Safety Net Programme (PSNP). 2008 Assessment Report commissioned by the PSNP Donor Group. Institute of Development Studies, Brighton.

Fenn, B, 2009. Legambo Child Caring Practices Project Legambo Woreda, Amhara, Ethiopia. Save the Children, London.

Fenn, B, Bulti, AT, Nduna, T, Duffield, A & Watson, F, 2012. An evaluation of an operations research project to reduce childhood stunting in a food-insecure area in Ethiopia. Public Health Nutrition 15(9), 1746–54.

Gilligan, DO, Hoddinott, J, Tafesse, AS, Dejene, S, Tefera, N & Yohannes, Y, 2007. Ethiopia Food Security Program: Report on the 2006 Baseline Survey. IFPRI (International Food Policy Research Institute), Washington, DC.

Handa, S, Devereux, S & Webb, D (Eds), 2010. Social Protection for Africa's Children. Routledge, London.

Hoddinott, J, Gilligan, D & Tafesse, AS, 2010. The impact of Ethiopia's productive safety net program on schooling and child labour. In Handa, S, Devereux, S & Webb, D (Eds), Social Protection for Africa's Children. London, Routledge, pp. 71–95.

ILO (International Labour Organization), 2007. Child Labour and Conditional Cash Transfer Programmes in Latin America. ILO, Geneva.

Jacoby, H & Skoufias, E, 1997. Risk, financial markets, and human capital in a developing country. Review of Economic Studies 64(3), 311–35.

Jones, N & Holmes, R, 2010. The politics of gender and social protection. ODI Briefing Paper 62. Overseas Development Institute, London.

Kamerman, SB, Neuman, MJ, Waldfogel, J & Brooks-Gunn, J, 2003. Social policies, family types and child outcomes in selected OECD countries. OECD Working Paper. Organization for Economic Cooperation and Development, Paris.

Lanjouw, P, Milanovic, B & Paternostro, S, 1998. Poverty and economic transition: How do changes in economies of scale affect poverty rates of different households? Working Paper, World Bank, Washington, DC.

Lindert, K, Linder, A, Hobbs, J & De la Brière, B, 2007. The nuts and bolts of Brazil's Bolsa Família Program: Implementing conditional cash transfers in a decentralized context. World Bank Social Protection Discussion Paper 709. http://siteresources.worldbank.org/INTLACREGTOPLABSOCPRO/Resources/BRBolsaFamiliaDiscussionPaper.pdf Accessed 1 November 2012.

MoARD (Ministry of Agriculture and Rural Development), 2006. Productive Safety Net Programme: Programme Implementation Manual (Revised). Government of Ethiopia, Addis Ababa.

MoARD (Ministry of Agriculture and Rural Development), 2009. Food Security Program 2010–2014. Government of Ethiopia, Addis Ababa.

MoFED (Ministry of Finance and Economic Development), 2007. Productive Safety Net Programme: Interim Unaudited Financial Report, 9 January–8 April 2007. Government of Ethiopia, Addis Ababa.

Nigussa, F & Mberengwa, I, 2009. Challenges of productive safety net program implementation at local level: The case of Kuyu Woreda, North Shewa Zone, Oromia region, Ethiopia. Journal of Sustainable Development in Africa 11(1), 248–67.

Psacharopoulos, G, 1997. Child labour versus educational attainment: Some evidence from Latin America. Journal of Population Economics 10(4), 377–86.

Roelen, K & Sabates-Wheeler, R, 2011. A child sensitive approach to social protection: Serving practical and strategic needs. In Proceedings of the International Conference on Social Protection for Social Justice, 13–15 April, Institute of Development Studies, Brighton.

Roelen, K, Edström, J, Butters, S, Sabates-Wheeler, R & Davies, M, 2011. Documentation of Child and HIV Sensitive Social Protection in the Eastern and Southern African Region. Centre for Social Protection, Institute of Development Studies, Brighton.

Shaffer, P, 2003. Social Protection: Lessons from a Save the Children Research Project Report. Save the Children, London.

Tafere, Y & Woldehanna, T, 2012. Beyond food security: Transforming the Productive Safety Net Programme in Ethiopia for the well-being of children. Working Paper No. 83, Young Lives. ODID (Oxford Department of International Development), University of Oxford.

Victora, CG, Adair, L, Fall, C, Hallal, PC, Martorell, R, Richter, L & Sachdev, HS, 2008. Maternal and child under-nutrition: Consequences for adult health and human capital. The Lancet 371(9609), 340–57.

Woldehanna, T, 2010. Productive Safety Net Program and children's time use between work and schooling in Ethiopia. In Cockburn, J & Kabubo-Mariara, J (Eds), Child Welfare in Developing Countries. Springer, Ottawa, pp. 157–209.

Woldehanna, T, Tafere, Y & Tefera, B, 2011. The impact of the Productive Safety Net Program on child work and education in Ethiopia. In Proceedings of the Seventh Annual Conference of the Ethiopian Society of Sociologists, Social Workers and Anthropologists, 26–27 March 2010, Addis Ababa.

World Bank, 2005. Education in Ethiopia: Strengthening the Foundation for Sustainable Progress. World Bank, Washington, DC.

Tackling child poverty in South Africa: Implications of *ubuntu* for the system of social grants

Adam Whitworth[1] & Kate Wilkinson[2]

In South Africa both liberal and more communitarian and relational discourses of citizenship can be seen – the latter in the form of the southern African idea of ubuntu. *Policy for assisting children, however, is dominated by the framework of liberal citizenship, most clearly through the Bill of Rights and in particular the Child Support Grant. Using analyses from a purpose-built microsimulation model we show how a neglect of children's broader relationships in the current liberal citizenship inspired policy context limits the effectiveness of the child poverty strategy. The empirical analyses demonstrate how a greater recognition by policymakers of the relational principles of* ubuntu *could be expected to have more effect on reducing child poverty.*

1. Introduction

Although widely used, the term 'citizenship' is contested across several different strands of thinking (Jones & Gaventa, 2002), each with its own associated implications for policy approaches. This is particularly notable in South Africa with its combination of liberal (as found in the Bill of Rights) and more communitarian discourses of citizenship (in the form of the southern African idea of *ubuntu*). This paper uses original microsimulation modelling to question how effectively South Africa's social security package combats child poverty, given that it is based squarely on a foundation of liberal citizenship rights at the expense, in terms of policy, of *ubuntu*.

Within liberal approaches citizens and the state can be thought of as bound together in a 'contract' in which the individual is granted rights in return for fulfilling certain obligations towards the state and fellow citizens (e.g. obeying the law, participating in paid work), with the terms of that contract being keenly contested (White, 2003). The analytical starting point for discussions of liberal citizenship is often thought to be the work of Marshall (1964), yet South African discussions of liberal citizenship precede this work and continue to be central through the Bill of Rights and – in terms of social rights – the social grants. This liberal view of the detached rights-bearing individual can be counterbalanced by more communitarian citizenship thinking which sees the individual as inherently embedded in social relationships and networks which are key to facilitating identity, resource needs and belonging The concept of *ubuntu*, outlined below, is a specifically southern African communitarian philosophy and can be understood as a second historically rich strand of citizenship thinking in South Africa, emphasising that individuals are defined and understood primarily through their relationships with others rather than by their status as discrete individuals. These

---
[1] Lecturer, Department of Geography, University of Sheffield, UK.
[2] Data Analysis Manager, Children's Commissioning Services, Sheffield City Council, Sheffield, UK

two distinct approaches to citizenship lend themselves to different policy approaches. In current policy for tackling child poverty in South Africa, liberal notions of citizenship dominate (through the Bill of Rights and social grants), yet we would argue that a greater consideration of the principles, practices and policy implications of *ubuntu* could lead to more effective strategies for reducing child poverty.

In this paper we first describe child poverty in South Africa and the current system of social assistance. We then discuss liberal citizenship as it relates to South Africa, and then *ubuntu* and its implications for the current policy regime. We present original empirical analyses from microsimulation modelling of South African household data in order to provide new empirical evidence to show the relevance of the principles and practices of *ubuntu* to policies for reducing child poverty. In the final section of the paper we draw together the implications for South African policies for tackling child poverty.

2. Child poverty and social assistance in South Africa

South Africa is classified as a middle-income country (UN, 2010) yet poverty rates, and especially child poverty rates, are exceptionally high. Proudlock et al. (2008) use the 2006 General Household Survey (GHS) to estimate that about 68% of children live in households with an income of less than R1200 per month. Using the 2001 Census data, Barnes et al. (2009) find that 81% of children experience income and material deprivation while Streak et al. (2009), using the 2005/06 Income and Expenditure Survey (IES), find that about two thirds of children are poor on each of three separate measures – income, consumption and expenditure.

Behind these aggregate figures lie important differences between groups. First, there remains an extreme racial disparity in the distribution of poverty and wealth (Gelb, 2003), a disparity that consistently widened throughout the early 20th century (Leibbrandt et al., 2010). It is estimated that 63% of black children live in ultra-poor[3] households while this is the case for only 4% of white children; by contrast, only 1% of black children live in the most affluent households with earnings of more than R16 000 per month, compared to 29% of white children (Monson et al., 2006). In terms of geography, Leibbrandt et al. (2010) observe that poverty rates in rural areas (77%) are about twice as high as those in urban areas (39%) but that the problem of urban poverty accounts for a growing share of all poverty because of ongoing processes of urbanisation and migration. Finally, the high rate of HIV/AIDS in particular has led to a rapid increase in the number of child-headed households since the mid-1990s and although this group comprises less than 1% of all children they are highly vulnerable to acute poverty (Richter & Desmond, 2008).

For most of the apartheid era little support was provided by the government to those living in poverty and the social assistance system was highly racialised and focused on the elderly and disabled. The State Maintenance Grant (SMG) was the main source of social assistance for children but in the early 1990s less than 1% of SMG recipients were black despite the group representing more than 80% of the population. After apartheid ended the new Government of National Unity established the Lund Committee in 1995 to explore income support provision for children. The deliberations and recommendations of the Lund Committee were inevitably shaped both by political negotiation and by the economic context of the time, particularly constraints on expenditure resulting from the shift to the Growth, Employment and Redistribution (GEAR) strategy, which placed greater emphasis on

---

[3]Ultra-poor households are households earning less than R800 per month.

fiscal constraint and a growth-driven approach to poverty alleviation than had previously been the case (Lund, 2008). It was made clear to the committee that universal expansion of the SMG to the whole population was (along with other possible reform ideas) ruled out as prohibitively expensive (Lund, 2008:18). In the end the Lund Committee proposed that a grant of R100 per month be provided to all children under the age of seven whose caregiver satisfied the means test.

Despite criticisms of the CSG, in particular because of its low value and the application of a means test (Martin & Rosa, 2002), its implementation in 1998 was an important step in embedding a social assistance transfer aimed at reducing child poverty in modern South Africa. The CSG differs from the previous SMG in many respects, one notable aspect being the shift to a child-based rather than household-based grant so that the funds can (in theory) follow the child even if the child moves to another household or as the parental situation changes (e.g. due to death of a parent as a result of HIV/AIDS) (Lund, 2008:52–3). Between 1998 and 2009 the nominal value of the grant increased to R260 per child per month (from April 2011) and the CSG has gradually been made available to older children so that those up to 18 will become eligible from January 2012. The income test was raised considerably in 2008 so that about 60% of all children in South Africa are now eligible and uptake has increased dramatically, standing at 86% in 2007 (Children Count, 2009).

The support for children through the CSG sits within the context of a broader social security regime. South Africa currently has a range of social grants besides the CSG, with the main ones in terms of claimant numbers being the Disability Grant (DG) for working age adults unable to work due to ill-health and the Old Age Grant (OAG). Both are means tested grants with a value of up to R1140 per month in April 2011. In August 2009 there were about 9.1 million child beneficiaries of the CSG, compared to about 1.3 million beneficiaries of the DG and 2.5 million beneficiaries of the OAG (SASSA, 2009). The CSG is thus received by several million more individuals than the DG or OAG but its value is much smaller.

Despite the introduction of these grants a notable gap in the country's social security regime is that there remains no provision for adults who are fit to work but unable to find work. This is a significant problem in the context of persistently high rates of unemployment – put at 24% in December 2009 (according to the more restrictive official definition[4]) – and there is inevitably a strong link between child poverty and parental or caregiver unemployment. Nationally 41% of children live in households where there is no adult in work, and in the province of Limpopo, which has the highest child poverty rate at 83%,[5] only 28% of children live in a household where there is an employed adult (Children Count, 2008).

3. Two approaches to dealing with child poverty in South Africa

3.1 Liberal citizenship

The work of Marshall (1964) is often taken as a starting point for discussions of liberal citizenship. Marshall's account sees citizenship rights and obligations as a means to

---

[4]The South African government publishes both narrow (or official) and expanded unemployment statistics. The official figure includes those economically active individuals who were out of work in the past week, would like to work and could start within the next two weeks, and who have taken active steps to find work in the past month. The expanded version drops the active work seeking criterion.
[5]Calculated using data from the GHS 2005 based on a household poverty line of R1200 per month.

generate a sphere of equality between all citizens in order to compensate for the inequalities in outcomes inherent in capitalism (Barbalet, 1988). Marshall saw citizenship as bringing with it a triad of civil, political and social rights[6] that developed during the 18th, 19th and 20th centuries. Despite being criticised for its historically Anglocentric focus (Turner, 1993), Marshall's framework remains analytically useful in thinking about citizenship in South Africa and has been applied explicitly to the South African context (Whitworth & Noble, 2008).

Indeed, liberal citizenship thinking in South Africa precedes the work of Marshall and has a long and distinguished history throughout the struggle movement of the 20th century. The idea of a package of rights for all South African citizens has its origins in the historic 1943 Africans' Claims in which the African National Congress (ANC) set out explicit claims for civil, political and social rights for all South African citizens irrespective of race or class. The response of the Smuts government to Africans' Claims was dismissive and the beginning of apartheid created a policy environment openly hostile to such debates for equality of citizenship, yet the 1954 Women's Charter and the ANC's 1955 Freedom Charter again set out such demands for universal civil, political and social rights. In many ways this historical legacy of liberal citizenship sits at the heart of current social policy reform and debate in modern South Africa. After the transition to democracy in 1994 a liberal approach to citizenship thinking became central to the vision of the post-apartheid nation through the work of the Taylor Committee and especially through the creation of the 1996 Bill of Rights in the South African Constitution, a document that is crucial in articulating a vision for the sort of society that South Africa aims to become (Motala, 2009:1), as well as giving justiciable 'teeth' to that vision in terms of citizenship rights.

After much political debate over the nature of social rights, Section 27 of the Bill of Rights was phrased thus: 'Everyone has the right to have access to ... social security, including, if they are unable to support themselves and their dependants, appropriate social assistance'. However, the statement contains the final caveat that 'The state must take reasonable legislative and other measures, *within its available resources*, to achieve the *progressive realisation* of these rights' (RSA, 1996:Section 27, 1 and 2; authors' emphasis). The Bill of Rights also contains a separate section relating specifically to the rights of children. Section 28 states that 'Every child has the right to basic nutrition, shelter, basic health care services and social services' (RSA, 1996:Section 28, 1.c) and here the clause relating to 'available resources' and 'progressive realisation' is, interestingly, not included. This has been interpreted by some to imply that the realisation of children's rights is not subject to limitations on available resources and therefore that children have a higher and undisputable claim on state funds (Liebenberg, 2001; Sloth-Nielsen, 2001). Others argue, however, that parents rather than the state have the primary duty and that the priority of children's rights is elevated only in instances where the parent is clearly unable to fulfil this duty (Creamer, 2002; Liebenberg, 2002), most commonly because of parental death or where the child is removed from the household for protective reasons.

The rights that the Constitution sets out specifically for children provide considerable support to policies that target children. These rights have been shown to be justiciable

---

[6]In citizenship theory, examples of civil rights are the right to free speech and the right to hold property, examples of political rights are the right to vote and to form political associations, and examples of social rights are rights to cash transfers or services such as health and education. The distinctions between the three types are of course not always completely clear in practice.

in court, notably in the *Grootboom*, *TAC*, *Khosa* and *S vs M* cases. Through these legal actions real progress has been made in defending children's rights and these should not be underestimated. However, the liberal approach also has drawbacks in that rights are separated and delivered as discrete packages to different citizens. Crucially, the separation of children's and adults' rights in the Bill of Rights – and the social grants which flow from them for children, but not for unemployed adult parents or caregivers – illustrates the Constitution's individualistic and somewhat atomised view of citizens. This is at odds with the more communitarian view expressed through *ubuntu* – and with the reality of children's lives – that relational bonds between citizens are also crucial to tackling child poverty.

3.2 *Ubuntu*

With links to the communitarian tradition of citizenship thinking, *ubuntu* is a southern African philosophy that understands the individual as embedded in and defined by broader relational ties of family, community and society (Bhengu, 1996; Coetzee & Roux, 1998; Coertze, 2001). At the centre of the concept is the Zulu saying *umuntu ngumuntu ngabantu* – 'a person is a person through people' (Shutte, 2001:23). *Ubuntu* sees the community as providing the relational context and support through which individuals develop and live, and it emphasises those values which forge bonds and build networks: sharing, compassion, understanding, reciprocity, kindness, solidarity and sensitivity. This philosophy is distinct from liberal conceptions of citizenship in that it is based on the emotional and relational bonds within which citizens exist and on which all citizens depend in order to fulfil their own potential rather than on the notion of a detached rights-bearing individual (Held, 1990). As citizens are conceived of as being related to and depending on each other, all are responsible for ensuring that others have everything they need.

The differences between these two notions of citizenship have practical policy implications. Of particular relevance to the effectiveness of social security policies to tackle child poverty is the way *ubuntu* recognises the inter-connectedness of children and adults. This is in contrast to current liberal-based policy which lacks a broader conceptualisation of children's relationships and inter-connectedness with a wider household, network and community which, in turn, have their own needs and resources. These differences suggest a need for greater recognition of the fact that children are relational beings and that households, communities and other networks may themselves act to pool resources and risks, in contrast to (and perhaps as a result of) the individualism assumed by current social security policy. It also suggests a need for more explicit recognition of the links between children's and adults' rights when seeking to tackle child poverty in South Africa. One strand of the literature on child-centred notions of citizenship has argued that children's rights are enhanced by increased autonomy (Therborn, 1993), yet the interdependence of children and adults cannot be ignored and they cannot be so easily separated that the welfare of one group can be improved independently of the other.

In many instances the principles of *ubuntu* have been used by the courts – either implicitly or explicitly – to interpret the principles set out in the Constitution (Keep & Midgley, 2007), yet the fragmentation of relational networks into discrete individuals is evident in the fulfilling of citizens' rights to social assistance through social grants. Thus, it could be argued that the liberal citizenship philosophy that underpins the Bill of Rights simultaneously advances and constrains the country's ability to tackle child poverty effectively. The Bill of Rights provides a valuable framework through which individuals can receive and fight for key social security transfers, but it also sees the world through the lens of liberal citizenship, which encourages the artificial separation of social security policies for children and for their network of adult caregivers.

4. Assessing welfare outcomes using microsimulation

Using original evidence from a purpose-built South African microsimulation model,[7] the remainder of the paper compares evidence for the efficacy of the liberal and the *ubuntu* philosophies for tackling child poverty. Microsimulation is widely used as a method of analysing the impact of changes to tax and benefit policies on different groups in society (see for instance Mitton et al., 2000, for a review) and has been applied specifically to studying the impact of policy on child poverty in a number of countries (Brewer et al., 2006; Figari et al., 2009). The South African Microsimulation Model (SAMOD)[8] is a static microsimulation model which tailors the EUROMOD model to the tax-benefit system and demographic context of South Africa. The model draws on the IES (2000 and 2005), the Labour Force Survey (2000, 2006 and 2007) and the Community Survey (2007) to simulate the South African population in 2007 and builds in the eligibility criteria for South Africa's key social assistance and tax policies. The model then allows detailed micro-level analyses of the impact of policy changes (both real and potential) on children and other groups.

4.1 Household composition, income pooling and child poverty

Given the differences in the availability and value of social transfers across individuals, household composition becomes a central consideration for any anti-poverty programme. Household structures for poor and non-poor households in the IES 2000 are shown in Table 1. There is no official poverty line in South Africa but a threshold of R462 per month (in 2007 prices) has been recommended by Statistics South Africa and the National Treasury (Stats SA, 2007) and is used here. The table shows that only about 4% of children in poor households do not live with a working age adult. Clearly the fact that few children live in households where there is no one of working age means that in theory most children should have access to wage income. However, in the context of high unemployment, under-employment and (for those with work) low wages, many children cannot gain much, if any, benefit from wage income generated by their working age caregivers.

Table 1 also shows how income might itself influence household formation decisions in the policy context where social assistance is provided only to certain individuals. Previous research has found evidence to suggest that for the poor, household formation may, at least in part, be an active response to economic need in the context of high unemployment and a partial system of social grants (Klasen & Woolard, 2008). From this perspective, children and particularly old people become valuable income sources for the wider household and family. This is supported by the table, which shows that in poor households working age adults generally live with children, old people or both of these groups (88% of working age adults live with another age

---

[7]SAMOD was developed by Kate Wilkinson.
[8]Further details of SAMOD can be found in Wilkinson (2009).

Table 1: Household composition for poor and non-poor households

	\multicolumn{5}{c}{Percentage living with}	
	Children	Working age	Old age	Three generations	Total %	Number of persons
Poor households						
Children	1.1	64.3	2.7	31.9	100	10 891 863
Working age	56.3	11.8	4.4	27.5	100	10 862 809
Old age	8.2	14.6	12.2	65.0	100	2 010 070
Non-poor households						
Children	0.2	84.9	0.3	14.6	100	7 302 943
Working age	53.0	33.6	4.2	9.2	100	14 202 371
Old age	1.2	24.7	40.2	34.0	100	1 521 622

group). By contrast, in non-poor households only 66% of working age adults live in a household also containing another age group. While not conclusive, these data support the notion that those living below the poverty line are more likely to form household configurations in which at least one person is likely to be able to access some form of social transfer.

Previous research on income pooling within households also supports the idea that income is shared between household members rather than being 'ring-fenced' for the eligible recipient and may therefore encourage particular household configurations (Bertrand et al., 2003; Ardington et al., 2009). For example, while most households state that the CSG is spent directly on the child, about 20% of households say they pool the grant for wider household needs (Guthrie, 2002). Other social grants such as the OAG are also pooled by the household for a variety of reasons – sustaining the household, substituting for missing incomes of unemployed household members, and cushioning the household against unexpected economic shocks – and thus the OAG also frequently benefits children (Sagner & Mtati, 1999; Duflo, 2000). Indeed, evidence suggests a positive link between household OAG receipt and child outcomes in areas such as education, health and nutrition (Duflo, 2000; Aguero et al., 2006). Given that the value of the OAG is approximately four times that of the CSG, its potential to benefit children is clearly greater than the CSG's in the context of household income pooling.

More broadly, a household's equivalised income[9] is influenced by many factors besides eligibility for social grants, such as market income (i.e. earned income), remittances and the number of people with whom any income must be shared. This point is illustrated further in Figure 1, which shows the average income derived from three main income sources (market income, social transfers and remittances) for each type of household, assuming full uptake of social grants. One issue common to poverty studies is the paucity of information about *intra*-household resource allocations, with equal sharing typically being assumed. A second issue in South Africa specifically is the lack of evidence about the nature and cost of adult and child needs, an issue which relates directly to the choice of equivalisation scale selected (although previous research finds

---

[9]Equivalised income is used to create comparable household incomes across households of different sizes.

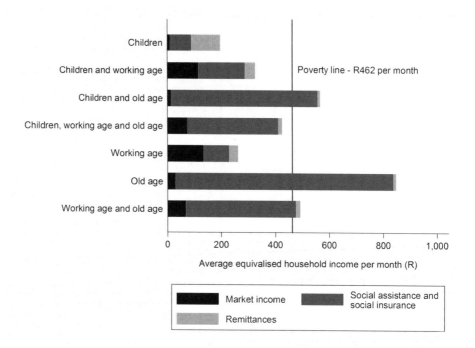

Figure 1: Average equivalised household income from different sources for individuals in different household types (R per month)

that which scale is chosen makes little material difference to child poverty results in South Africa – Streak et al., 2009). The present study follows Cutler & Katz (1992) in calculating the number of adult equivalents in each household on the basis of previous South African research,[10] which gives an approximate mid-point in the range of equivalence scales that have been used in South Africa.

Figure 1 shows that while households containing working age individuals typically have higher market incomes (as might be expected), the social transfer system creates even more significant differences between different types of household. In particular, only children living in households with older people have a reasonable chance of moving above the poverty line. Yet, as noted above, only about one third of children live in such households, which means that the OAG is not an effective mechanism for addressing child poverty in the aggregate.

The overall impact of each social transfer in turn on different age groups is presented in Figure 2. Assuming that every household pools all its income, the figure shows that the CSG has roughly the same impact on the proportion of children living in poverty as most other social transfers – despite the CSG being by far the largest social grant explicitly directed at children – and as intra-household transfers. For other groups the impact of the OAG on poverty rates among the elderly is particularly striking, a combination of its relatively generous level and the fact that about 40% of non-poor elderly

---

[10] In this scale, adult equivalents per household = $(a + (c * b))^d$ using values $c = 0.75$ and $d = 0.86$, which align with the implicit equivalence scales derived by Potgieter (Woolard & Leibbrandt, 1999).

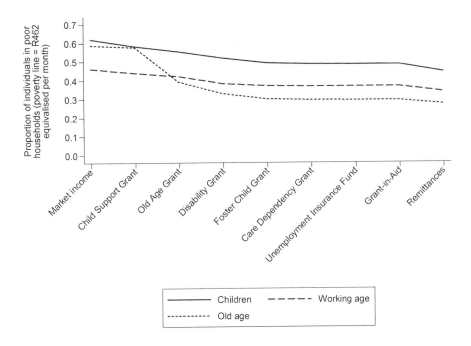

Figure 2: Impact of 2008 system of social transfers on the proportion of individuals living in households with incomes below the poverty line

households do not contain any children or working age adults with whom the OAG is shared (see Table 1).

The above analyses illustrate the importance that income pooling and household structures have for the effectiveness of policies to tackle poverty for different age groups. The individualistic view of the right to social assistance creates some inequality, with a small proportion of children benefiting more than others by virtue of living with elderly household members.

Turning to broader strategies to tackle child poverty, in Figure 3 we evaluate the effectiveness of seven policy reforms that have been considered by the South African government: a basic income grant paid at R180 per month, an extension to the CSG to children up to the age of 18, an extension to the CSG to all children and removal of the means test, a means tested grant of R180 to the low-income working age individual, a means tested grant to the low-income working age individual of between R100 and R360 depending on existing income, an extension to the current OAG to cover men from the age of 60 (rather than 65 as at present), and an extension to the OAG and removal of the means test to make the grant universal (and taxable for those paying tax). Of these reforms only one has been implemented – the extension of the CSG to age 18.

Comparing each reform with the existing system, we find that the variable-rate low-income grant paid to the working age poor and the basic income grant have the greatest impact on poverty rates for all age groups, including children. Figure 3 suggests therefore that greater recognition of children's broader relationships provides

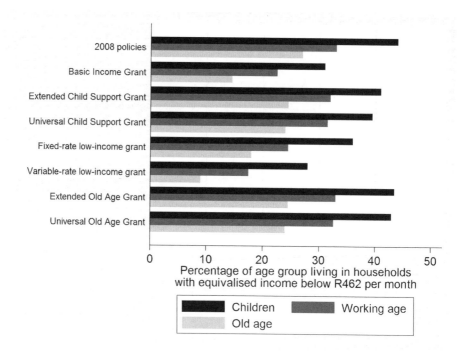

Figure 3: Percentage of each age group living in households with post-tax and transfer equivalised incomes below the poverty line

a significantly more effective mechanism to reduce child poverty than either the current social grants regime or a range of alternative policy options. It is of course also necessary to consider the cost as well as the impact of any potential policy reform. Figure 4 shows the overall cost of each of these potential reforms as well as the cost per individual to remove them from poverty. The variable-rate grant to the working age individual is the most expensive scheme but, interestingly, is also the most cost effective in terms of the average cost of removing an individual from poverty.

The analyses in Figure 3 and Figure 4 present a simplified view of the costs and benefits of policy reforms. The microsimulation modelling demonstrates that the current individualistic approach to tackling child poverty does not necessarily generate the most efficient or effective policies for reducing child poverty. Two points are of particular note. First, greater recognition in policy of the principles and practices of *ubuntu* and of children's relationships and inter-connectedness with adults offers an alternative, and arguably more effective, means of addressing child poverty. Second, there are various ways in which a greater recognition of *ubuntu* can be implemented, with each having positive – though differing – impacts on reducing child poverty. Particularly effective (in terms of reducing child poverty) and efficient (in terms of average cost per person removed from poverty) appear to be a basic income grant, a fixed low income grant and a variable low income grant. Moreover, while the focus here is only on potential social assistance reforms, the broader and more important message is the need to address poverty in the working age population in order to reduce child poverty more effectively, irrespective of the policy instrument used. The policy focus thus need not, and indeed should not, be restricted to social assistance

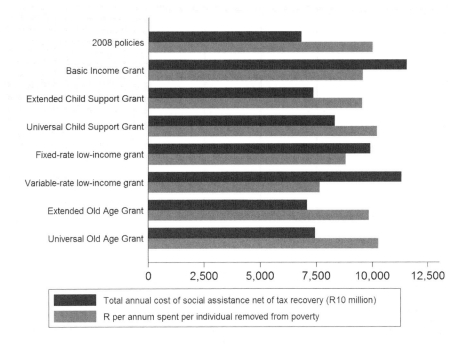

Figure 4: Total annual cost of reform and average cost per individual removed from poverty

reforms but should also consider employment generation policies to assist the working age poor and, as a consequence, poor children.

Naturally, further factors would need to be considered to assess the true cost of the reform and any possible unintended consequences or incentive effects. One issue is the potentially large administrative costs of any means tested scheme, and in particular of the highly effective, though administratively much more complex, variable low income grant. A second issue is the potential incentive effects or unintended consequences resulting from any such income support policies aimed at poor children or poor households. The South African debate has seen a great deal of attention paid to concerns that the CSG encourages teenage pregnancy, something which a grant targeted at households rather than children might avoid.[11] Such concerns seem ill-founded, however, in that research (Makiwane et al., 2006; Steele, 2006; Moultrie & McGrath, 2007) has repeatedly found no evidence of any link between CSG and teenage pregnancy in South Africa. Thus child-based policies remain firmly on the table, though greater recognition of *ubuntu* highlights the point that extensions to the CSG without income support or employment generation strategies to help other household or broader network members are unlikely to alter overall child poverty levels dramatically.

---

[11] Assuming that means tests are applied on non-equivalised household incomes as is currently the case.

5. Conclusions

In this paper we have argued that in South Africa the dominance – yet demographically partial implementation – of the liberal citizenship perspective and the relative neglect of the communitarian principles and practices of *ubuntu* has serious implications for the effectiveness of current government policy to tackle child poverty. While the enshrinement of rights in the Bill of Rights has significant advantages in South Africa, our analyses suggest that the system of social grants needs to take a broader, more collective and more grounded approach than is currently the case in the liberal model of citizenship and as set down in the Bill of Rights and operationalised in the current package of social grants. In particular, in seeking to tackle child poverty through the CSG the current policy formulation seems limited in that children are granted individualised rights as autonomous beings abstracted from familial and social relations and from patterns of household behaviour in terms of household formation and resource pooling. This ignores the fact that child poverty is situated in the broader context of the needs and structures of families, households and relationships. The social assistance programmes to tackle child poverty need to recognise this.

Using original microsimulation modelling, we have highlighted ways in which grants not directed at children nevertheless have important implications for tackling child poverty. Extensions to the age eligibility within the CSG are welcome, as would be increases to its real value. Despite this progress, however, the CSG continues in reality to be used to support broader household needs. Policies for reducing child poverty would be more effective if the principles of *ubuntu* and its application in practice were better recognised in the package of policy supports available, whether via social assistance programmes or employment generation policies or both. The fact that most children live in households that remain poor even after receiving social assistance shows that child poverty and working age poverty cannot be separated as easily as the current liberal citizenship inspired policy framework would suggest. Rather, there is a need for the principles and practices of *ubuntu* to be better recognised in the government's anti-poverty strategy. The government has various options available for implementing *ubuntu* inspired policy reforms – each with its own measurable level of cost, effectiveness and efficiency. Reform in this direction seems essential if child poverty is to be reduced in the new South Africa.

Acknowledgements

The authors are grateful to Professor Holly Sutherland and colleagues at the University of Essex for sharing the EUROMOD model.

References

Aguero, J, Carter, M & Woolard, I, 2006. The Impact of Unconditional Cash Transfers on Nutrition: The South African Child Support Grant. SALDRU (Southern Africa Labour and Development Research Unit), University of Cape Town.

Ardington, C, Case, A & Hosegood, V, 2009. Labor supply responses to large social transfers: Longitudinal evidence from South Africa. American Economic Journal 1(1), 22–48.

Barbalet, J, 1988. Citizenship: Rights, Struggle and Class Inequality. Open University Press, Milton Keynes.

Barnes, H, Noble, M, Wright, G & Dawes, A, 2009. A geographical profile of child deprivation in South Africa. Child Indicators Research 181–99.

Bertrand, M, Mullainathan, S & Miller, D, 2003. Public policy and extended families: Evidence from pensions in South Africa. The World Bank Economic Review 17(1), 27–50.

Bhengu, M, 1996. Ubuntu: The Essence of Democracy. Novalis Press, Cape Town.

Brewer, M, Browne, J & Sutherland, H, 2006. Micro-simulating Child Poverty in 2010 and 2020. Joseph Rowntree Foundation, York.

Children Count, 2008. Facts about Children: Children in Households without an Employed Adult. Children's Institute, Cape Town.

Children Count, 2009. Take-up of the Child Support Grant. Children's Institute, Cape Town.

Coertze, R, 2001. Ubuntu and nation building in South Africa. South African Journal of Ethnology 24(4), 113–18.

Coetzee, P & Roux, A (Eds), 1998. The African Philosophy Reader. Routledge, New York.

Creamer, K, 2002. The Impact of South Africa's Evolving Jurisprudence on Children's Socio-economic Rights on Budget Analysis. IDASA (Institute for Democracy in Africa), Pretoria.

Cutler, D & Katz, L, 1992. Rising inequality? Changes in the distribution of income and consumption in the 1980s. The American Economic Review 82(2), 546–51.

Duflo, E, 2000. Grandmothers and granddaughters: Old age pension and intra-household allocation in South Africa. Working Paper 8061, National Bureau of Economic Research, Cambridge, MA.

Figari, F, Paulus, A & Sutherland, H, 2009. Measuring the size and impact of public cash support for children in cross-national perspective. EUROMOD Working Paper EM6/09, Institute for Social and Economic Research, University of Essex, Colchester.

Gelb, S, 2003. Inequality in South Africa: Nature, Causes and Responses. The EDGE Institute, Johannesburg.

Guthrie, T, 2002. Assessing the Impact of the Child Support Grant on the Well-being of Children in South Africa: A Summary of Available Evidence. Children's Institute, University of Cape Town.

Held, V, 1990. Feminist transformations of moral theory. Philosophy and Phenomenological Research 50 (Suppl), 321–44.

Jones, E & Gaventa, J, 2002. Concepts of Citizenship: A Review. Institute of Development Studies, University of Sussex, Brighton.

Keep, H & Midgley, R, 2007. The emerging role of *ubuntu-botha* in developing a consensual South African legal culture. In Bruinsma, F & Nelken, D (Eds), Explorations in Legal Culture. Elsevier, Amsterdam.

Klasen, S & Woolard, I, 2008. Surviving unemployment without state support: Unemployment and household formation in South Africa. Journal of African Economies 18(1), 1–51.

Leibbrandt, M, Woolard, I, Finn, A & Argent, J, 2010. Trends in South African income distribution and poverty since the fall of apartheid. Social, Employment and Migration Working Papers No. 101, OECD (Organization for Economic Cooperation and Development) Publishing, Paris.

Liebenberg, S, 2001. The right to social assistance: The implications of Grootboom for policy reform in South Africa. South African Journal on Human Rights 17(2), 232–57.

Liebenberg, S, 2002. South Africa's evolving jurisprudence on socio-economic rights: An effective tool in challenging poverty? Law, Democracy and Development 6(2), 159–91.

Lund, F, 2008. Changing Social Policy: The Child Support Grant in South Africa. HSRC (Human Sciences Research Council) Press, Cape Town.

Makiwane, M, Desmond, C, Richter, L & Udjo, E, 2006. Is the Child Support Grant Associated with an Increase in Teenage Fertility in South Africa? Evidence from National Surveys and Administrative Data. HSRC (Human and Sciences Research Council), Pretoria.

Marshall, TH, 1964. Citizenship and social class. In Marshall, TH (Ed.). Class, Citizenship and Social Development: Essays by T.H. Marshall. Doubleday, New York.

Martin, P & Rosa, S, 2002. Childhood Poverty in South Africa. Alliance for Children's Entitlement to Social Security. Plumstead, Cape Town.

Mitton, L, Sutherland, H & Weeks, M (Eds), 2000. Microsimulation Modelling for Policy Analysis. Cambridge University Press, Cambridge.

Monson, J, Hall, K, Smith, C & Shung-King, M (Eds), 2006. South African Child Gauge 2006. Children's Institute, University of Cape Town.

Motala, M, 2009. South Africa's slippery slope: Beefing up the implementation of bad policies. The South African Civil Society Information Service, 5 March, Johannesburg.

Moultrie, T & McGrath, N, 2007. Teenage fertility rates falling in South Africa. South African Medical Journal 97(6), 442–3.

Proudlock, P, Dutschke, M, Jamieson, L, Monson, J & Smith, C, 2008. South African Child Gauge 2007/2008. Children's Institute, University of Cape Town.

Richter, L & Desmond, C, 2008. Targeting AIDS orphans and child-headed households? A perspective from national surveys in South Africa, 1995–2005. AIDS Care 20(9), 1019–28.

RSA (Republic of South Africa), 1996. The Constitution of the Republic of South Africa, Act No 108 of 1996. Government Printer, Pretoria.

Sagner, A & Mtati, R, 1999. Politics of pension sharing in urban South Africa. Ageing and Society 19, 393–416.

SASSA (South African Social Security Agency), 2009. Statistical Report on Social Grants: Report No. 21. SASSA, Pretoria.

Shutte, A, 2001. Ubuntu: An Ethic for a New South Africa. Cluster Publications, Pietermaritzburg.

Sloth-Nielsen, J, 2001. The child's right to social services, the right to social security, and primarily prevention of child abuse: Some conclusions in the aftermath of Grootboom. South African Journal on Human Rights 17(2), 210.

Stats SA (Statistics South Africa), 2007. A National Poverty Line for South Africa. Stats SA & National Treasury, Pretoria.

Steele, M, 2006. Report on Incentive Structures of Social Assistance Grants in South Africa. Department of Social Development, Pretoria.

Streak, J, Yu, D & Van der Berg, S, 2009. Measuring child poverty in South Africa: Sensitivity to the choice of equivalence scale and an updated profile. Social Indicators Research 94, 183–201.

Therborn, G, 1993. The politics of childhood: The rights of children in modern times. In Castles, F (Ed.), Families of Nations: Patterns of Public Policy in Western Democracies. Dartmouth Publishing, Aldershot.

Turner, B (Ed.), 1993. Citizenship and Social Theory. SAGE, London.

UN (United Nations), 2010. Social indicators. http://unstats.un.org/unsd/demographic/products/socind/inc-eco.htm Accessed 9 February 2011.

White, S, 2003. The Civic Minimum. Oxford University Press, Oxford.

Whitworth, A & Noble, M, 2008. A safety net without holes: An argument for a comprehensive income security system for South Africa. Journal of Human Development 9(2), 247–63.

Wilkinson, K, 2009. Adapting EUROMOD for a developing country: The case of South Africa and SAMOD. EUROMOD Working Paper EM5/09, Institute of Social and Economic Research, University of Essex, Colchester.

Woolard, I & Leibbrandt, M, 1999. Measuring Poverty in South Africa. Development Policy Research Unit, University of Cape Town, Cape Town.

The South African disability grant: Influence on HIV treatment outcomes and household well-being in KwaZulu-Natal

Lucia Knight[1], Victoria Hosegood[2] & Ian M Timæus[3]

This paper explores the implications of the disability grant for household members' well-being and adults' success on ART (antiretroviral therapy). It uses case studies based on data from an in-depth qualitative study of 10 households in KwaZulu-Natal. Receipt of the disability grant ensured that the basic needs of the HIV-infected adult could be met by other household members, especially when the grant was received when the person first met the qualifying criteria and in conjunction with ART. Where treatment was effective, HIV-infected adults were able to make substantial contributions to the well-being of other members in addition to the financial support provided by the grant itself. Thus, early access to financial support in conjunction with commencing ART may lead to improved health outcomes and reduce poverty and vulnerability associated with illness in poor households. This synergistic relationship between social welfare and treatment may in turn contribute to greater cost-efficiency.

1. Introduction

Many South African households are faced with the dual challenges of HIV and poverty. The social security system in South Africa was designed to reduce deprivation and vulnerability in poor households by providing a range of means-tested cash grants (Lund, 2008). The child support grant and old age pension are the most common of these. The old age pension, in particular, is redistributed within households (Case & Deaton, 1998; Seekings, 2002; Duflo, 2003). However, despite their potential for redistribution and the benefits that grants have for poor households, including those affected by HIV, the design of the current system fails to account adequately for HIV.

The disability grant was originally designed to provide for those who were, as a result of severe disability, rendered unable to work and to supplement their household income (Seekings, 2002). Neither the Social Assistance Act of 1992 nor the 2001 amendment to it make any mention of HIV (Nattrass, 2005). Despite the high prevalence of HIV in South Africa, the ill-health and loss of work that results from this and the repercussions for households' socioeconomic status, the government currently does not provide a targeted grant for poor HIV-infected individuals or affected households. Those assessed as impaired or disabled because of chronic illness and therefore unable to work should,

---
[1] Postdoctoral Fellow, HIV/AIDS, STI and TB Unit, Human Sciences Research Council (HSRC), Durban, South Africa.
[2] Reader in Demography, Faculty of Social Sciences, University of Southampton and Africa Centre for Health and Population Studies, University of KwaZulu-Natal, Mtubatuba, South Africa
[3] Professor of Demography, Department of Population Health, London School of Hygiene & Tropical Medicine, London, UK

according to the guidelines, qualify for this cash transfer either on a 'permanent' (i.e. for five years) or 'temporary' (less than one year) basis before their eligibility is reviewed (Nattrass, 2005). The problem is that until 2008 when the policy was explicitly changed many provinces used a CD4 count of below 200 cells/mm^3, regardless of impairment or disability, as the main criterion for eligibility (Simchowitz, 2004). Policymakers have therefore not adequately considered the differences between illness and disability and designed the grants system accordingly; this has led to criticisms (Simchowitz, 2004; Nattrass, 2005; Hardy & Richter, 2006).

The disability grant was worth R1200 in April 2012.[4] Research in the Free State shows that, like the old age pension, which is the equivalent amount, it can contribute substantially to income and reduce the depth and severity of poverty in affected households (Booysen & Van der Berg, 2005). Despite not being designed to target those affected by HIV, the disability grant is likely to make a greater contribution to affected households, and particularly the sick person's socioeconomic status, than the smaller child support grant. While other cash transfers may play a role similar to that of the disability grant in affected households, because the disability grant is paid to an individual the focus in much of the literature is on whether receiving it may affect their adherence to antiretroviral therapy (ART). Specifically, the wish to meet the qualifying criteria for the disability grant may represent a disincentive to adhering to ART (Hardy & Richter, 2006; Leclerc-Madlala, 2006; Phaswana-Mafuya et al., 2009).

Instead of focusing on whether a negative relationship exists between the disability grant and ART, we explore the way in which access to both treatment and the disability grant can positively influence personal and therefore household well-being. Specifically, we investigate the impact of disability grant receipt on poor households affected by HIV in South Africa. We show that the timing of grant receipt plays a role in the contribution the grant makes to health outcomes for individuals on ART. The analysis compares case studies where the grant was received when the person qualified, a case where the receipt of the grant was delayed and another where, despite applying and qualifying for the grant, the applicant failed to receive it. The case studies also document the benefits that timely receipt of both the disability grant and treatment can have for the well-being of the rest of the household. The case study where receipt of the grant was delayed and the case where the grant was not awarded illustrate some of the barriers to more widespread uptake of the grant by eligible individuals.

We first review the principal debates about the disability grant and HIV, and then provide some empirical evidence for the benefits of the disability grant from a small qualitative study of HIV-affected households in KwaZulu-Natal. We conclude with recommendations that may help to maximise the personal and household-level benefits and outcomes of access to a disability grant and ART.

2. ART and the disability grant in South Africa: Debates and developments

The literature dealing with both the disability grant and HIV/AIDS has, to date, largely focused on a perceived trade-off between access to ART and the disability grant (Hardy & Richter, 2006; Leclerc-Madlala, 2006; Phaswana-Mafuya et al., 2009; Venkataramani et al., 2010). Prior to 2008, the qualifying criteria for ART initiation and access to a disability grant were both based on a minimum CD4 count of 200 cells/mm^3 or a

---

[4] 1 USD = 8.17 ZAR (on average) in 2012.

medical assessment showing that the person was at stage 4 of the illness as defined by the World Health Organisation (Lawn et al., 2008). These identical eligibility criteria fuelled claims that the disability grant was a disincentive to continuing ART, i.e. that poor, largely unemployed people in receipt of a disability grant might not adhere to the therapy, or might even stop completely, to ensure that they would keep receiving the grant and not lose it (Nattrass, 2005). Despite this concern, however, no subsequent empirical research has provided evidence of a substantial trade-off. Recent research raises concerns instead about the impact of withdrawal of the disability grant from those whose health has improved with ART and points to the inappropriateness of the use of the CD4 count or the viral load as criteria for access to the grant (Hardy & Richter, 2006; Leclerc-Madlala, 2006; Phaswana-Mafuya et al., 2009).

Perhaps influenced by an outcry from researchers, civil society and the public (Heywood, 2008), the eligibility criteria for the disability grant were changed in 2008, disallowing its review or removal on the basis of the CD4 count (DSD, 2008). Instead, the major qualifying criteria for receipt are physical or mental impairment or disability that renders the person unfit for work or employment (SASSA, 2010). In addition, recent health policy changes mean that those with a CD4 count of less than 350 cells/mm^3 qualify for ART (DoH, 2011). This change is recent and the bulk of adult patients currently on ART, including those enrolled in our study, qualified for treatment at 200 cells/mm^3. These changes in eligibility criteria, along with little evidence for any disincentive, suggest that new research should abandon the focus on disincentives.

Despite changes to the review and renewal guidelines, concern does remain, however, about the consequences of grant loss for households. Some quantitative research in the Western Cape and Free State has indicated that the time limits on receipt of the grant have been poorly monitored and that grant receipt continued after the review period elapsed (Booysen & Van der Berg, 2005; Venkataramani et al., 2010). These findings suggested that fewer grants may have been terminated than anticipated on the basis of earlier literature (Hardy & Richter, 2006; Leclerc-Madlala, 2006; Phaswana-Mafuya et al., 2009). One third of those receiving the grant in the Western Cape sample were also working, demonstrating a possible failure to implement the means test which requires those applying to be unable to work (Venkataramani et al., 2010). In addition, the results show no change in self-reported health in those who lost the disability grant. The threat of grant loss and the disincentive effect associated with the loss may therefore be less significant than has been commonly assumed.

While some research points to the valuable role that the disability grant plays in the health, nutrition and income of households affected by HIV, these studies fail to consider when the grant is accessed and whether a potentially beneficial relationship exists between this grant and ART (Phaswana-Mafuya et al., 2009; Venkataramani et al., 2010). This paper therefore examines the relationship between receipt of the disability grant and successful ART and considers the benefits of timeous grant receipt.

3. Methods

3.1 Background

The households enrolled in this study were from rural and peri-urban communities in the Umkhanyakude district of northern KwaZulu-Natal and were part of the Africa Centre Demographic Surveillance Survey (DSS) population. The DSS population is very mobile and 33% were non-resident (Tanser et al., 2008). Fluid and multiple household memberships and a generational mix contribute to household complexity. Households are often poor and unemployment is high. Social grant receipt is fairly widespread and the DSS data from 2006 suggest that 90% of those eligible receive an old age pension. In addition, 27% of rural households and 43% of urban households with eligible children were getting at least one child support grant (Muhwava, 2008). For the purpose of this study, a 'household' was defined as people who consider themselves to be members of the same household; this includes resident members and, in some cases, non-resident members who live elsewhere but maintain social ties with the household.

Antenatal HIV prevalence in the district in 2008 was 40%, the fourth highest rate in KwaZulu-Natal (DoH, 2009). ART has been available since 2004, through government clinics, supported by an HIV Treatment and Care Programme run by the Africa Centre, and an estimated 7500 people in the area were receiving treatment by the end of 2008 (Hontelez et al., 2011). The community is fairly well-serviced by clinics staffed weekly by Africa Centre doctors. Cause-specific mortality data collected using verbal autopsies[5] between 2000 and 2009 showed that 50% of adult deaths in the DSS were HIV-related (Herbst et al., 2011). Access to ART has resulted in a substantial reduction in mortality – approximately a 22% reduction for women and 29% for men between 2002 and 2006 (Herbst et al., 2009). But despite increased access to treatment, improved health and reduced mortality, late presentation for HIV testing and delayed initiation of ART because of the CD4 count guidelines means that many households nevertheless have some experience of illness or death.

3.2 Data collection and analysis

The study was conducted in 10 households that included either an adult HIV death or a member living with symptomatic or treated HIV. All the households were poor, with limited access to formal employment, and relied heavily on social grant income. A local home-based care project and the verbal autopsy staff at the Africa Centre were identified as being able to share information about this type of household. These sources were useful because they could put us in contact with households where people were aware of the HIV status of their members and were comfortable with talking about the sensitive issues relating to HIV. The study enrolled five households identified by the local Catholic Church home-based care programme, one household identified by verbal autopsy staff, and one that was a chance contact. The study also included three households that had been part of an earlier Household Dynamics study investigating the socioeconomic impact of HIV/AIDS on households and their members in the same district prior to the advent of public ART (Montgomery et al., 2006; Hosegood et al., 2007).

For logistical reasons all households selected had to have an adult respondent who was present during the day to be interviewed. This meant that available respondents were likely to be too old or sick to be working, unemployed, studying, on holiday or doing shift work. Our respondents were therefore mostly women and mostly 55 years and above, potentially introducing gender and age bias. On the other hand, the 10 households reflected a variety of social and economic situations and were broadly representative of other households in Umkhanyakude. All respondents provided informed consent and the Humanities and Social Sciences Research Ethics committee

---

[5]Verbal autopsies analyse symptoms to determine cause of death and are particularly useful where cause-of-death data are poor (Herbst et al., 2011).

at the University of KwaZulu-Natal and the Research Ethics Committee at the London School of Hygiene and Tropical Medicine granted the study ethical approval.

We collected in-depth ethnographic, retrospective and contemporary information about the experience of illness and death. The data were collected using multiple semi-structured interviews and non-participant observation in the household over a six-month period beginning in January 2008. Each interview dealt with a particular topic but prospective data about the current household situation were also collected at each visit. Household genograms and event maps were used to collect information about household composition, relationships and important episodes and events relating to illness and death (Adato et al., 2007).

Data from genograms, household event maps, transcripts of translated interviews and observation field notes were used to create household case studies covering the five years preceding fieldwork and the six-month period of research. All names used in the analysis and this paper were changed to pseudonyms. The case study approach enabled a detailed description of household experience in context and the analysis of socioeconomic changes at household and individual level (Mikkelson, 1995; Russell, 2005). The case studies were compared and interview transcripts and field notes were also analysed cross-sectionally using framework analysis (Mason, 2002). Although limited in their generalisability to different contexts, these in-depth qualitative case studies revealed the complexity of the respondents' experience and they offer important insights into social policy (Ritchie & Spencer, 1994). We coded the research questions according to themes and added to these as further themes were identified in multiple reading and coding iterations.

4. Findings

The focus of this paper is on adult illness, ART and the disability grant. We chose four case studies to summarise for this paper, as examples of four typical scenarios. Two had members receiving both ART and a disability grant during the study period. The Dlamini household had a member benefiting concurrently from the disability grant and ART. The Nkosi household had a member who had started treatment before the study began but received her disability grant later – this provided an example of the effect of a new grant on the well-being of a person on ART and their household. The other two had members receiving ART but no disability grant. The Dube household had a member on ART who had received a temporary disability grant but lost it before the study began – this was an example of the effect of grant loss and also of the importance of timeous receipt of both the grant and ART. The Bhengu household had a member who had made an incomplete application for a grant – this was an example what can happen to a household and its sick members when disability grant applications fail.

Although the households in these studies were in receipt of other grants, particularly child support grants, these grants were smaller and targeted at other members of the household. In addition, all these other grants had been accessed for some time before the study and their use was well-established prior to both the illness of the adult and the receipt of the disability grant.

4.1 Dlamini household

The Dlamini household was a very large four-generation household. Gugu, the eldest living daughter, aged 33, was HIV-positive but had been on treatment since late 2006 and was well. Although her mother was the household head, the responsibilities for financial decision-making and ensuring the household met its basic needs fell to Gugu. The household survived on the income from a number of social grants. Seven of the younger children in the household qualified for child support grants and this income was spent on their basic needs and their mothers'. The elderly household head, Gugu's mother, received an old-age pension, but Gugu explained that the bulk of this was spent on her mother's health care expenses for diabetes and high blood pressure. Despite a fairly large total monthly household income, the size of the household meant that it was quickly spent on the basic needs, particularly food for the children and the health care of the household head.

Gugu received a disability grant for herself one month after starting ART. She attributed the improvement in her health as much to the grant as to the treatment:

> When I started taking treatment, I went to register for my disability grant. Everything went quickly and I got it in November. I have seen a big difference. I can see that my body is much better.

The improvements that Gugu observed in her own health and her psychological and financial welfare were not only crucial for herself and her child but had implications for the rest of the household. As the decision-maker, she controlled the purchase of food, ensured that the household members' basic needs were met and cared for her mother. The disability grant income meant that she could invest some capital in the informal family business, which had stopped operating while she was severely ill. Gugu therefore made substantial contributions to the household's income and well-being as a result of receiving the disability grant.

Limited data are available from this study about the possible disincentive that receiving a disability grant presents to adherence to ART. The respondents seldom spontaneously initiated reports of their concerns about the loss of a disability grant. It was only when asked that they mentioned such concerns. Gugu was one respondent who articulated her fear of losing the grant:

> They told us that we could lose the [disability] grant. I don't know how I feel about that. That is why I want to register [my son for a care dependency grant], because when [my disability grant] gets cut off I will need help. .... I went to look for a job before but I had a problem because [he] was not staying with me and he didn't take his treatment well. I am afraid to leave him again [to look for work] because maybe he won't take it again and will get sick.

When asked to explain her concerns in more detail, Gugu said she was particularly concerned about losing the grant because she was caring for her sick child and would have to leave home to seek employment if she lost this grant.

4.2 Nkosi household

Thobela and Bheki were a cohabiting couple living with their two children. Both were HIV-positive and Thobela, aged 36, was extremely ill, unable to walk and required ongoing physical care. She had been on ART for about four months at the start of fieldwork. Although Thobela and her family believed that her health had improved slightly because of the treatment, they continued to struggle to afford adequate food and transport to the clinic. They were also concerned about how cut off they were becoming from their neighbours and community. These social and economic problems experienced by the household appeared to contribute to Thobela's failure to make a better recovery.

The household was poor before Thobela started treatment: Bheki had lost his job and was neither employed nor looking for work because he needed to care for Thobela and Thobela had stopped informal trading because of her illness. This meant that they were surviving financially on a child support grant, worth R210 in 2008,[6] for their youngest child and a very small piecemeal income that Bheki earned doing herding or weeding when Thobela could be left alone. Thobela and Bheki both spoke about being poor and their feeling of desperation about their financial situation. The household had no alternative source of income or support and were isolated from both family and the community. Their financial situation made it difficult to buy food and other necessities and get Thobela to the clinic:

> It's not enough [money] ... to go to the clinic I need money, it's all credit [she had to borrow money to pay for transport to the clinic]. If I got a [disability] grant it would be better.

Thobela applied for a disability grant soon after starting ART but did not receive it immediately. Despite visiting the Department of Social Development and the South African Social Security Agency to follow up on the progress of her application, she failed to find out why she was not receiving it, although some officials suggested her application might have been lost. Then, after four months of investigation, with no explanation, Thobela's disability grant was suddenly paid out. The reaction of the household was one of great joy – the grant of R1140 almost quadrupled their monthly income.

Thobela's receipt of the disability grant subsequently had clear benefits for both the household's well-being and her own health. Bheki confirmed that he was under less pressure to provide resources for his family and felt generally better, more rested and healthier. The first disability grant payment enable the family to purchase new school uniforms for the children, thereby ensuring they could remain in school. Thobela felt a dramatic improvement in her health:

> It's not like it was before. We are not suffering now. You can see that now I can walk. A person can die, if they are not eating and taking pills [ART]. I will be fine now.

Thobela attributed the improvement in her health to being able to afford different food. Whereas before the household survived largely on staples such as maize meal, after the grant they were able to expand their diet to include some tinned fish for protein and more vegetables.

Thobela's return to health meant she was able to resume her domestic chores. Towards the end of the study period, she was walking, albeit slowly and with some pain. She was able to work in her garden and was growing spinach for her family. The homestead became cleaner and tidier as Thobela was able to do more and the other members of the household had time to devote to activities other than her care and support.

4.3 Dube household

The Dube household was headed by a 90-year-old woman who lived with her 34-year-old daughter-in-law, Thembilihle, her daughter Lungile and three grandchildren.

---

[6] 1 USD = 8.25 ZAR (on average) in 2008.

Thembilihle was HIV-positive, had been on treatment since 2004 and was well in 2008. Like Gugu, she found that her health improved on the combined receipt of ART and the disability grant:

> When I went on treatment I became better, I gained weight again and the marks I had on my body are not there anymore.

Like all the sick household members in our sample, she was severely ill and unable to work when she started ART and the disability grant supported her and her household financially while she recovered.

Thembilihle's disability grant was discontinued. She had recovered on treatment and at a review with her doctor in 2007 she was considered well enough to work and her doctor therefore refused to fill in another application for the grant. She had since requested another review but was informed that her health had improved, her CD4 count had normalised and that she was able to work and therefore would not be considered. Since losing the grant she had obtained a formal job working full-time at a grocery shop in town. She continued taking her medication and had negotiated working hours with her employer enabling her to attend the clinic or hospital without jeopardising her employment.

Thembilihle, like Gugu, was the primary decision-maker in her household. Her income from her job went into the communal pot, along with her mother-in-law's old age pension and extra income from selling beer, to support the rest of the household, none of whom contributed financially.

Thembilihle planted and tended the household garden and fruit trees that provided the household with seasonal produce. She was also a member of a stokvel[7] along with other women in the community. This stokvel was not merely a saving scheme: the money pooled was lent to others and the interest generated added to the group's income.

4.4 Bhengu household

Nomsa, aged 56, was the head of a multi-generational household of 11. Her adult daughter, Zinhle, was HIV-positive and extremely ill. Prior to her illness Zinhle had been working in Richards Bay, which enabled her to remit money home to build a structure on her mother's property. When she became very ill she stopped working and returned to live there. No other household member was employed and they relied on the income from three child support grants (which in 2008 had a combined value of R630) collected for Nomsa's youngest child and two grandchildren. Nomsa described the household's financial situation since the loss of Zinhle's support:

> I try, with this R600, to buy groceries, pay the school fees and also the school transport for R100. I am left with R500, I went and bought 25 kg [of maize meal], it doesn't last the month, I also buy a bag of beans and I pay for [funeral] insurance ... As I have explained, we are hungry. Last month I had to get R200 credit because I didn't have any maize meal left.

Zinhle was unable to walk and needed company when leaving the household. This increased the household's transport costs, which they struggled to afford, and made access to treatment and health care difficult. Nomsa expressed her despair at her household's situation and concluded that to pay for the required trips to the clinic for Zinhle she would need to borrow the money. Transport problems also affected

---

[7] A stokvel is an informal communal savings or rotating credit union.

Zinhle's ability to access a disability grant. Although she had applied at the clinic, her approval required assessment by the medical examiner at the Department of Social Development offices, as Nomsa explained:

> I haven't been able to take her [to the medical examiner] because I don't have any money left. I have to hire a car [to get to town].

Despite their difficulties getting access, health care was an unspoken priority for the household and the journey to the clinic was shorter and thus cost less than getting to town. Zinhle therefore failed to complete her application and receive a grant.

It is possible that had Zinhle been able to access a disability grant the household's experience of illness would have been different. Zinhle should also have qualified for food parcels from the clinic and these, had they managed to get them, might have made a small difference to the household. Access to a disability grant would have more than doubled the household's small income from the child support grant, thus dramatically improving not only the household income but also Zinhle's personal situation. Unfortunately, although Zinhle started treatment, her condition did not improve, she was eventually hospitalised and died without receiving a disability grant. A combination of health and financial problems that a disability grant might have gone a long way to ameliorating trapped Zinhle in illness and her household in poverty.

5. Discussion

Our case studies appear to indicate an important relationship between ART and the receipt of a disability grant. It seems that, in similar situations, access to targeted financial support, in this case the disability grant, can help to ensure successful health outcomes for those on ART, and also contribute to household's well-being more generally. To recover their health while receiving treatment, household members living with HIV depend on the ability of the household to provide sufficient care, nutrition and other necessities (Zachariah et al., 2006). Like many poor households in South Africa with limited access to other sources of income or sustainable livelihood activities, those in our study depended on the disability grant, and other grants, to meet basic needs, particularly for food and health care.

Quantitative research in the Eastern Cape (Phaswana-Mafuya et al., 2009) produced similar findings, particularly about the food needs of the sick. Households with members receiving the disability grant reported significantly fewer shortages of food in the preceding 12 months than HIV-affected households without the grant. Additional household income in the form of a disability grant has major implications for both the sick person and their household. Evidence from Malawi suggests that inadequate nutrition is linked to greater mortality within the first three months of ART (Zachariah et al., 2006). Botswanan and South African research shows that where household income is lost as a result of illness, replacement income, such as social grants, is key for meeting basic needs, food and economic security, thereby supporting individuals' well-being (Booysen, 2004; Rajaraman et al., 2006). Other research agrees that household poverty and hunger may hinder long-term adherence to treatment, suggesting that the ability to provide for the basic needs of sick adults may support adherence to ART (Hardon et al., 2007; Coetzee et al., 2011).

Besides helping to meet basic needs and thus improving nutrition and health, the different outcomes in our case studies suggest that the relative timing of receipt of the disability grant and beginning ART is important. In contrast to those on ART who received the grant in good time, those who received it late recovered health more slowly. Our case studies therefore suggest that a synergistic relationship may exist between timeous receipt of this grant and improved health outcomes on ART. Several studies have shown that the first six months to a year of treatment is crucial and determines whether the treatment will be successful; those who survive this period have a reduced risk of both morbidity and mortality (Bussmann et al., 2008; Lawn et al., 2008). Our case studies show that timely receipt of the disability grant enabled household members to respond to the nutritional and health care needs of the sick member during this decisive period.

In the case study households where sick members received a disability grant and ART in good time, the respondents spoke about the substantial contribution to household livelihood that the sick member was able to make on returning to health: bringing money into the household through formal or informal employment, investing time and labour in diversifying the household's activities, and taking on additional responsibilities in the home so as to free other members for additional domestic and income generating activities. The timeous receipt of the grant thus had benefits not just for the sick member but also for the household as a whole.

The HIV/AIDS and STI National Strategic Plan 2007–2011 proposes the creation of a new grant targeted at those with chronic illness (DoH, 2007). This has yet to be implemented, despite hearings for an amendment to the Social Assistance Bill in 2010, and is not addressed in the 2012–2016 plan (PMG, 2010; DoH, 2011). Although the plan does not supply much detail about the proposed grant, civil society organisations have actively supported the proposal and suggest further that a chronic disease grant should be designed and targeted towards all those who are chronically ill, not just persons living with HIV (Silber, 2009; Black Sash, 2010). We support further exploration and consideration of such a grant. By improving access to basic needs, it would promote adequate access to health care and better health outcomes for individuals and households, and possibly longer-term adherence to ART (SANAC, 2008). The need to remove remaining barriers to accessing the disability grant and the confusion about qualifying criteria, as well as the need for timely access in combination with ART, support the case for a better targeted and managed cash transfer for severely ill individuals. A chronic illness grant that was separate from the disability grant would be easier to administer and would obviate some of the problems with review and adherence raised in the literature and assumed by general opinion (PMG, 2010), and it would fill the current gap in social welfare provision for those with HIV and other chronic illness such as tuberculosis.

The establishment of a new grant would make it possible to develop eligibility criteria that would enable the applicant to receive it at diagnosis or the start of treatment, thereby acting as an incentive for early VCT (voluntary counselling and testing) and timely treatment. The amount currently provided by the disability grant could also be reduced to ensure its longer-term fiscal viability. Booth & Silber (2008) argue that these changes could remove any current threat of loss currently associated with the disability grant and the possible temptation to stop treatment in favour of the grant; themes that dominate the literature and rhetoric around this grant. A chronic illness grant could also reduce stigma and public misunderstanding about the way in which people with chronic illness qualify for the current disability grant and highlight the differences between chronic long-term illness and disability (Silber, 2009). In addition, it would be possible to make ART adherence a condition of grant receipt, therefore maximising health outcomes. This condition would also support contact with testing, treatment and health care services.

A limitation of this study is that the selection of households was limited to those who were available, had some experience of illness and consented to be interviewed. The convenience sample that resulted is of course not representative of all households. Despite the potential bias towards disclosed households[8] and those willing to participate, the sample reflects a range of household types and contexts. While the method of selecting the sample potentially undermines the external validity of the study, it is likely that the findings would be similar in similar contexts.

Another limitation of the research is the small sample size. Case studies of a few households have limited generalisability, but can provide valuable in-depth insight into the experiences of households and are recognised as an important method of analysing data in qualitative research (Mikkelson, 1995). Case studies allow for the collection of retrospective and prospective data over a long time and we would argue that this detailed contextual and historical household information helps us to understand how processes work and therefore develop explanations that help us to suggest possible causality (Mason, 2002).

6. Conclusions

The findings of our four case studies show that the disability grant helps households to provide for their sick members who are on ART, and can enable those members to attend clinics. It can successfully cushion households against the loss of the sick person's employment and help them to respond to the sick person's needs until that person returns to health and can contribute once more. Those with successful ART outcomes are able to make substantial contributions to the well-being of the household. The most important finding is that *combined access* to the disability grant and ART, especially where the grant is received *in good time*, has particular benefits for the health of those receiving treatment. The importance of prompt receipt of the disability grant by those on ART suggests that measures to ensure its prompt delivery could improve the cost-effectiveness and long-term efficiency of South Africa's ART programme.

These findings demonstrate the role that social welfare payments can play in supporting the provision of other services, in this case the provision of health care by the Department of Health. We recommend that government further consider and explore the feasibility of a chronic illness grant, thereby providing a cash transfer tailored to the needs of this client group instead of conflating their needs with those of the disabled. Although this proposal needs further investigation, it has the potential to better target poor individuals and households affected by HIV, to act as an instrument to reduce the problems of late diagnosis and initiation of treatment and to allow for more efficient and effective administration of access to the grant.

Acknowledgements

This research was conducted while L Knight was a PhD student at the London School of Hygiene and Tropical Medicine. The research was funded by a UK Economic and Social

---

[8]These are households where the members have disclosed their status to one another and in some cases to people outside the household.

Research Council (ESRC) postgraduate studentship linked to an ESRC/Department of International Development funded research project (grant number RES-167-25-0076). The authors are grateful to the Africa Centre for Health and Population studies for logistical and administrative support. Comments on a draft of the paper were provided by the facilitators of a SANPAD-funded Writing for Scientific Publication workshop. An early version of this paper was presented at the 4th SA AIDS Conference in 2009.

References

Adato, M, Lund, F & Mhlongo, P, 2007. Methodological innovations in research on the dynamics of poverty: A longitudinal study in KwaZulu-Natal, South Africa. World Development 35, 247–63.

Black Sash, 2010. Black Sash Submission to the Portfolio Committee of the Department of Social Development. Black Sash, Cape Town.

Booth, P & Silber, G, 2008. A Draft Briefing Document for the Establishment of a Chronic Diseases Grant. South Africa National AIDS Consortium – Treatment. Care and Support Technical Task Team, Johannesburg.

Booysen, F, 2004. Social grants as safety net for HIV/AIDS-affected households in South Africa. SAHARA-J: Journal of Social Aspects of HIV/AIDS 1, 45–56.

Booysen, F & Van der Berg, S, 2005. The role of social grants in mitigating the socio-economic impact of HIV/AIDS in two Free State communities. South African Journal of Economics 73, 545–63.

Bussmann, H, Wester, CW, Ndwapi, N, Grundmann, N & Gaolathe, T, et al., 2008. Five-year outcomes of initial patients treated in Botswana's National Antiretroviral Treatment Program. AIDS 22, 2303–11.

Case, A & Deaton, A, 1998. Large cash transfers to the elderly in South Africa. The Economic Journal 108, 1330–61.

Coetzee, B, Kagee, A & Vermeulen, N, 2011. Structural barriers to adherence to antiretroviral therapy in a resource-constrained setting: The perspectives of health care providers. AIDS Care 23, 146–51.

DoH (Department of Health), 2007. HIV and AIDS and STI Strategic Plan for South Africa, 2007–2011. DoH, Pretoria.

DoH (Department of Health), 2009. National HIV and syphilis antenatal prevalence survey in South Africa 2008. DoH, Pretoria.

DoH (Department of Health), 2011. National Strategic Plan for HIV and AIDS, STIs and TB, 2012–2016. DoH, Pretoria.

DSD (Department of Social Development), 2008. Minister Skweyiya responds to National Association of People with AIDS (NAPWA) claims of social grants cancellations. Department of Social Development Statement. www.dsd.gov.za/index.php?option=com_content&task=archivecategory&id=46&Itemid=107 Accessed 10 May 2010.

Duflo, E, 2003. Grandmothers and granddaughters: Old-age pensions and intrahousehold allocation in South Africa. World Bank Economic Review 17, 1–25.

Hardon, AP, Akurut, D, Comoro, C, Ekezie, C & Irunde, HF, et al., 2007. Hunger, waiting time and transport costs: Time to confront challenges to ART adherence in Africa. AIDS Care 19, 658–65.

Hardy, C & Richter, M, 2006. Disability grants or antiretrovirals? A quandary for people with HIV/AIDS in South Africa. African Journal of AIDS Research 5, 85–96.

Herbst, AJ, Mafojane, T & Newell, ML, 2011. Verbal autopsy-based cause-specific mortality trends in rural KwaZulu-Natal, South Africa, 2000–2009. Population Health Metrics 9, 47.

Herbst, K, Cooke, G, Barnighausen, T, KanyKany, A, Tanser, F & Newell, ML, 2009. Adult mortality and antiretroviral treatment roll-out in KwaZulu-Natal, South Africa. Bulletin of the World Health Organization 87, 754–62.

Heywood, M, 2008. Civil Society Report Back to SANAC Plenary Session. SANAC (South African National AIDS Council), Pretoria.

Hontelez, JAC, De Vlas, SJ & Tanser, F, et al., 2011. The impact of the new WHO antiretroviral treatment guidelines on HIV epidemic dynamics and cost in South Africa. PLOS ONE 6, e21919.

Hosegood, V, Preston-Whyte, E, Busza, J, Moitse, S & Timæus, IM, 2007. Revealing the full extent of households' experiences of HIV and AIDS in rural South Africa. Social Science & Medicine 65, 1249–59.

Lawn, SD, Harries, AD, Anglaret, X, Myer, L & Wood, R, 2008. Early mortality among adults accessing antiretroviral treatment programmes in sub-Saharan Africa. AIDS 22, 1897–908.

Leclerc-Madlala, S, 2006. 'We will eat when I get the grant': Negotiating AIDS, poverty and antiretroviral treatment in South Africa. African Journal of AIDS Research 5, 249–56.

Lund, F, 2008. Changing Social Policy: The Child Support Grant in South Africa. HSRC (Human Sciences Research Council) Press, Cape Town.

Mason, J, 2002. Qualitative Researching. SAGE, London.

Mikkelson, B, 1995. Methods for Development Work and Research: A Guide for Practitioners. SAGE, London.

Montgomery, CM, Hosegood, V, Busza, J & Timæus, IM, 2006. Men's involvement in the South African family: Engendering change in the AIDS era. Social Science & Medicine 62, 2411–19.

Muhwava, W, 2008. Trends in Economic Status of Households in the ACDIS. Monograph Series No. 3. Africa Centre for Health and Population Studies, Mtubatuba, South Africa.

Nattrass, N, 2005. Trading off income and health? AIDS and the Disability Grant in South Africa. Journal of Social Policy 35, 3–19.

Phaswana-Mafuya, N, Peltzer, K & Petros, G, 2009. Disability grant for people living with HIV/AIDS in the Eastern Cape of South Africa. Social Work in Health Care 48, 533–50.

PMG (Parliamentary Monitoring Group), 2010. Social Assistance Amendment Bill: Public hearings. Black Sash, NAPWA and AIDS Law Project, Parliamentary Monitoring Group, Cape Town. www.pmg.org.za/report/20100420-public-hearings-social-assistance-amendment-bill-b5-2010 Accessed 5 December 2011.

Rajaraman, D, Russell, S & Heymann, J, 2006. HIV/AIDS, income loss and economic survival in Botswana. AIDS Care 18, 656–62.

Ritchie, J & Spencer, L, 1994. Qualitative data analysis for applied policy research. In Bryman, A & Burgess, R (Eds), Analyzing Qualitative Data. Routledge, London.

Russell, S, 2005. Illuminating cases: Understanding the economic burden of illness through case study household research. Health Policy and Planning 20, 277–89.

SANAC, 2008. A Draft Briefing Document for the Establishment of a Chronic Disease Grant. SANAC (South African National AIDS Council), Pretoria.

SASSA (South African Social Security Agency), 2010. You and Your Grants 2010/11. SASSA, Pretoria.

Seekings, J, 2002. The broader importance of welfare reform in South Africa. Social Dynamics 28, 1–38.

Silber, G, 2009. A Chronic Disease Grant for South Africans. Equal Treatment: Magazine for the Treatment Action Campaign. Treatment Action Campaign, Cape Town.

Simchowitz, B, 2004. Social security and HIV/AIDS: Assessing 'disability' in the context of ARV treatment. CSSR Working Paper No. 99. Centre for Social Science Research, Cape Town.

Tanser, F, Hosegood, V & Bärnighausen, T, et al., 2008. Cohort profile: Africa Centre Demographic Information System (ACDIS) and population-based HIV survey. International Journal of Epidemiology 37, 956–62.

Venkataramani, A, Maughan-Brown, B, Nattrass, N & Ruger, J, 2010. Social grants, welfare, and the incentive to trade-off health for income among individuals on HAART in South Africa. AIDS and Behavior 14, 1393–400.

Zachariah, R, Fitzgerald, M, Massaquoi, M, Pasulani, O, Arnould, L, Makombe, S & Harries, AD, 2006. Risk factors for high early mortality in patients on antiretroviral treatment in a rural district of Malawi. AIDS 20, 2355–60.

Index

Note:
Page numbers in **bold** type refer to figures
Page numbers in *italic* type refer to tables
Page numbers followed by 'n' refer to notes

ACCION International 9
activism: civil society 22; policy 56
Adato, M.: *et al* 72, 80
administrative structure 26
adult labour 115–16, 117, 118
Africa 6; agriculture 33; Charter on the Rights and the Welfare of the Child 103; social protection 13–23
Africa Centre: Demographic Surveillance Survey (DSS) population 137
African National Congress (ANC) 55, 56, 124; Freedom Charter (1955) 124
African Peer Review Mechanism (APRM) 102
Africans' Claims (1943) 124
agrarian economy 16, 20
agriculture 33
aid: conditionality 118; food 13, 16, 17, 18, 20, 30; revenue 47–8
AIDS *see* HIV/AIDS
Angola 50; education services 46; health services 46; taxes 46
antiretroviral therapy (ART) 135–47
apartheid 47, 49, 55, 56, 122
Armstrong, B. 3
Asia 5, 15
asset building 1
assistance *see* social assistance
audits: social 13, 22
autopsies: verbal 138, 138n

Bailey, S.: *et al* 112
balancing principle 14
banks: bail-out 37
Barrientos, A.: *et al* 54–68
basic income 57
Bastagli, F. 31, 32
behavioural effects 26–7
beneficiaries 21, 22
benefits: child 4; disability 10; form 26; payment 26; universal categorical 26, 34, 35
Beveridge Report (1942) 15

Bhengu household 139, 142–3
Booth, P.: and Silber, G. 144
Botswana 2, 18, 40, 44, 50; Banking Act (1995) 91; burial societies 91; Christian AIDS Intervention Programme 90; community home-based care model 89–90; community support networks 89–90; family and kin support systems 88–9; Family Strengthening Programme 90; formal social protection 91–3; Ipelegeng Programme 93; mutual aid associations 90; National Development Plan 85; non-formal social protection 84–97; Orphan Care Programme 92; poverty 87; Programme for Destitute Persons 92; Regional Hunger and Vulnerability Programme (RHVP) 88; Remote Area Development Programme 93; savings and credit associations 91; social development 84–97; social protection programmes 48–9; social services 46; Social Welfare Unit 85–6; taxes 46, 49; unemployment 87; Universal Old Age Pension Scheme 92–3; Vulnerable Group and School Feeding Programmes 92
Brazil 1, 2, 6, 8; *Bolsa Escola* 59, 60; *Bolsa Familia* 32, 59, 60, 61, 62, 63, 66; Constitution 56, 57; GDP growth 56; inequality 62–4, **62**; minimum wage 63–4; non-contributory pensions 56, 57, 59, 60, 61; old age poverty 64–5, **64**; population 55; poverty 62–5, **62**, **64**; Programme for the Eradication of Child Labour 59; social assistance programmes *58*, 59–60; social insurance 55, 57, 60, 66; social protection expansion 54–68; social protection systems 57–9; unemployment 63; United Social Assistance System 61
Bryden, J. 30
burial societies 91

capital: human 10, 24, 27, 28–9, 31–2, 66, 114; types 28

INDEX

care: community home-based model 89–90; economy 73; and gender 77–8, 80
case studies 145
cash transfers 1, 8, 13, 16, 20, 33, 72, 75, 108, 113, 136, 145; conditional 9, 10, 31–2; Lesotho 102; Mexico 80
cash vs food debate 17
child benefit 4
child labour 59, 111; Ethiopia 114–18
child maintenance grants 45
child poverty 71, 75, 111; and policy 126; and race 122; reduction 130; South Africa 121–34
child sensitive social protection 111–20
child-sensitive social programming (CSSP) 111–12
child(ren): bearing 27; HIV/AIDS 99–100, 112; living arrangements 78–9, **79**; mortality 99–100; orphaned and vulnerable children (OVCs) 101, 102–3, 108; rights 124–5; social protection programmes 111–20; South Africa 69–83; well-being 72, 73, 78–9, 80
China 8, 28
chronic disease grants 144–5
citizenship 121, 124, 125; liberal 121, 123–5, 132; rights and obligations 123–4
civil rights 124n
civil servants 5, 15
civil society activism 22
claimants 21, 22
clients 21
Coates, J.: et al 78
Cockburn, J. 116; and Dostie, B. 116
cohesion: family 78; social 27, 30
community 5, 7; development projects 6; home-based care model 89–90; support networks 89–90
community-based organisations (CBOs) 87, 90
conditional cash transfers 9, 10, 31–2
conditionality 26
Congo, Democratic Republic 15, 112
contracts: social 13–14, 21–2, 39, 40, 43–4, 47, 50, 66
contributory social insurance schemes 54
Crawford, P.J. 112
credit associations: and savings 91

Dafuleya, G.: Zibagwe, S. and Nduna, T. 111–20
De Dominicis, L.: et al 33–4
death 139; benefits 10
decent work principles 16
decision making: household financial 76, **76**, 79–80
Dekker, A.H.: and Olivier, M. 85

democracy 99; political 30
Democratic Republic of Congo 15, 112
democratisation 56, 65, 66
Department for International Development (DFID) 33
dependency syndrome 14, 17
development: aid 41, 43; economic 6, 10, 24–5, 60, 65, 87; institutional 57–62; policy 6; studies 3, 5, see also social development
developmental social welfare 56
Devereux, S. 13–23, 48, 49, 50; et al 114; and Sabates-Wheeler, R. 7, 8
direct support programmes: Ethiopia 112–13, 114
disability 135–47; benefits 10; pensions 45
Dlamini household 139–40
domestic taxes 45, 46
Donne, J. 28
donors 39, 41, 43, 44, 88, 101; international 8
Dostie, B.: and Cockburn, J. 116
Drahokoupil, J. 14
Drèze, J.: and Sen, A. 29
drought 17, 99
Dube household 139, 141–2
Duflo, E. 31
duty-bearer 21, 22

economic development 10, 60, 65, 87; social dimensions 6; and social security 24–5
economic growth 1, 8, 10, 18, 20, 24–38, 54; and inequality 33–4; measurement 27; and social protection 27–8; theories 28
economic planning 6
economic power 30
economy: agrarian 16, 20; care 73; local 30, 32–3; macro- 24
education 57, 75, 76, 98, 127; services 46, see also schooling
Egypt 15
employer liability 104, 105
employment 27; policies 54; women 72–3
empowerment: women 69, 70, 72, 77, 80
English Poor Law 3
entitlement failure 16
equality: gender 1
equivalised income 127, 127n, **128**, **130**
Esping-Andersen, G. 15
Ethiopia: child labour 114–18; direct support programmes 112–13, 114; Employment Generation Scheme 19; food aid 18; Gratuitous Relief 19; National Nutrition Programme (NNP) 118; NGO Law 22; Productive Safety Net Programme (PSNP) 17, 19–21, 33, 111–20; public works programme 113, 114, 115, 116, *117*; schooling 113–14, 115, **115**, 116, 117, 118; Young Lives study 114–15

150

INDEX

Eurocentric welfare state 1, 2, 5
Europe: social security 13, 15
European Report on Development (2011) 25
exceptionalism: South African 18
exclusion: social 9
expenditure: and financing 39–51; and revenue sources 44, *45*

faith-based organisations (FBOs) 9, 87
family: cohesion 78; and kin support systems 88–9
famine 27
farming 15, 16; subsistence 100
feminisation: social assistance 69
finance: microfinance 8, 9
financial decision-making: household 76, **76**, 79–80
financing: and expenditure 39–51; politics 40–1; social 49
food: intake 31; transfers 114; vs cash debate 17
food aid 13, 16, 17, 18, 20, 30
food insecurity 13, 16, 20, 78, 99, 103, 113
food security 20, 44, 78, 98, 113
formal social protection 14, 85, 86, 87, 91–4; initiatives 85, 86, 87
Foundation for International Community Assistance (FINCA) 9
funding 11
funds: social 8

Gambia 31
gatherings: international 11
gender 71–3; and care 77–8, 80; and child sensitive social protection 69–83; equality 1; inequality 80; and poverty 70–1; projects 6
governments 7, 88; trust 27, 34
Grameen Bank 9
grants 63; access 1; chronic disease 144–5; old age (OAG) 57, 59–60, 61, 123, 127, 128; social 18, 19, 22, 31, 121, 122, 125, 127, 130, 138; social assistance 10
Gray, M. 87
Great Recession 8
grievance procedures 22
growth *see* economic growth

Handa, S.: *et al* 111
Harmonised Approach to Cash Transfers 102
health 57, 76, 78, 127; care 111, 143, 144; services 46
HIV 99; mortality rates 138, 143; South Africa 135–47; Treatment and Care Programme 138; treatment outcomes 135–47

HIV/AIDS 77, 78, 84, 86–90, 94; children 99–100, 112; Lesotho 99–100; South Africa 122, 123; voluntary counselling and testing (VCT) 144
Hochfeld, T.: Moodley, J. and Patel, L. 69–83
home-based care model: community 89–90
Hosegood, V.: Timæus, I.M. and Knight, L. 135–47
Household Food Insecurity Access Scale 78
households 5, 7, 66; asset building programme 20; composition 126–31, *127*, 139; financial decision-making 76, **76**, 79–80; formation 26; risk management 8; and women 76–7
Hujo, K.: and McClanahan, S. 40
human capital 27, 31–2, 66, 114; formation 10, 24, 28–9
Human Development Index (HDI) 84, 99, 100
Human Poverty Index (HPI) 100
humanitarian relief 13, 16

illness 139
income: basic 57; equivalised 127, 127n, **128**, **130**; market 127; non-contributory pension 65; pooling 126–31; security 29; sources 75; statutory maintenance programmes 3; transfers 6
India 6; National Rural Employment Guarantee Scheme 2; social audits 22
indigenous practices 88
industrialisation 14, 88
inequality 30, 33–4, 36, 55; Brazil 62–4, **62**; gender 80; reduction 66; South Africa 62–4, **62**, 70
informal social protection 14
innovation 29–30, 54, 55, 62, 65
insecurity: food 13, 16, 20, 78, 99, 103, 113
institutional development 57–62
institutional reform 59–60
insurance *see* social insurance
insurance: microinsurance 8, 9–10
International Food Policy Research Institute (IFPRI) 19
international gatherings 11
International Labour Organisation (ILO) 3, 85, 100–1, 104; conventions 7; Maternity Protection Convention (2000) 105; Social Security Convention (1952) 106; Social Security Minimum Standards Convention (1952) 4
International Monetary Fund (IMF) 6
international organisations 101
International Social Security Association (ISSA) 3
investment 29–30, 32; and risk 29, *29*; social 10

151

INDEX

iron rice bowl system 28
Islamic countries 9

Johannesburg University 74, 80

Kenya: Hunger Safety Net Programme 17, 22
kin support systems: and family 88–9
Knight, L.: Hosegood, V. and Timæus, I.M. 135–47
knowledge: local 30
KwaZulu-Natal 135–47

labour: adult 115–16, 117, 118; child 59, 111, 114–18; force 15, 100; migrant 78, 80
labour market 27; Africa 16; flexibilisation 16; intervention 21; linkages 19–21; policies 54
Latin America 2, 5, 15, 31; social protection programmes 117
learning policy 7–10
Leibbrandt, M.: et al 63, 122
Lesotho 1, 2, 17, 18, 40, 44, 49, 50, 88, 98–110; Cash and Food Transfer Pilot Project 22; cash transfers 102; child grants programme (CGP) 102, 103; child mortality 99–100; Children's Protection and Welfare Act (2011) 101, 103; Consolidated Fund 104; contribution based social security scheme 98; democracy 99; domestic taxes 45; Education Act (2010) 101; employer liability 104, 105; food insecurity 99; Free Primary Education programme 103; GDP 100; HIV/AIDS 99–100; human development indicators 99; Labour Code 106; labour force 100; maternity 104–5; national strategic development plans 101; National Vision 2020 strategy 101; OAP Act (2005) 101; Old Age Pension 48, 98, 101–2, 108; Pensions Proclamation (1964) 101, 104, 106; population 99; poverty 99, 100; Public Officers' Defined Contribution Pension Fund Act (2008) 101, 107; Public Service Regulations (2008) 105; retirement 104, 106–7; sickness 104, 106; social assistance initiatives 101–4; social insurance framework 104–8; social pensions 48; social protection floor initiatives 101–4; unemployment 100; Workmen's Compensation Act (1977) 101, 101n
liberal citizenship 121, 123–5, 132
Lieberman, E.S. 42
livelihood: inputs 1; rural 16
living arrangements: children 78–9, **79**
Livingstone Declaration (2006) 21
London School of Economics (LSE) 4
Lund Committee 122, 123

Lund, F. 56, 123

McClanahan, S.: and Hujo, K. 40
macro effects 30, 33–4
macroeconomy 24
Malawi 17, 44, 50, 88; Dowa Emergency Cash Transfer 33; Farm Input Subsidy programme 44
malnutrition 59
market: income 127; labour 16, 19–21, 27, 54; pathology 14; self-regulating 14
Marshall, T.H. 121, 123–4
maternity 104–5; leave 15
Mauritius 46, 49, 50, 84; domestic taxes 46; social welfare 46–7
Mberengwa, I.: and Nigussa, F. 114, 117
Mexico 2, 6, 8; cash transfer programme 80; *Oportunidades* programme 9, 33; PROGRESA 31, 32, 33
microfinance 8, 9
microinsurance 8, 9–10
microsimulation 126, 130, 132
Midgley, J. 2–12, 86; and Tang, K. 24–5, 86–7; Ulriksen, M. and Patel, L. 1
migrant labour 78, 80
Millennium Development Goals (2000) 6, 98, 100, 103, 109, 112
minimum wage 3, 19; Brazil 63–4
Mkandawire, T. 33, 36, 44
Moodley, J.: Patel, L. and Hochfeld, T. 69–83
mortality 27; child 99–100; HIV rates 138, 143
Moss, T. 41
Mozambique 88
Multi-Fibre Agreement 100
Mupedziswa, R.: and Ntseane, D. 84–97
mutual aid associations 90

Namibia 2, 18, 44, 50; Basic Income Grant (BIG) 26, 32, 45; child maintenance grants 45; disability pensions 45; domestic taxes 45; old age pensions 45; taxes 46
nation state 5, 14
Nattrass, N.: and Seekings, J. 18
natural resources 48–50; revenue 41, 43
Nduna, T.: Dafuleya, G. and Zibagwe, S. 111–20
neighbourhoods 7
networks: community support 89–90
New York: Opportunity NYC-Family Rewards 9
Nicaragua: school enrolment 31–2
Nigussa, F.: and Mberengwa, I. 114, 117
Nkosi household 139, 140–1
non-contributory pension income 65
non-contributory social assistance programmes 54

INDEX

non-formal social protection 84–97; Botswana 84–97
non-governmental organisations (NGOs) 21, 22, 87, 88, 103
non-profit organisations 5, 7
Ntseane, D.: and Mupedziswa, R. 84–97
nutrition 27, 71, 127, 143, 144

old age: pensions 2, 45, 48, 98, 101–2, 108; poverty 64–5, **64**; social assistance transfers 66
Olivier, M. 98–110; and Dekker, A.H. 85; *et al* 85, 93, 94
Organisation for Economic Co-operation and Development (OECD) 25, 32
organisations: community-based (CBOs) 87, 90; faith-based (FBOs) 9, 87; international 101; non-governmental (NGOs) 21, 22, 87, 88, 103; non-profit 5, 7
orphaned and vulnerable children (OVCs) 101, 102–3, 108

Palesa Peko v The National University of Lesotho (1995) 106
Paraguay 33
Partnership for African Social & Governance Research (PASGR) 85
Patel, L. 87; *et al* 88; Hochfeld, T. and Moodley, J. 69–83; Midgley, J. and Ulriksen, M. 1
path dependence 54, 55, 62, 65
payments: Southern African Customs Union 108
Peer Review Mechanism: African 102
pensions 4, 13, 15, 31, 45, 101, 104, 106, 107; disability 45; non-contributory 56, 57, 59, 60, 61, 65; old age 2, 45, 48, 98, 101–2, 108; social 13, 48, 50
Piachaud, D. 24–38
planning: economic 6
Polanyi, K. 14
policy 34; activism 56; exchanges 7–10, 10–11; learning 7–10; making 40–1; migration 100; social 2, 3–5, 11, 36; social assistance 34, 35
political democracy 30
political rights 124n
politics 54, 55, 56–7, 65; financing 40–1; spending 40–1
population 55, 99, 137
Posel, D.: and Rogan, M. 70
poverty 18, 20, 30, 34, 36, 37, 45, 55, 59, 61, 89; Botswana 87; Brazil 62–4, **62**; child 71, 75, 111, 121–34; and gender 70–1; Lesotho 99, 100; old age 64–5, **64**; reduction 8, 35, 54, 65, 66, 80, 85, 112; South Africa 62–4, **62**; women 77

power: economic 30; purchasing power parity (PPP) 55n
pregnancies: teenage 18, 131
privatisation: social security 5
property rights 42
public works programmes 1, 13, 19, 20, 21; Ethiopia 113, 114, 115, 116, *117*
purchasing power parity (PPP) 55n

race: and child poverty 122
Ranis, G.: *et al* 31, 33
Rawlings, L.B. 10
reciprocity 43, 85
redistribution 1, 24–38, 63
reform: institutional 59–60
regionalisation 88
remittances 127
rents 44, 50
resources: natural 41, 43, 48–50
retirement 104, 106–7
revenue: aid 47–8; domestic 48–50; natural resources 41, 43; sources 41–2, *43*; sources and expenditure 44, *45*; Southern African Customs Union 100; tax based 50
rights: children 124–5; citizenship 123–4; civil 124n; committees 22; holder 21; political 124n; property 42; social 1, 121, 124, 124n; workers 19
risk: and investment 29, *29*
risk management: household 8
Roelen, K.: *et al* 112
Rogan, M.: and Posel, D. 70
Ross, M. 42
rural livelihoods 16
Rwanda 21; Ubudehe Credit Scheme 20; Vision 2020 Umurenge Programme (VUP) 19, 20

Sabates-Wheeler, R.: and Devereux, S. 7, 8
Save the Children (UK) Ethiopia 113
savings: and credit associations 91
school enrolment: Nicaragua 31–2
schooling 31, 111; attendance 71, 78; Ethiopia 113–14, 115, **115**, 116, 117, 118
Schweinitz, K. de 3
security: food 20, 44, 78, 98, 113; income 29, *see also* social security
Seekings, J.: and Nattrass, N. 18
selective social assistance 25
self-help 85
self-regulating markets 14
Sen, A. 16; and Drèze, J. 29
Seychelles 84
Shutte, A. 125
sick leave 15
sickness 104, 106
Silber, G.: and Booth, P. 144

INDEX

Soares, S.: et al 63
social assistance 4, 6, 21, 26, 36, 98; Brazil 58, 59–60; expansion 54–68; feminisation 69; initiatives 101–4; Lesotho 101–4; non-contributory programmes 54; policies 34, 35; selective 25; South Africa 2, 55, 58, 59–60, 61, 66, 122–3; trajectories 60–2; transfers (old age) 66
social audits 13, 22
social cohesion 27, 30
social contracts 13–14, 21–2, 39, 40, 43–4, 47, 50, 66
social development 1, 10, 36, 45, 65; Botswana 84–97; features 6; literature 11; perspective 5–7; and social protection 2–12, 86–8
social exclusion 9
social financing 40
social funds 8
social grants 22, 127, 130; and human capital 31; South Africa 18, 19, 125, 138
social insurance 4, 6, 25, 26, 35, 37, 99, 101; Brazil 55, 57, 60, 66; contributory schemes 54; Europe 3; Lesotho 104–8; policies 34; South Africa 60
social investment programmes 10
social pensions 13, 48, 50
social policy 2, 3, 5, 11, 36; academic study 4; perspective 3–5
social protection: academic study 3–7; affordability 8; cultural basis 93; definition 24, 71; demand 14; economic impact 10; effects 24–38; expansion 54–68; floor 98, 98n, 101–4, 108; supply 14; types 25–6, 34–5
social reproduction 14
social rights 1, 121, 124, 124n
social safety net 8
social security 2, 3, 4, 6, 7, 9, 11, 15, 54n, 106; affordability 8, 10; and economic development 24–5; Europe 13, 15; Islamic countries 9; literature 2–3; privatisation 5
social services 1, 46
social spending 40
social transfers 18, 127, 128–9, **129**
social welfare 42, 46–7, 54n, 145; developmental 56
solidarity 85
Somalia 15
South Africa 1, 6, 8, 40; Bill of Rights 121, 122, 124, 125, 126, 132; child poverty 121–34; Child Support Grant (CSG) 17, 26, 31, 47, 56, 59, 69–83, 121, 127, 131, 136, 139; children 69–83; civil society activism 22; Constitution 56, 125; Disability Grant (DG) 47, 123, 135–47; domestic taxes 46; Doornkop 73; economic policy 63; economy 18; exceptionalism 18; Extended Public Works Programme 18; GDP growth 56; grants 63; Growth, Employment and Redistribution (GEAR) strategy 122–3; HIV/AIDS 122, 123, 135–47; HIV/AIDS and STI National Strategic Plan 144; inequality 62–4, **62**, 70; Johannesburg University 74, 80; Lund Committee 122; migrant labour 78, 80; migration policy 100; National Development Plan 22; National Planning Commission 49; Old Age Grant (OAG) 57, 59–60, 61, 123, 127, 128; Old Age Pension 47, 49, 69, 71; old age poverty 64–5, **64**; population 55; poverty 62–4, **62**; social assistance 2, 55, 66, 122–3; Social Assistance Act (1992) 135; Social Assistance Bill 144; social assistance grants 10; social assistance programmes 58, 59–60, 61; social development 87; social grants 18, 19, 121, 122, 125, 138; social insurance 60; social protection 49, 57–9; social protection expansion 54–68; social protection programmes 49, 57–9; social security 54n; Social Security Commission (1943) 14; social welfare 54n; State Maintenance Grant (SMG) 122, 123; taxes 49; teenage pregnancies 18, 131; unemployment 63, 70, 123; Unemployment Insurance Fund 18; women 69–83; Women's Charter (1954) 124; workers' rights 19
South Africa Netherlands Research Programme on Alternatives to Development (SANPAD) 80
South African Microsimulation Model (SAMOD) 126, 126n
Southern Africa: social protection 44–7
Southern African Customs Union (SACU) 39, 43, 44, 45, 46, 47–8, 102; payments 108; revenues 100
Southern African Development Community (SADC) 84; Code on Social Security 105
spending: politics 40–1; priorities 41–2, 43; social 40
state-buidling 42
states 7
statutory income maintenance programmes 3
stokvel 142, 142n
subsistence farming 100
support networks: community 89–90
support programmes: direct 112–13, 114
Swaziland 17, 18, 44, 45, 48, 50, 88

Tafere, Y.: and Woldehanna, T. 118
Tang, K.: and Midgley, J. 24–5, 86–7

INDEX

taxes/taxation 41–2, 44, 45, 46, 49; base 39, 42, 50; -based revenue 50; cuts 40; direct 42; domestic 45, 46; and state-building 42

teenage pregnancies 18, 131

Timæus, I.M.: Knight, L. and Hosegood, V. 135–47

Titmuss, R. 4

transfers 57, 60; conditional cash 9, 10, 31–2; food 114; and service provision 61

Tunisia 15

ubuntu 121–2, 125–6, 130, 131, 132

Ulriksen, M. 39–51; Patel, M. and Midgley, J. 1

unemployment 18, 89, 100; Botswana 87; insurance 13, 15, 19; South Africa 63, 70, 123

United Kingdom (UK): Department for International Development (DFID) 33

United Nations (UN) 6; Children's Fund (UNICEF) 72, 100, 102, 112; Convention on the Rights of the Child (UNCRC) 103, 117; Development Assistance Framework (UNDAF) 100; Development Programme (UNDP) 99; International Covenant on Economic, Social and Cultural Rights (ICESCR, 1966) 4, 21, 104; Research Institute for Social Development (UNRISD) 24; Universal Declaration on Human Rights (UNDHR, 1948) 21, 48; World Food Programme (WFP) 100; World Summit for Social Development (1995) 6

United States of America (USA): Social Security Act (1935) 3

universal categorical benefits 26, 34, 35

universalisation 61

urbanisation 14, 85, 88

verbal autopsies 138, 138n

Vij, N. 22

wage: minimum 3, 19, 63–4

Washington Consensus 6

Webb, B.: and Webb, S. 3

welfare: developmental social 56; social 42, 46–7, 56, 145

welfare state 3, 5; Eurocentric 1, 2, 5; Western 11

well-being: child 72, 73, 78–9, 80

Woldehanna, T. 114–15; and Tafere, Y. 118

women 124; care burden 80; employment 72–3; empowerment 69, 70, 72, 77, 80; groups 9; and households 76–7; poverty 77; South Africa 69–83, 124

work: decent work principles 16

workers: rights 19

World Bank 6, 85, 113

World Health Organisation (WHO) 137

Zambia 40, 44, 47, 49–50; donor funded programmes 47–8; Kalomo Social Cash Transfer Scheme 33; Public Welfare Assistance Scheme 44

Zibagwe, S.: Nduna, T. and Dafuleya, G. 111–20

Zimbabwe 88

www.routledge.com/9780415508322

Related titles from Routledge

Democratization in Africa
Challenges and Prospects
Edited by Gordon Crawford and Gabrielle Lynch

Two decades have passed since the 'third wave' of democratization began to roll across sub-Saharan Africa in the early 1990s. This book provides a very timely investigation into the progress and setbacks over that period, the challenges that remain and the prospects for future democratization in Africa. It commences with an overall assessment of the (lack of) progress made from 1990 to 2010, exploring positive developments with reasons for caution. Based on original research, subsequent contributions examine various themes through country case-studies, inclusive of: the routinisation of elections, accompanied by democratic rollback and the rise of hybrid regimes; the tenacity of presidential powers; the dilemmas of power-sharing; ethnic voting and rise of a violent politics of belonging; the role of 'donors' and the ambiguities of 'democracy promotion'.

Overall, the book concludes that steps forward remain greater than reversals and that typically, though not universally, sub-Saharan African countries are more democratic today than in the late 1980s. Nonetheless, the book also calls for more meaningful processes of democratization that aim not only at securing civil and political rights, but also socio-economic rights and the physical security of African citizens.

This book was originally published as a special issue of *Democratization*.

May 2012: 234x156: 304pp
Hb: 978-0-415-50832-2
£85 / $145

For more information and to order a copy visit
www.routledge.com/ISBN 9780415508322

Available from all good bookshops

www.routledge.com/9780415819657

Related titles from Routledge

Language Planning in Africa
The Cameroon, Sudan and Zimbabwe

Edited by Nkonko Kamwangamalu, Richard B. Baldauf Jr. and Robert B. Kaplan

This volume focuses on language planning in the Cameroon, Sudan and Zimbabwe, explaining the linguistic diversity, the historical and political contexts and the current language situation (including language-in-education planning), the role of the media, the role of religion and the roles of non-indigenous languages. The authors are indigenous to the situations described, and draw on their experience and extensive fieldwork there. The materials on the three polities contained in this volume draw together the literature on each of the polities to present an overview of the research available about each of them, while providing new research-based information. The purpose of the volume is to provide an up-to-date overview of the language situation in each polity based on a series of key questions in the hope that this might facilitate the development of a richer theory to guide language policy and planning in other polities where similar issues may arise.

This book comprises case studies originally published in the journal *Current Issues in Language Planning*.

June 2013: 246 x 174: 240pp
Hb: 978-0-415-81965-7
£85 / $145

For more information and to order a copy visit
www.routledge.com/9780415819657

Available from all good bookshops